PRAISE FOR

You Are Not Your Brain

"A testament to mind over brain. . . . It's the truth of the matter that sheer willpower can truly make you break free."

—*Leonardo DiCaprio*

"Operating on the highly rational perspective that we are not our brains but rather substantial free agents who exercise control over our brains, Schwartz and Gladding develop a simple yet profoundly insightful approach for developing a flourishing life. The result is truly life-giving, and it will bring healing and hope to all who read it and practice its wisdom."

—*J. P. Moreland, author of* The God Question

"How can the brain, which is just a complex network of interconnected nerve cells, give rise to consciousness and to thought? Dr. Jeffrey Schwartz and Dr. Rebecca Gladding argue, persuasively, that the mind actually has massive causal effects on the functioning of the brain. In other words, you can not only change the way you think, feel, and behave through conscious effort when you're upset, but you can also change the programming and chemistry of your brain. A compelling and important message."

—*David D. Burns, M.D., author of* Feeling Good: The New Mood Therapy

"The idea that we can deliberately and systematically change our brains with our minds was once thought ridiculous. But now, largely due to Jeffrey Schwartz and his UCLA research on neuroplasticity and OCD, this once revolutionary idea is well accepted. Rebecca Gladding and Jeffrey Schwartz adapt Schwartz's extraordinarily successful program for a mainstream audience, giving simple, self-directed tools to help achieve greater happiness, emotional balance, and overall well-being."

—*Susan Kaiser Greenland, author of* The Mindful Child

"The book *You Are Not Your Brain* will be very helpful to those who want to improve their outlook on life and enhance their quality of life. As this book shows, and most every musician knows, *You Are Not Your Brain*. The Heart and the Spirit are the source of real creativity. The brain is a vehicle to express that creativity."

—*Kenny Burrell, jazz guitarist, National Endowment for the Arts*
Jazz Master Professor of Music and Ethnomusicology, UCLA

You Are Not Your Brain

The 4-Step Solution for Changing Bad Habits, Ending
Unhealthy Thinking, and Taking Control of Your Life

Jeffrey M. Schwartz, M.D., *and* Rebecca Gladding, M.D.

AVERY | a member of Penguin Group (USA) Inc. | New York

Published by the Penguin Group
Penguin Group (USA) Inc., 375 Hudson Street, New York, New York 10014, USA •
Penguin Group (Canada), 90 Eglinton Avenue East, Suite 700, Toronto, Ontario M4P 2Y3, Canada (a division
of Pearson Penguin Canada Inc.) • Penguin Books Ltd, 80 Strand, London WC2R 0RL, England • Penguin
Ireland, 25 St Stephen's Green, Dublin 2, Ireland (a division of Penguin Books Ltd) • Penguin Group
(Australia), 250 Camberwell Road, Camberwell, Victoria 3124, Australia (a division of Pearson
Australia Group Pty Ltd) • Penguin Books India Pvt Ltd, 11 Community Centre, Panchsheel Park,
New Delhi–110 017, India • Penguin Group (NZ), 67 Apollo Drive, Rosedale, North Shore 0632,
New Zealand (a division of Pearson New Zealand Ltd) • Penguin Books (South Africa) (Pty) Ltd,
24 Sturdee Avenue, Rosebank, Johannesburg 2196, South Africa

Penguin Books Ltd, Registered Offices: 80 Strand, London WC2R 0RL, England

First trade paperback edition 2012
Copyright © 2011 by Jeffrey Schwartz and Rebecca Gladding

Excerpts from *Mindfulness in Plain English* by Bhante Henepola Gunaratana (2002) are reprinted with
permission from Wisdom Publications, 199 Elm Street, Somerville, MA, 02144 USA. www.wisdompubs.org.

Most Avery books are available at special quantity discounts for bulk purchase for sales
promotions, premiums, fund-raising, and educational needs. Special books or book excerpts
also can be created to fit specific needs. For details, write Penguin Group (USA) Inc.
Special Markets, 375 Hudson Street, New York, NY 10014.

THE LIBRARY OF CONGRESS CATALOGUED THE HARDCOVER EDITION AS FOLLOWS:

Schwartz, Jeffrey, date.
You are not your brain : the 4-step solution for changing bad habits, ending unhealthy thinking, and taking
control of your life / Jeffrey Schwartz and Rebecca Gladding.
p.   cm.
Includes bibliographical references and index.
ISBN 978-1-58333-426-3
1. Behavior modification.   2. Habit breaking.   3. Brain.   4. Change (Psychology).
I. Gladding, Rebecca.   II. Title.
BF637.B4S35   2011   2011006684
158.1—dc22

ISBN 978-1-58333-483-6 (paperback edition)

Printed in the United States of America
5   7   9   10   8   6

BOOK DESIGN BY NICOLE LAROCHE

To my mom, who has been my biggest advocate and ally—
I couldn't have written this without you; and in memory of
my grandmothers, Bertha E. Dow and Virginia Gladding

—Rebecca Gladding

To the people of Pacific Crossroads Church

—Jeffrey M. Schwartz

To all in need of faith, hope, love, and courage

CONTENTS

PART TWO

The Skills

PART THREE

Applying the Four Steps to Your Life

Habit, if not resisted, soon becomes necessity.

—Saint Augustine

INTRODUCTION

There are only a few true necessities in life, but for many of us, it doesn't feel that way. A lifetime of habits, ingrained by repetition, can seemingly make us slaves to a not always beneficial master—our own brain.

Nothing is more confusing or painful than when your brain takes over your thoughts, attacks your self-worth, questions your abilities, overpowers you with cravings, or attempts to dictate your actions. Have you ever felt that something is compelling you to "go" places, mentally or emotionally, where you don't want to be? Do you find yourself acting in uncharacteristic ways or doing things you don't really want to be doing?

The reason is simple: *Deceptive brain messages* have intruded into your psyche and taken over your life. Left to its own devices, your brain can cause you to believe things that are not true and to act in any number of self-destructive ways, such as:

- Overthinking problems and fretting over things that are out of your control
- Getting stuck or panicked by unfounded fear and worries

- Blaming and chastising yourself for things that are not your fault
- Engaging in unhealthy behaviors to escape life's daily stresses
- Reverting to past patterns when you are trying to make a change

The more often you act in these unhealthy ways, the more you teach your brain that what is simply a habit (a learned behavior) is essential to your survival. Your brain does not distinguish whether the action is beneficial or destructive; it just responds to how you behave and then generates strong impulses, thoughts, desires, cravings, and urges that compel you to perpetuate your habit, whatever it may be. Unfortunately, more often than not, these behaviors are not ones that improve your life.

Clearly, the brain can exert a powerful grip on one's life—*but only if you let it.* The good news is that you can overcome the brain's control and rewire your brain to work for you by learning to debunk the myths it has been so successfully selling you and by choosing to act in healthy, adaptive ways. That's the mission of this book and the cornerstone of our approach: to share our innovative, empowering method of learning how to identify and demystify deceptive brain messages, so that you develop healthy, adaptive brain circuits that enable you to live a fulfilling life free from these unwanted, unhelpful, and false intruders.

It will be *your* life, the life *you have chosen,* with the brain *you have sculpted*—not the old path of troubling actions and behaviors imposed upon you by deceptive brain messages.

How can you achieve this? With our Four Step method, which teaches simple skills you can use and *practice* every day and apply to any unsatisfactory part of your life. The result will be a lasting change in perspective, courtesy of a source that has been seriously stifled by the deceptive brain messages: your intelligent, caring inner guide. This friend will help you counteract deceptive brain messages and act in concert with your own goals, values, and interests. You will finally see *who you really are*—not who your brain has been *telling* you that you are—and put your true self in the driver's seat for the rest of your life.

Sound difficult to accomplish? You won't think so after you read the stories of others who have successfully employed our Four Step method to turn their lives around. *You Are Not Your Brain* touches on intimate personal journeys of several people whose lives were once plagued by deceptive brain messages and who managed to break the cycle—like Sarah, who struggled with depression and self-doubt; Ed, who was paralyzed by fears of rejection; Steve, who used alcohol to relieve stress; Liz, who worried about her future; Kara, who felt she was unlovable unless she was physically perfect; John, who repetitively checked e-mail as a way to assuage his fear that his girlfriend was leaving him; or Abby, who constantly worried that something bad would happen to someone she loved.

While your situation may not be as dramatic or intense, some form of deceptive brain messages impacts almost everyone at some point in life. Even if our lives usually run smoothly, when we are stressed or feeling down these false thoughts and unhealthy actions find a way to sneak in and cause havoc. They can shake our confidence, make us find ways to escape reality, use drugs or alcohol, overeat, spend money we don't have, avoid people we care about, become angry, develop excessive expectations of ourselves, not say what we really think or feel, limit our range of experiences, worry excessively . . . you name it. Even in the most benign situations, giving in to deceptive brain messages causes us to lose time that would have been better spent elsewhere. At its worst, we end up acting impulsively—in ways that are not representative of who we really are—and falling into grief and regret.

Most encouragingly, however, this powerful approach will help you identify and deal with the majority of your problems, not just one symptom, because we focus on the underlying, unifying cause of your distress: deceptive brain messages. In short, *You Are Not Your Brain* will empower you to approach life's ups and downs in a skillful way, using just four easily learned steps. You will find that repeated practice with the Four Steps will transform your life—and your brain—giving you the power to become the person you want to be.

How This Book Is Unique

A critical component to getting better—in the long term—is to understand that these highly deceptive intruders are coming from the brain (not you!) and that these false messages are not indicative of who you are or of the life you could lead. Other popular therapies have failed to focus on this crucial distinction between who you *are* and the *symptoms* you are experiencing. Although some methods may teach how to change the meaning of your thoughts (as in cognitive-behavioral therapy) or how to become aware of your thoughts (mindfulness), they do not emphatically tell you that these brain-based messages are not representative of who you really are and that you do not have to act on them.

In contrast, this book combines the best of cognitive-behavioral therapy and mindfulness while simultaneously helping you bolster your belief that you deserve to be free of these unwanted intruders. In so doing, you learn that to truly change your life and your brain, you must reevaluate the deceptive brain messages and *engage your mind to focus your attention on new, healthy actions and behaviors.*

So, not only do we teach you *how* to notice your deceptive brain messages and how to change your relationship to the deceptive brain messages, we also empower you by showing you that you have within yourself an intelligent, loving guide (your Wise Advocate) that knows that your *brain* has been the problem, not you or your mind.

The Four Steps Change Your Brain Wiring in Healthy, Adaptive Ways

The goal of the Four Steps is to teach you how to sharply focus your attention so that you rewire your brain in healthy, positive ways. How do we know this happens? We've already done the research at UCLA and proven it in people with obsessive-compulsive disorder.

Drawing on Dr. Schwartz's strong belief that the mind can change the brain, the UCLA researchers asked people with OCD to participate in a research study where they either took medication or learned our Four Step approach to dealing with the intrusive, negative messages they were bombarded with on a daily basis. The team scanned people's brains before treatment and ten to twelve weeks after they had been following our method or taking medications.[1] Much to our delight, they found that the people who used our Four Step method had the same positive changes in their brains as the people who took medications to treat their OCD. These incredible brain changes occurred because of our mind's ability to change our brains (i.e., how we focus our attention). You can see the results for yourself in the images in figure I.1 below.

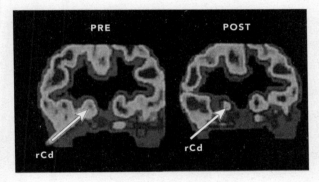

Figure I.1. Success with the Four Steps

PRE shows the brain before using the Four Steps and POST shows the brain ten weeks after using the Four Steps. Notice the decrease in the size of the rCd (a part of the brain that is overactive in OCD) once participants had been using the Four Steps for ten weeks. Copyright © 1996 American Medical Association[2]

---

1. Jeffrey M. Schwartz, Paula W. Stoessel, Lewis R. Baxter, Jr., Karron M. Martin, and Michael E. Phelps, "Systematic Changes in Cerebral Glucose Metabolic Rate After Successful Behavior Modification Treatment of Obsessive-Compulsive Disorder," *Archives of General Psychiatry* 53, no. 2 (February 1996): 109–13.

2. Ibid.

Encouragingly, recent research in Germany replicated our findings. Those researchers found that OCD patients' symptoms decreased significantly *when they simply listened to an audio CD* that explained our treatment method. That bears repeating because it is key to the path you are about to embark on: No other interventions were given to these participants—just an audio CD, their commitment, and their effort to make progress by following the Four Steps.

THE FOUR STEPS

Step 1: Relabel—Identify your deceptive brain messages and the uncomfortable sensations; call them what they really are.

Step 2: Reframe—Change your perception of the importance of the deceptive brain messages; say why these thoughts, urges, and impulses keep bothering you: They are *false brain messages* (It's not ME, it's just my BRAIN!).

Step 3: Refocus—Direct your attention toward an activity or mental process that is wholesome and productive—even while the false and deceptive urges, thoughts, impulses, and sensations are still present and bothering you.

Step 4: Revalue—Clearly see the thoughts, urges, and impulses for what they are, simply sensations caused by deceptive brain messages that are not true and that have little to no value (they are something to dismiss, not focus on).

With our Four Step method, you will learn how to focus your attention in beneficial ways—just like these people did—so that you can retrain your brain while simultaneously bolstering and empowering your true self.

Whom This Book Is For

Given that deceptive brain messages affect all of us at some point, this book can help anyone with excessive nervousness, worry and anxiety, tension, depression, anger, substance abuse, other addictions (including gambling, gaming, and sex), relationship problems, or other automatic behaviors and habits that are causing problems in your life, such as overeating, repeatedly checking things like texts/e-mail, excessively researching information, overthinking and overanalyzing situations and events, or avoiding important aspects of your life.

You do not have to be diagnosed with a disorder for the Four Steps to help you. Rather, you just need to have had the experience of being stressed out and overrun by your brain—which can include thoughts, urges, impulses, repetitive behaviors, or uncomfortable physical or emotional sensations—and want things to be different in some way. Wherever deceptive brain messages surface and cause you to not trust reality or to do something you do not want to be doing (i.e., it is bad for you in the long run), the Four Steps can help.

As a self-treatment method, the Four Steps work extremely well in those with mild to moderate symptoms—people who are functioning in the world to some extent (e.g., working, volunteering, going to school, caring for others) and are bothered by what their brains are doing. For example, you may get easily distracted and may have trouble getting through your day, but you can focus your attention some of the time, are able to consider the fact that your brain is causing these symptoms, and are ready, at least to some extent, to put forth effort to make changes in your life. If you are already in therapy, you can work with your therapist to integrate the Four Steps into your therapeutic plan.

The Four Steps do not work well enough on their own (i.e., self-treatment) in people with debilitating symptoms—those that severely limit their ability to focus their attention and function in their day. People with severe symptoms likely need extra help by using medications or more intensive therapy (including weekly therapy or a structured program). Why? With severe symptoms, people are not able to focus their attention well enough to use the Four Steps and do not have the ability or insight to see that the deceptive brain messages *might* be false. The whole point of the Four Steps is to take you from believing so strongly in your deceptive brain messages to seeing their falsehood, so if your symptoms are at the point where you cannot even entertain the possibility that the deceptive thoughts are created by your brain, you will need some extra help. Similarly, we want to make sure you understand that the Four Steps do not treat severe psychiatric disorders where insight is severely compromised in a chronic fashion, such as schizophrenia, where the brain's influences are too strong, such as mania in bipolar disorder, or when chronic thoughts of suicide are present.

Structure of the Book

We have chosen to divide this book into three parts so that we can emphasize how your sense of self gets fused with the deceptive brain messages (Part One), the skills you need to learn to untangle that unhelpful web of thoughts, emotions, and actions (Part Two), and how to apply the Four Steps to your life (Part Three). Note: If learning the skills, rather than knowing the theory and science, is your primary goal, you may want to read chapters 1 and 2, then skip to Part Two (chapter 6). You can always come back to the rest of Part One later.

PART ONE. A SENSE OF SELF
Given our emphasis on separating your sense of self from deceptive brain messages, we begin by teaching you what deceptive brain messages are and help you identify the ones that are bothering and impairing you. Then, you will see how the mind can powerfully and unexpectedly change the brain in positive ways when you intentionally direct your attention. From there,

we explain why habits are so hard to break on a biological level and what happens inside your brain whenever deceptive brain messages surface. We also discuss how your sense of self fused with the deceptive brain messages.

PART TWO. THE SKILLS

We begin by discussing where many of your deceptive brain messages likely came from, then provide you with a brief overview of the key points you need to keep in mind as you begin learning the Four Steps. These are the tips and tricks our patients wished they had known from the start and that they thought we should share with you. With that background, we teach you each of the Four Steps, including how to become more aware of your deceptive brain messages with Step 1: Relabel; why deceptive brain messages bother you so much and lead to thinking errors with Step 2: Reframe; how to sharply focus your attention with Step 3: Refocus; and how to change your perspective of yourself with Step 4: Revalue. In these chapters, we will include many exercises to help you learn how to use the Four Steps effectively, and we discuss the major stumbling blocks others have encountered when trying to learn the Four Steps.

PART THREE. APPLYING THE FOUR STEPS TO YOUR LIFE

In this final section, we review various ways the Four Steps can be creatively applied to your life and explain the difference between true emotions (those that reflect your true self) and unhelpful emotional sensations (emanating from deceptive brain messages). We also explain how Step 3: Refocus can be used to help you deal with deceptive brain messages in relationships, when you are experiencing powerful cravings (such as stress eating), when you feel depressed or fatigued, when you are not getting out into the world because of fear of rejection, or when you have excessive expectations of yourself (i.e., perfectionism). The final chapter of the book is devoted to helping you develop your Four Step plan and living your life in accordance with your true self.

The encouraging message from our more than twenty-five years of research and clinical practice is that you *do* have control over your responses to these deceptive brain messages and you can use your understanding of how the brain works to your advantage by using our Four Step approach.

Let's begin!

PART ONE

A Sense of Self

CHAPTER 1

You Are Not Your Brain

Nothing is more confusing or painful than when your brain takes over your thoughts, attacks your self-worth, questions your abilities, overpowers you with cravings, or attempts to dictate your actions. "It's like the invasion of the brain snatchers," says Ed, a talented Broadway performer whose career was on hold for years because of his intense stage fright and fears of rejection. Running on autopilot in a most unhelpful way, Ed felt like his "brain just took over," filling him with self-doubt and anxiety. "It was horrible and humiliating . . . it told me all these things about me that just weren't true. That I was no good, a second-class citizen, that I didn't deserve anything."

What's worse, those deceptive brain messages about Ed were dead wrong. The truth is that Ed is an accomplished performer who is revered and loved for his wit, ability to engage a crowd, and unshakable confidence on the stage. People are always excited to see him and are moved by his performances, yet his deceiving brain would not let him accept their rave reviews. Rather than believing in his inherently wonderful qualities and impressive skills, Ed's brain was programmed to ignore his positive attributes and instead focus on what he *might* have done wrong or how people *might* perceive his mistakes—in essence, to home in on his minute flaws and imperfections.

Where did these negative beliefs and doubts come from? Although he sees that most of his deceptive brain messages took root in childhood, one specific experience changed everything for him. It all began, he remembers, when he was standing before a famous Broadway producer at age twenty. As he prepared to run the scene, Ed became dazed and paralyzed. "I just left my body," he says. "It was the most horrifying experience." The event haunted his dreams and, by the time he was thirty, it began to plague his days. "I was no longer having nightmares about being onstage naked, I was having that feeling more or less whenever I went to an audition. I felt exposed and raw." Beneath that competent and tranquil façade, Ed was gripped by a fear of rejection and was in turmoil. Taking his deceptive brain messages completely at face value, Ed avoided auditions altogether, believing that his career was over—that his anxiety and fear had won.

DECEPTIVE BRAIN MESSAGES

Any *false or inaccurate* thought or any *unhelpful or distracting* impulse, urge, or desire that takes you away from your true goals and intentions in life (i.e., your true self).

Even if you are not dealing with overwhelming anxiety, you may recognize the feeling of being assailed by deceptive brain messages. Consider the case of Sarah, a twenty-nine-year-old public relations specialist who struggled with depression and perfectionism for many years before starting our program.

Like so many of us, she was afraid of not living up to expectations and questioned her abilities often. Even more troubling, Sarah was exquisitely sensitive to others' comments and actions, which caused her to often over-personalize interactions with friends, family, and coworkers. For example, if she was talking with a friend and he "paused, even for a second," she says, she would assume that she had said something wrong or upset the other person in some way. She would not be able to step back from her deceptive brain messages and look for an alternate explanation for why her friend responded as he did or realize that it had nothing to do with her. Instead, she would become instantly anxious and replay the seemingly botched interaction over and over in her head, hoping to come to some sort of resolution. Her brain would run in endless loops, asking numerous questions and envisioning various scenarios in a desperate attempt to control her anxiety.

No matter what she did, Sarah couldn't figure it out or make the terrible feelings of anxiety go away. Inside, she felt like a failure and somehow ended up believing she was the problem. She hoped and pleaded with herself: If only she could figure out what had happened, she could prevent a similar situation in the future and avoid this uncomfortable feeling and the associated negative thoughts. Unfortunately, she never did. Instead, she would get more anxious and continually overanalyze the situation until she was exhausted.

What Sarah didn't know at the time was that her brain was sending her the destructive message that to receive love, acceptance, and adoration, she had to be perfect and take care of everyone else. In essence, she had to ignore her true self and focus on others, no matter the cost to her.

TRUE SELF

Living according to your true self means seeing yourself for who you really are based on your sincere striving to embody the values and achieve the goals you truly believe in.

It includes approaching yourself, your true emotions and needs, from a loving, caring, nurturing perspective that is consistent with how your loving inner guide (Wise Advocate) sees you.

Sarah's deceptive brain messages became so overwhelming at times that she would stay in bed and try to shut out the world. She developed physical symptoms, including headaches, body pains, and a complete lack of motivation. It was as if a blanket of sleepiness had descended upon her and coated her entire being. As the depression progressed, Sarah stopped interacting with her family and friends, lost interest in her normal activities, and stopped exercising.

The more her brain churned out these negative messages, the more Sarah believed, as she says, that she was "a loser." Unable to resist those false thoughts or believe in herself, she fell deeper and deeper into despair until she was convinced that she was utterly worthless and that life was hopeless. Her depression came to inaccurately and inappropriately define her. "This is me," she thought, "a depressed, negative person who is not worthy of anything."

Similar to Sarah, Abby also struggled with a tendency to overanalyze. Rather than questioning her self-worth, Abby's deceptive brain messages caused her to constantly worry about the safety of her friends and family—and then repeatedly doubt whether she should say or do anything. Although she was fully capable of stating her views with clarity and conviction at work, Abby couldn't ever quite tell the important people in her life what she really thought or how she felt. "I just never know if I am doing the right thing," Abby said when she was in the thick of her symptoms. "How can I ensure the best for my family without making them feel like I am being overprotective or smothering them? What if someone gets hurt or makes a mistake and I knew it was a bad idea? How could I live with that, knowing that I could have done something to prevent that outcome?"

Abby's "guilt machine" often kicked into high gear when she did state her concerns, views, and opinions. For instance, if she put her foot down and forbade her children to do something, she would feel that she was disappointing them or depriving them in some way. As she explained, "I don't like conflict, but I don't like the results of staying quiet or being passive either." It was a veritable catch-22: She could not live with the guilt, yet she felt anxious and scared when she did state her views and beliefs.

At some level, Abby knew she was living an incomplete life by neglecting her true self, yet she saw no way out. Beholden to her deceptive brain messages and paralyzed by indecision, she often felt guilty and anxious. No matter how she tried, she could not pull herself out of her excessive thoughts, alter her assumption that she had to protect everyone, or use her Wise Advocate to help her see the bigger picture.

WISE ADVOCATE

The aspect of your attentive mind that can see the bigger picture, including your inherent worth, capabilities, and accomplishments.

The Wise Advocate knows what you are thinking, can see the deceptive brain messages for what they are and where they came from, understands how you feel (physically, emotionally), and is aware of how destructive and unhealthy your habitual, automatic responses have been for you.

The Wise Advocate wants the best for you because it loves and cares for you, so it encourages you to *value your true self* and *make decisions in a rational way* based on what is in your overall best interest in the long term.

Equally devastating were Steve's deceptive brain messages that kept him from being able to truly connect with his wife, children, and coworkers.

In his case, Steve's deceiving brain tried to convince him that everyone in his life wanted something *from* him and that they were not spending time or talking with him because of who he was or because they genuinely cared for him. This false perception caused Steve to become easily annoyed and excessively angry with anyone he perceived was indirectly asking him to do something. Of course, Steve's deceptive brain messages were clouding his ability to invoke his Wise Advocate to help him see the truth: that the people in his life really liked and respected him because he is smart, funny, caring, and insightful, which draws people to him and his ideas. Contrary to what his deceptive brain messages were saying, the people in his life didn't want him to do their work or take care of him—they wanted to spend time with and learn from a genuinely interesting and charismatic man.

Sadly, believing in and relying on his deceptive brain messages caused Steve to live in a state of chronic stress. No matter where he looked, he saw needy, helpless people everywhere, which drained his energy and fueled his frustration further. Unfortunately, his response to these unsettling surges of anger and disappointment in others was to avoid people whenever possible and to seek solace and relaxation each night in a few glasses of wine. While drinking definitely helped dissolve the stress, it created worsening problems at home and at work: Steve became ever more emotionally distant from the important people in his life, which made him feel alone and deeply sad.

Ed, Sarah, Abby, and Steve are just a few examples of the devastating toll deceptive brain messages can take on people's lives and how listening to such false messages can lead to depression, anxiety, relationship difficulties, isolation, addictions, unhealthy habits, and more. When they were not able to use their Wise Advocate to look at the bigger picture and did not align their actions with their true self, our patients were stuck in an endless cycle of deceptive brain messages.

The Cycle of Deceptive Brain Messages

How do deceptive brain messages manifest and what do they cause you to do? To find out, let's follow the case of Kara, a twenty-five-year-old woman who had been dieting, bingeing, and purging since her teens. If you met Kara today, you would have no idea she held such distorted views of her body as a teen. Confident and vibrant, she seems to have it all. She is successful in her career as an analyst and has a large network of friends. Yet for most of high school and college, she was overwhelmed by deceptive brain messages related to her appearance.

Kara describes the process of how deceptive brain messages impacted her in this way. First, a false, negative thought would strike, telling her she was "no good" and "unlovable" because she was not physically perfect. Although it was not true, Kara would take this missive at face value and accept it as reality. What happened next was excruciating, she says. "I would get an intensely uncomfortable sensation," she remembers, "a feeling that I could not stand being in my own skin." She felt "gross" and "disgusted" with herself, both emotionally and physically. The sensations were unbearable and all Kara wanted to do was get away from these feelings as fast as she could. Her distress would rise, reaching a crescendo that she could no longer tolerate. Although she would sometimes try to resist them, the uncomfortable sensations, including strong anxiety and self-loathing, were too strong. Eventually, she would relent and engage in an unhealthy behavior (e.g., purging, bingeing, dieting excessively). Once she gave in, a sense of calm would wash over her and she would feel all right again. That momentary relief—and that's all it ever was—was better than nothing.

Or so she thought. What Kara learned with experience was that once she completed the behavior, the deceptive brain messages and uncomfortable sensations came back in full force. "No matter what I did, I always ended up right back where I started. Nothing ever worked," she recalled recently. Her life was consumed by her deceptive brain messages and its mandates of how she should act. "I was wasting my life," she laments. She lost important time that she could have spent with her family and friends, on her career, or on pursuing activities she truly enjoyed.

Kara felt horrible about engaging in these cycles to try to make the terrible feelings of inadequacy go away. Deep down, she wanted to figure out how to stop the behaviors and not buy into the deceptive brain messages, but she had no idea how to do it. She had tried almost every diet and had been to numerous therapists and nutritionists. Nothing helped. Even worse, Kara eventually realized that the problem was intensifying, not getting better: "The more I paid attention to food and to how I looked, the worse I felt about myself and the stronger those negative thoughts became."

What was happening to Kara when she was immersed in following her deceptive brain messages? She was stuck in an unrelenting pattern where destructive thoughts and impulses led to distress and unhealthy behaviors.

If we simplify the process of what transpired whenever Kara gave in to her deceptive brain messages, we see a cycle unfold in which the negative thoughts or urges were followed by intensely uncomfortable physical or emotional sensations that she desperately wanted to get away from. As a consequence, Kara would engage in some unhealthy or unhelpful behavior to relieve her distress. While they provided a momentary reprieve, these actions ultimately were detrimental to her because her body and brain learned to associate these behaviors with relief (despite the fact that they were causing her harm in the long term).

What Kara described is a universal phenomenon that applies to you and all of your deceptive brain messages, regardless of what initiates them. As shown in figure 1.1, the process begins when a deceptive brain message surfaces and causes you to experience some kind of distress or discomfort. You might experience a physical sensation, like your heart pounding, a pit in your stomach or overwhelming cravings, or an emotional state, such as fear, dread, anxiety, anger, or sadness. No matter what it is, your primary

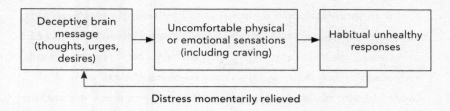

Distress momentarily relieved

Figure 1.1. Cycle of Deceptive Brain Messages

This figure depicts the process of how a deceptive brain message progresses to unhealthy behaviors and habits. After a deceptive brain message arises, you experience intensely uncomfortable sensations that can be physical or emotional. Because of how unpleasant and powerful the sensations are, you feel an urgent desire to make these sensations go away. As a result, you respond in an *automatic* (habitual) way that is ultimately unhelpful or unhealthy for you.

goal at this point is to get rid of that sensation as fast as you can, so you act in an automatic, habitual way.

As you've seen from Ed, Sarah, Abby, Steve, and Kara, the harmful strategies used to avoid and escape those uncomfortable sensations vary depending on the content of the deceptive brain messages and the patterns you have developed to attempt to deal with distress. The range of possible responses is endless and includes feeding an addiction, getting into an argument, avoiding a situation, shutting out the world, or endlessly checking something. In many cases, you are not even aware of what you are doing, but somewhere inside you, likely below the level of conscious awareness, you instinctively believe you have to complete the behavior to get rid of the intense and unpleasant feeling you're experiencing.

EMOTIONAL SENSATIONS VERSUS EMOTIONS

Something that confuses many people when we talk about the uncomfortable sensations that arise from deceptive brain messages is the difference between an *emotional sensation* and an *emotion or true feeling.*

Whenever we talk about emotional sensations, we are referring specifically to those feelings that are *evoked by deceptive brain messages and are not based in the truth*. For example, if you are feeling sad because you lost someone you care about, that is an emotion based on a real event. In all likelihood, your reaction is what most people would experience and is proportional to the event. Thus, it is an *emotion,* not an *emotional sensation.* These kinds of emotions should not be avoided; rather, you should experience and constructively deal with them as they arise.

In contrast, if you were feeling sad because you had the thought that no one cared about you and that you were unlovable—despite evidence to the contrary, such as having good connections with a variety of loving family and friends—then your sadness would be based on a deceptive brain message. We would consider this an *emotional sensation* (not an emotion) that could lead you to act in a way that is not helpful to you, such as isolating from people who really do care about you, using food or substances as an escape, or engaging in another unhealthy behavior.

Throughout the book, we will use the term *emotional sensation* to refer to feelings that are caused by deceptive brain messages. These are the sensations we want you to focus on as you use the Four Steps because they are the ones that you need to learn how to dismiss and see as being caused by deceptive brain messages. Ultimately, they are not true and are leading you to act in ways that are not helpful or constructive.

We will continue to discuss the difference between emotions and emotional sensations caused by deceptive brain messages and help you learn how to differentiate them. For now, keep the following distinction in mind: *Emotions* should be felt and constructively dealt with because they honor your true needs and your true self, whereas *emotional sensations* should be Relabeled and Reframed with the Four Steps because they are destructive and false, and cause you to act in ways that are not healthy or beneficial to you.

Although it is natural to want to avoid distress, seek out pleasure, or feel relief, the problem with satiating these cravings or quelling that upset is that your brain then becomes hardwired to automatically choose unhealthy behaviors to calm you down. In essence, indulging these habitual responses causes your body and brain to begin to associate something you do, avoid, seek out, or repetitively think about with *temporary* relief or pleasure. These actions create strong and enduring patterns (circuits) in your brain that are difficult to change without considerable effort and attention. As this process unfolds, the deceptive brain messages occur more frequently and the uncomfortable sensations grow more intense, making it harder for you to resist them or change your behaviors.

Therefore, whenever you repeatedly do something pleasurable or avoid some kind of overtly painful sensation, your brain "learns" that these actions are a priority and generates thoughts, impulses, urges, and desires to make sure you keep doing them again and again. It does not care that the action ultimately is bad for you.

As you will learn throughout the book, what you do now and how you focus your attention influence your brain and how it is wired. This means that if you repeat the same act over and over—regardless of whether that action has a positive or negative impact on you—you make the brain circuits associated with that act stronger and more powerful. So, if you avoid something that causes you anxiety (like Ed), hide from people who love you when you are depressed (like Sarah), continually worry about others (like Abby), or drink to reduce your stress level (like Steve), your brain is going to strengthen the circuits supporting those actions—meaning that your brain will be far more likely to repeat the behavior or habit automatically whenever a similar situation arises.

You will learn more about why habits are so hard to break and the biology behind deceptive brain messages in chapters 3 and 4. For now, keep in mind the cycle Kara described: The take-home message is that deceptive brain messages lead to uncomfortable sensations (both physical

and emotional) that cause you to act in automatic ways that are not beneficial to you.

HABITUAL RESPONSES

When someone mentions the word *habit*, most people think of repetitive physical actions. While those certainly are habits, we consider a larger range of responses to be habits as well. For example, if you constantly avoid a situation, person, or location because of how uncomfortable it makes you feel, you also are acting in a habitual way.

The same goes for engaging in repetitive thoughts caused by deceptive brain messages that do not lead to a solution or any forward progress. Re-member Abby's overactive "guilt machine" that caused her to worry about every little thing related to her family members and Sarah's struggle to try to figure out solutions for interacting with her friends and coworkers? They each described repetitively thinking about and analyzing situations to try to *rid themselves of the horrible sensations they were experiencing.* In Abby's case, the sensation was guilt and for Sarah it was anxiety and de-pression. Although the content of their deceptive brain messages and their uncomfortable emotional sensations were different, their responses and goals were the same: repetitively thinking about something for which there was no solution and desperately trying to get rid of the uncomfortable sensation caused by a deceptive brain message. (Note: Other words for repetitively thinking about something include *rumination, mental compul-sions,* and *overthinking.*)

We consider overanalyzing and overthinking to be habitual responses. Therefore, when we talk about the Habit Center and habitual responses, we are referring to repetitive thoughts, actions, or inaction—anything that you do *repeatedly* that is caused by a deceptive brain message and takes you away from focusing on something that is beneficial to you.

Identifying Your Deceptive Brain Messages

Now that you have a sense of what deceptive brain messages are, you can begin to think about how they are negatively impacting you. Some things, like behaviors and cravings, are easier to identify because you can see or feel them physically. What is harder for many people to identify at first are the thoughts associated with specific actions.

Although it is often difficult initially to see your deceptive thoughts at the beginning, we do not want you to feel discouraged or give up. Through case stories, explanations, and exercises, we will help you recognize the kinds of deceptive, negative messages your brain sends you. The point right now is for you to start becoming aware that these deceptive messages likely are lurking in your brain.

How can you begin to recognize the false, negative thoughts associated with your actions and uncomfortable sensations? One of the best ways to "see" the deceptive thoughts is to be attentive to your "negative self-talk"— those things you automatically say to yourself without awareness that are not true and that others might never even suspect were present inside your head. You may have already been exposed to the idea of such deceptive brain messages, just under a different name. Some therapists or authors might refer to them as "cognitive distortions," "automatic thoughts," "negative thinking," or "scripts." The main point is that these are the disparaging stories you tell yourself—the inaccurate explanations you give for why something is happening the way it is—that cause you to act in habitual ways that are not beneficial to you.

Often, seeing what others have described and experienced can be helpful in identifying your deceptive brain messages. On pages 16 and 17 are examples of deceptive brain messages, uncomfortable sensations, and unhealthy habitual responses we've heard over the years.

False Thoughts/Impulses/Urges
(i.e., Deceptive Brain Messages)
- I'm not good enough.
- I should have/I shouldn't have.
- I'm crazy/I'm a sick person.
- I'm a bad person/I am not as good as . . .
- I don't matter/Everyone else is more important than me.
- I will be rejected/Everyone thinks I am . . .
- There's something wrong with me.
- I have no control.
- No one likes me/I am unlovable/I will be alone.
- All of my worth is in taking care of others.
- I don't deserve to be happy—I deserve to suffer or be punished.
- Everyone else seems to be doing things correctly; what's wrong with me?
- I want unrealistic or unattainable things, like always feeling "good."
- I have a repetitive craving for something that ultimately is not beneficial to me.
- I have an urge to escape reality.

Uncomfortable Sensations
- Anxiety
- Pit in my stomach
- Butterflies
- Tightness or pounding in my chest
- Sweating
- Heart beating fast
- Excessive anger
- Heat in my chest, arms, or face
- Sadness/depression
- Fatigue

- Feeling scared/frightened
- Feeling helpless/hopeless
- Having a physical craving for something pleasurable

Habitual Responses
- Using drugs or alcohol
- Shopping/spending money I do not have
- Wasting time on things I do not need to do
- Fighting/arguing
- Compulsive sex
- Excessive eating, dieting, or purging
- Avoiding people, places, events
- Smoking
- Eating things that are not good for me
- Repeatedly checking something (e.g., e-mail, text, facts, information)
- Avoiding unpleasant (but beneficial) things like exercise
- Overthinking or overanalyzing situations, events, problems

Think about your deceptive brain messages and the cycles you go through. What are the false messages your brain sends to you and what do you do as a result of those negative messages? It could range from negative thoughts about yourself to feelings of inadequacy to the desire to escape your reality, indulging in a pleasurable craving, or something else that wastes your precious time and money. What we are getting at are the thoughts, urges, desires, and impulses that cause you to act in ways that take you away from your true goals and values.

Here are examples of how the cycle of deceptive brain messages played out for some of our patients. Read across each row to get a sense of what the person's thoughts, sensations, and responses were. After you review these examples, we'll have you come up with some of your own.

EXAMPLES OF THE CYCLE
OF DECEPTIVE BRAIN MESSAGES

Deceptive Brain Message	Uncomfortable Sensations	Habitual Responses
I'm not good enough.	Pit in my stomach	Get reassurance from someone that I am okay.
I'm a bad person.	Tightness in chest	Isolate/withdraw from people.
I should have listened to Joe, not argued with him.	Heart beating out of my chest, sweating	Repeatedly apologize to Joe, even though he keeps saying it was not a big deal.
I am so stressed out, I just need to get out of my head.	Overwhelmed, "amped up"	Use alcohol, pot, or other drugs to escape.
They are not going to hire me for this position.	Butterflies in my stomach, scared	Make up an excuse to not go to the interview; avoid the situation.
I am going to mess up this presentation.	Ringing in my ears, feeling a little dizzy	Ask someone else to give the presentation or move it to another day.
She's going to leave me!	Scared, nervous energy, light-headed	Check my e-mail again to see if she responded (and that everything is okay).
I am so angry at him—it's all his fault!	Surging heat in my chest and arms	Get into an argument, even though it really wasn't his fault.
I really want to eat something sweet.	Hunger, salivation	Eat some cake even though I don't need it and am trying to lose weight.
I have an urge to eat fried food (even though I have high cholesterol).	Craving—it tastes so good—I want it!	Eat some fried chicken and increase my cholesterol levels further.

The clear message in the examples above is that all of the people doubted themselves and their truth, could not see what was really happening, or craved something so strongly that they were unable to follow the path of their true goals and values. To deal with the uncomfortable sensations (both physical and emotional), they did *something* to alleviate the distress, including looking for reassurance, repeatedly apologizing, checking e-mail, avoiding a situation, using a substance to dull their senses, or indulging a craving to bring themselves momentary pleasure, such as eating sweets or fried food. In all cases, the actions were harmful to them and did not get them any closer to their true goals in life.

With this background, use the table below to figure out your pattern of deceptive brain messages, uncomfortable sensations, and habitual responses. Don't worry about doing this perfectly or having an all-inclusive list. This is just a jumping-off point—there will be many more opportunities along the way to refine your list. For now, just see what comes to mind. Remember: We're trying to increase your awareness of what your brain is doing automatically, without your knowledge. For now, write down some of your deceptive thoughts, uncomfortable sensations, and what they cause you to do or avoid.

EXAMPLES OF THE CYCLE
OF DECEPTIVE BRAIN MESSAGES

Deceptive Brain Message	Uncomfortable Sensations	Habitual Responses

Deceptive Brain Message	Uncomfortable Sensations	Habitual Responses

Throughout the book, we will help you identify what kinds of deceptive brain messages are causing problems in your life and figure out ways to deal with them. For now, we simply want you to start becoming aware of all the times during the day that your brain tries to tell you one thing, whereas your goals or intentions would guide you to do something else.

You Are Not Your Brain

Now that you understand what deceptive brain messages are and how much damage they can cause, you likely want to know the solution: *constructively focusing your attention with your mind*. What do we mean?

We've shown you that the *brain* is capable of sending out false, deceptive messages in an unrelenting fashion and that these unwanted thoughts and destructive urges can overrun your life. They can take you away from your true self (i.e., your true goals and values) and cause you to live a life devoid of direction. And, as long as you remain unaware of what your brain is doing or believe that there is no way to alter how your brain functions, you are essentially powerless to live life on your terms. There's no place from which to make a change because the very thing that is generating the deceptive brain messages appears to be running the show.

The good news is that you have an ally that can help you sculpt your brain to work for you, rather than against you: *the mind*. Although there are many different concepts and definitions of the mind out there, ours is straightforward: The mind is involved in helping you constructively focus your attention. Why is this important? When you learn how to focus your attention in positive, beneficial ways, you actually rewire your brain to support those actions and habits. In this way, the mind gives *you* the power to determine your actions, decide what is important (and what is not), and reassess the value or meaning of situations, people, yourself, and events.

THE DIFFERENCE BETWEEN THE MIND AND THE BRAIN

The brain receives inputs and generates the *passive* side of experience, whereas the mind is *active*, focusing attention, and making decisions.

Another way to think about the difference between the mind and the brain is this: The brain receives information from the environment, including images, verbal communication from others, emotional reactions, bodily sensations, and so on, and then processes that information in an automatic and rote way. No thought or awareness is involved (at least initially). Once it processes these inputs, the brain presents the information to our conscious awareness.

This is where the mind comes in. At this point, the mind has the ability to determine whether it wants to focus either on that information coming from the brain or on something else. In comparison to the mind, then, the brain is passive—it does not take a long-term, values-based approach to actions. In other words, the brain does not incorporate your true self or Wise Advocate into its processes, but merely reacts to its environment in habitual, automatic ways.

In the case of Kara, her brain was wired to falsely associate bingeing, purging, or excessive dieting with being thinner and loved. As long as she believed in these deceptive brain messages and responded with the same unhealthy behaviors, *Kara's brain was running the show.* She would be stuck in unending loops of deceptive thoughts, rising anxiety, and unhealthy actions—and her brain wiring and unhealthy habits would only get stronger and more entrenched. She would not break this cycle until she could begin to engage her Wise Advocate to help her see how destructive those acts were (even though they brought her momentary relief or pleasure). As her Wise Advocate grew stronger, she would *actively* change how she focused her attention and how she responded to the deceptive brain messages. This would allow her to resist the strong urges to excessively diet, binge, or purge in the future when deceptive brain messages surfaced.

As you can see from Kara's example, what makes the mind unique is that it has the ability to consider many options and can weigh short-term actions against longer-term goals. In essence, the mind is the agent that ensures you are following the path to achieving your goals as defined by your true self. How does the mind align these goals and actions? By integrating the view of the Wise Advocate and using insight, awareness, morals, and values to guide your responses and empower you to make choices that are in your long-term best interest. The brain, in contrast, tends to act in an automatic way that ensures momentary survival and a sense of safety. Remember Darwin? You can think of the brain as working in the survival-of-the-fittest mode—trying to ensure safety, comfort, or relief in this moment, no matter what the future costs.

Just to be very clear: The brain and the mind work together, as a team. Neither is "better" than the other. We certainly need the brain's quick actions to survive if we are confronted with a dangerous situation, such as being attacked or about to be hit by a car. That fight-or-flight response is what ensured the survival of our species to this point. In the end, it's really about balancing the necessary, energy-efficient, and quick actions originating in the brain that ensure momentary survival with the longer-term, considered decisions coming from the mind (assisted by your Wise Advocate).

WHEN THE SYSTEM GOES AWRY

On the surface, it seems like this division of labor between the mind and the brain is ideal. When we are dealing with thoughts, emotional sensations, and actions that are consistent with our true self (who we aspire to be), all is fine. But what if we actually have unhealthy or maladaptive routines programmed into those automatic neural structures and we are not aware that they are happening? For example, what if we've taught the brain's Habit Center to perform an action that is not good for us, like excessively drinking alcohol when we're stressed or eating ice cream every night (even though we are trying to lose weight) because it makes us feel good?

We'll talk more about how this happens in later chapters, but for now believe us when we say that the automatic parts of the brain are so efficient that their routines can become wired into our brain without us realizing it and can lead to devastating consequences. That's why learning how to *focus your attention* is so important—it is the one variable you have power over that *can change your brain.* This is why, when the stakes are high, such as continuing to use a drug that is destroying your life, repeatedly eating something that causes your health to suffer, or giving in to anxiety to the point that you avoid things that are beneficial to you, you need to engage the Wise Advocate to recruit the mind to make important long-term decisions.

Unfortunately, many people, when in the grips of sadness, desire, anger, urges, anxiety, fear, or addiction, cannot and do not make this distinction between the mind and the brain. They cannot see what is happening and tend to blindly follow the impulse-laden brain wherever it wants to take them. They accept momentary relief or pleasure at the price of future pains. It makes sense from a biological perspective—we are all wired to use the automatic, energy-efficient parts of our brain first, with the primary goal of survival or safety in that moment. But choosing momentary relief and placing your attention on an unhealthy behavior come at a steep price because these choices can end up shaping the brain in detrimental ways.

We'll talk more about the mind's ability to change the brain, known as Self-Directed Neuroplasticity, in chapter 2, but first we want to address one other fact: Biology is *not* destiny. To succeed with the Four Steps and sculpt your brain in the ways you want, you need to believe that you are not destined to live a predetermined life based on your genetics. You have the ability to overcome many of the obstacles you inherited and to influence the ways in which your brain and body function.

BIOLOGY IS NOT DESTINY

Many of us feel powerless to make a change. We think, "I am these thoughts, I am these urges, this is *who* I am." Some feel that even if they seek out treatment and improve, the fact that they have been depressed, anxious, or addicted in the past means they will always be *that* person, the one with the problem. Or they worry that the symptoms are destined to recur. They believe they were dealt a bad genetic hand at birth and are sentenced to a life of misery and chronic struggle. They often end up thinking, "What's the point? I can't beat this thing. I've tried before and nothing has ever worked. I might as well give up."

This is a sad and tragic way to approach life, especially when there is so much we can do about many of our problems and challenges. Granted, we are talking about genetic vulnerabilities or predispositions, not severe genetic diseases, such as Down's syndrome or Huntington's disease, that cannot be altered by lifestyle changes. Several examples of genetic vulnerabilities that often come to mind include alcoholism, high blood pressure, high cholesterol, and diabetes. What's most interesting—and applicable to you—is that in all of these cases, the underlying biology you were born with can be heavily influenced by how you act. In fact, *there really is no distinction between many physical and psychological ailments in terms of your ability to influence your body and brain to make positive changes in your life.*

Equally important, there also is no distinction in how hard it is to make those changes, even when your life depends on it. Yet people often do not make the changes, even when they know it is best for them. This is because *change demands considerable effort and a strong commitment.* Often, the knowledge that we need to change isn't enough and shaming us into submission doesn't help, either. In fact, it usually causes us to react in the opposite way: We become entrenched in our behaviors rather than liberated from them. This is perhaps the most important reason why we must never capitulate to confusing our biology with our true self. What we need instead is to use our awareness of the crucial difference between biology and who we want to be to *motivate* and *empower* us to truly believe we are in control of our lives and our health.

The key to succeeding, then, is not merely education and fear tactics, but an awareness that overcoming rote, automatic neural pathways takes an incredible amount of effort, patience, and dedication. Not only do you have to clearly see that you are engaging in these actions and that they are hurting you, you have to expend the effort and energy to recruit different brain pathways and make different choices each time you are confronted with the urge to follow your old ways. It is the same struggle we talked about previously: giving in to short-term rewards and enticements at the expense of long-term gains. It is the dilemma of satiating the brain-based messages in the moment versus choosing actions that are aligned with your goals and values (i.e., your true self). The ultimate goal is seeing that you are far more than your deceptive brain messages and that you can make choices that are in your genuine best interest.

YOU ARE NOT A DISEASE OR DISORDER

If biology is not destiny and the brain is constantly sending out false messages, then it follows that you are not what your brain is trying to say you are. You are not a bad person just because those inaccurate and highly deceptive brain messages are present in your head. Rather, you are a person who is experiencing an onslaught of brain-based communications that are not true.

Accepting this fact, we know, can be challenging. Insidious and highly destructive, these types of false brain messages try to convince us that what we are feeling is the truth, that we are defined by our deceptive thoughts and feelings. Unfortunately, these messages can become so ingrained and inculcated in our lives that they begin to provide a sense of familiarity and comfort—which makes it all the harder to try to give them up.

If you don't believe it happens, consider this example from Ed. One day he posed a question to others he knew were also dealing with deceptive brain messages: "If you had a magic wand and could get rid of all your symptoms—be 'normal' right now—would you do it?" Surprisingly, some of the people hesitated in answering this question because their lives and identities had become so entwined with their symptoms. Despite improving considerably and having some knowledge that their brains were sending out these caustic messages, Ed's acquaintances still had trouble de-identifying with their symptoms and their current way of life. Although they wanted to be free from the deceptive brain messages, they were also scared. Who would I be, they asked, if I didn't have these thoughts, these feelings, these habits? After all, isn't this what defines me? Isn't this who I am?

Although difficult to believe at first, the fact is the brain is distorting reality by framing the majority of your experiences through the lens of deceptive brain messages. The truth is that you are a good person, worthy of love, attention, affection, and more.

With time and repeated practice with the Four Steps, Ed came to know that this was true. He triumphantly realized one day: "This is just a reality my brain is *creating*. It is not the truth and I don't have to believe it." With this eloquent insight and an ever-increasing belief in himself and his abilities, Ed was able to lift the veil of his deceptive brain messages by saying to himself: "Don't believe everything you think or feel!" Similarly, Sarah came to this empowering conclusion regarding her symptoms and identity: "This isn't *me*, this is *depression*."

Separating your identity, your true self, from the deceptive brain messages and unhealthy habits you're engaging in is critical. Therefore, we cannot overstate this point: *You are not a disease, problem, or disorder.* You are a *person* struggling with upsetting symptoms from which you want to find relief. This distinction is crucial because people who realize that they are more than their symptoms feel like they have the power to overcome them. Without this belief in yourself and your abilities, the path to healing will be much more challenging. We hope that this knowledge, along with specific help from us throughout the book, will help you increase your ability to dismiss the deceptive, brain-based messages, believe in yourself, and change your life for the better.

YOU CAN SUCCEED

From the stories of Ed, Sarah, Abby, Steve, and Kara, it is clear that the brain can lead you down a dangerous path resulting in depression, anxiety, troubled relationships, addiction, excessive anger, emotional isolation, and more. Their stories have highlighted a major roadblock you've likely been encountering: a lack of awareness that your brain was running the show.

The true message of this chapter is that you have the ability to define who you aspire to be (your true self) and align your behaviors with those goals. Let's face it: This is no easy task. We know that to really alter your behavior requires that you fundamentally modify the choices you make on a daily or even minute-by-minute basis. We also know that you are going to have to fight against powerful brain biology in the Habit Center, which acts in a very efficient and automatic way outside of our awareness. Ultimately, you succeed when you recognize that it is not your fault that you are struggling—it's just that your brain is simply doing what it does best—and resolve to make changes that are in your long-term best interest. That said, the fact that you are up against some intense brain biology does not get you off the hook or give you an excuse to give up—only you can free yourself from the tyranny of bad brain circuits.

Summary

- Your brain sends you false messages all the time throughout your day.
- These messages often are destructive and can prevent you from achieving your goals.
- Deceptive brain messages are any thoughts, impulses, or desires that take you away from your true goals and intentions in life.
- You are not defined by the thoughts in your head.
- The mind and the brain are distinct entities.
- The Wise Advocate can help you decide how to act and how you perceive/think about things.
- The mind chooses how you focus your attention.
- You have the ability to define your true self and align your actions with those goals and values on a moment-to-moment basis.

- You are not a disorder, disease, or problem.
- Biology is not destiny.
- Your Wise Advocate encourages you to make decisions that reflect your true self and that benefit you in the long term.
- YOU ARE NOT YOUR BRAIN.

CHAPTER 2

Using Your Mind to Change Your Brain

The Power of Self-Directed Neuroplasticity and Meaningful Goals

Imagine what it would be like to wake up one day and not be able to move half of your body. On the Saturday before Easter in 2001, Connie Smiley experienced that firsthand. An engaging, lively sixty-five-year-old outreach coordinator at the Cincinnati Zoo, Connie was driving to the zoo for a Safari pre-trip meeting. As an avid animal lover and former grade school teacher, Connie couldn't wait for this trip to Africa, which would be her fourth. This time she was going to visit the cheetah sanctuary—a lifelong dream—and tour parts of Africa she had never seen.

As she was driving to the zoo that day, she noticed that something was wrong. "I began to realize that I was having trouble keeping my car from going left," she says. A little later, while walking on the zoo grounds, she was dragging her left foot slightly and it felt like her left arm was "made out of a ton of bricks." She met her daughter there, who correctly identified that she was having a stroke and insisted she go to the hospital. Both she and her daughter knew the signs of stroke well because Connie's husband had a massive stroke ten years prior and lived out his days in a nursing home, unable to care for himself.

Connie was admitted to the hospital and at first her symptoms did not seem that bad. However, by Monday morning—three days after her symptoms began—she could not move the left side of her body at all. "Not a finger, not a toe, nothing," she recalls. When you have a stroke like that, you lose half of all your muscles, including those muscles involved in chewing, breathing, and speaking loudly. Connie didn't want to believe what was happening to her and was incredibly disappointed that she was about to miss this amazing opportunity to see her favorite animal in its natural habitat.

"Things went downhill from there," she remembers. Her physicians believed that her stroke was severe and that she would not recover the use of her left arm or leg. They certainly were not sugarcoating her prognosis, as Connie recalls: "My own doctor came in to see me and said, 'Well, you'll never walk again.'" Another doctor said she would pray for her. Images of Connie's husband flashed before her eyes. Would she end up like him, stuck in a nursing home for the rest of her life? Despite what the doctors were telling her, Connie did not give up hope: "I made a decision right then and there, knowing it might not be possible. If there was any way I could keep from ending up like that, I was going to do whatever it took." Unbelievably, seven weeks after her first symptoms began, the woman whose left side had been completely paralyzed was able to walk with assistance and go home.

Since her stroke, Connie has made incredible progress. Some of her abilities, such as walking, came back very quickly, whereas others, like holding heavy objects in her left hand, have yet to fully return. Throughout it all, she used Self-Directed Neuroplasticity powered by her meaningful goals to guide and fuel her recovery.

Why introduce you to Connie and her stroke, a physical problem, when we are focusing on overcoming deceptive brain messages? There are several reasons. First, physical struggles and the emotional toll they take often are easier to understand than purely emotional ones. You can see part of the struggle with your eyes and understand it in a more universal way. Second, Self-Directed Neuroplasticity—the underpinning of

Connie's recovery and yours—works in exactly the same way for the physical maladies Connie experienced and the psychological distress caused by deceptive brain messages. This means that everything Connie learned and did can be applied to you. Finally, the challenges Connie faced emotionally and the motivation she had to muster to achieve her goals are similar to what you will face as you work with the Four Steps.

Labeling Physical and Emotional Sensations

Connie's road to recovery was anything but easy. She spent a week in the hospital and then transferred to Drake Center, an acute rehabilitation facility in Cincinnati, Ohio. There she spent three weeks in the acute inpatient unit and another three weeks at their assisted living center. The days were long and intense. She was making progress every day, but she was not improving as fast as she had wanted or expected. As she remembers, "I think I originally thought I would be back to the way I was before. It took me a while to accept that, no, that's never going to be."

The discrepancy between her expectations and reality led to considerable frustration and anger—two emotional sensations that became Connie's biggest obstacles during her stay at Drake. Often, if she could not achieve what she wanted, she says her frustration would get "to the point where I would start throwing things and losing it." Her deceptive brain messages were telling her that she was not working hard enough and that she *should* be able to complete the task. As these negative messages took hold, Connie would be consumed with strong physical sensations—the surging heat of anger—and her thoughts would become clouded. No longer able to focus on the task at hand because her emotional sensations were taking over, she would become stuck.

Rather than stewing in the uncomfortable sensations of rising anger and frustration, Connie labeled her emotions so that they no longer held power over her. "By simply saying 'I'm mad,'" she recalls, "I wasn't mad anymore . . . it took care of the problem." Once she stated what was happening—by making mental notes—Connie was able to get outside of the sensations. Instead of being consumed with anger, frustration, and the powerful physical sensations that accompanied them, Connie would focus her attention toward the task at hand.

MAKING MENTAL NOTES

The process of becoming aware of and focusing your attention toward noticing the appearance of a thought, sensation, urge, response, or event as it arises.

Mental notes involve more than simply identifying a deceptive brain message, uncomfortable sensation, or habitual response—they also include focusing your attention on them long enough for you to encode, or *remember*, the experience without becoming ensnared by it. This allows you to start noticing patterns in your thoughts, urges, sensations, and responses that are unhelpful or harmful to you. When you repeatedly make mental notes, you start to "see" the unhealthy thoughts, urges, sensations, and responses faster and can dismiss them before they spiral out of control. We will teach you more about mental notes in Part Two of the book when we discuss Step 1: Relabel. For now, keep in mind that mental notes are a powerful way to identify your deceptive brain messages and the patterns they create so that you can more rapidly dismiss them and refuse to give in to their commands.

Saying No to False Brain Messages—
Reframing Their Content

Making mental notes was a key step for Connie, but it was not enough on its own. She also needed to evaluate the content of her deceptive brain messages so she could counter and veto them.

One day while at Drake's assisted living facility, Connie fell in the shower. She was not yet strong enough to walk on her own and was still using a wheelchair. Having no way to summon help, Connie knew she would have to figure out a way to get to the hall. As Connie lay there, she managed to get her upper body onto the seat of the wheelchair and propelled herself forward on her knees. She was making progress, but then her chair got stuck on the door frame. "I had this awful 'I can't do this' moment," she recalls, and she momentarily gave up.

Then, something miraculous happened. A few moments after saying "I can't," Connie realized that she was giving in to a deceptive brain message. She reminded herself of something she had learned years earlier: Whenever she said the phrase "I can't," what she was really communicating is "I won't." The minute she recognized what was really happening and called it like it was, she remembers, "I was totally empowered to do it." She turned the deceptive brain message on itself by discounting it and instead believing in herself by saying, "Of course I will! This is ridiculous." Once she labeled and Reframed the content of her deceptive brain message by looking at it rationally, Connie calmed down, collected her thoughts, and figured a way out of the bathroom, successfully receiving the help she needed.

Connie's process of Relabeling her negative brain messages (Step 1) and Reframing their content (Step 2) as self-punitive allowed her to veto the intended action (Step 3)—the one telling her to give up and accept defeat. To counteract those negative messages, she used a rational, supportive perspective to see reality as it truly was and believe in herself. In other words, she successfully invoked her Wise Advocate to reevaluate the deceptive brain messages. With its guidance, she chose a positive, healthy response that enabled her to get help.

Veto Power

Another one of Connie's assets was her ability to focus her attention away from deceptive brain messages and on to activities that helped her regulate her physical and emotional sensations. Struggling daily to make gains in therapy, Connie remembers crying and feeling overwhelmed whenever anyone would come visit her. While she wasn't depressed or demoralized, she would become flooded with physical and emotional sensations that were out of her control. At one point, a psychologist recommended that she consider taking an antidepressant to deal with her crying spells. The psychologist said to her, "If you are going to cry every time someone comes in, your friends won't want to come around anymore." Because of her strong belief in herself and strong alignment with her Wise Advocate, Connie declined the medications and responded by saying, "Look, my friends will come and if they don't, they're not friends. I will take care of it." And she did.

When those overwhelming physical and emotional sensations surfaced, Connie would "stop a second and swallow—then I could get over it." By focusing on a physical act like swallowing (i.e., Step 3: Refocusing away from the distressing false sensations), Connie was able to move forward. That ability to refuse to give in to her deceptive brain messages—what we call *veto power*—allowed her to choose new responses that enabled her to interact with her family and friends in the ways she wanted.

VETO POWER

The ability to refuse to act on a deceptive brain message, uncomfortable sensation, or habitual response.

Self-Directed Neuroplasticity

A large part of Connie's success was due to her ability to keep going forward even when she felt like giving up. By focusing her attention and efforts on things that mattered to her, Connie was able to persevere through almost any challenge. Peter G. Levine, a researcher at Drake Center and author of *Stronger After Stroke*, worked closely with Connie during parts of her recovery. As he explains, she used her passion for the animals and teaching—those things that gave meaning to her life—"to drive her nervous system towards recovery far beyond any expectations."

What Levine is referring to is a concept known as neuroplasticity, which is the ability of the brain to take on new functions based on a person's changing needs and actions.

PLASTICITY AND NEUROPLASTICITY

Plasticity comes from the Greek word *plastikos*, meaning "formed" or "molded."

Neuroplasticity includes any process that results in a change in the brain's structure, circuits, chemical composition, or functions in response to changes in the brain's environment. It is a property of the brain and is best understood as a *capacity* (or potential) for brain areas and circuits to take on new roles and functions.

How does neuroplasticity work? Let's take the hypothetical example of Sam, who was unable to walk after a stroke, to see what normally would happen when a person sustains damage to his brain that causes the left side of his body to be weak. When a stroke occurs, blood flow decreases in a specific part of the brain, which can result in permanent damage to that area. Where this damage occurs determines what kinds of deficits a person might have. For example, if someone has a stroke in the speech area, he may have trouble speaking, whereas if he has an injury to the motor cortex (where movements are initiated), he may not be able to move parts of his body.

For Sam, the part of his brain that controls movement was damaged—that's why he couldn't walk. There was nothing wrong with his muscles or other parts of his brain. Rather, it was that some of the nerve cells involved in moving the left side of his body had died. They would never come back and could not be used again. This means that for Sam to walk again, he had to "teach" another section of the brain to take over the function of walking. This is exactly what we mean by *neuroplasticity*—assigning new functions to areas in the brain that had previously been used for something else.

If one action is repeatedly needed or requested, the brain is "taught" that the new function is important and that previously allocated brain areas need to be redirected for novel uses. Therefore, to circumvent the damaged area and allow Sam to walk again, Sam's brain had to convert areas dedicated to other movements to the task of walking. By reallocating its resources in this way, the brain prioritized the functions that are used or needed most often. For Sam, *reassigning* how certain brain areas functioned allowed him to walk again. That's truly an example of neuroplasticity in action.

In Connie's case, her hard work and effort "rewired her own brain in a rather curious way," according to Levine. What Levine expected to find and what actually happened were quite different. Since neuroplasticity typically overtakes functioning of *adjacent areas of brain tissue—on the same side as the original damage*—and assigns that adjacent tissue with a new function, Levine assumed that he would see activity in an adjoining part of Connie's *right* brain when he asked her to move the fingers of her left hand in the MRI scanner. Shockingly, this was not what happened. "What made it even more curious," Levine recalled, "was that the scan showed that the left hand had essentially 'borrowed' neuronal firepower from the area of the brain that usually controls the right hand." In essence, the left side of Connie's brain was controlling *both* her left and her right hands!

At first, this created problems for Connie because her brain was not sure which side she wanted to move. As Connie recalls, "For a long time, if I was exercising my left thumb, my right thumb would be going right along and I could not stop it. It was like the two parts were tied together." In Connie's brain, they actually were. Eventually Connie learned how to disconnect the two sides so that only one thumb moved when she wanted it to. These incredible examples of neuroplasticity—the left side of her brain taking over control of moving both of her hands and her ability to learn to separate out movement of one hand versus the other—proved to Connie that all her hard work of focusing her attention truly was rewiring her brain.

What made this feat so remarkable was that everything gleaned from Connie's brain scans and her symptoms indicated to most of her doctors that she would *never* recover *any* use of her left side. In their opinion, the part of her brain that controlled movement of her left side had been severely damaged and there was no way she would be able to walk or use her left hand again. After all, there seemed to be no location where "traditional" neuroplasticity could have reassigned the task of moving her left hand. Although they knew neuroplasticity could work wonders, they just didn't see how it would be possible in Connie's case given the damage she sustained. What they did not count on was how determined Connie was, how sharply she could focus her attention on the task at hand, and how plastic or adaptable her brain could actually be.

NEUROPLASTICITY VERSUS SELF-DIRECTED NEUROPLASTICITY—IT'S IN THE FOCUS

On its own, neuroplasticity is neither good nor bad. It simply is a brain mechanism that developed to help us adapt to our environment and survive changing conditions. The real power is in the concept of Self-Directed Neuroplasticity, because it gives *you* a say in what happens to you and how your brain is wired.

SELF-DIRECTED NEUROPLASTICITY

Using the power of focused attention, along with the ability to apply commitment, hard work, and dedication, to direct your choices and actions, thereby rewiring your brain to work for you and with your true self.

In the absence of goals and values (i.e., when it is not self-directed), neuroplasticity can be either a helper or a hindrance, depending on how you are unconsciously choosing to act and focus your attention. As you've seen before, left entirely to its own devices, the brain can direct you to act in less than optimal or beneficial ways. This is why actively focusing attention on developing new, healthy circuits is necessary to most effectively change a behavior that is impairing you. The good news is that problems caused by or made worse by maladaptive neuroplasticity can be markedly improved or solved by focusing your attention in a positive way.

In Connie's case, when deceptive brain messages led to unhealthy behaviors (e.g., not engaging in physical therapy), neuroplasticity definitely worked against her: She could not rewire her brain in ways that she wanted and her progress was halted. However, when Connie directed her attention toward her physical therapy goals and made the effort to continue exercising her left side, Self-Directed Neuroplasticity was the agent of change that assisted in rewiring her brain.

The take-home point is that neuroplasticity is operating all the time, which means that if you repeatedly engage in the same behaviors (even something as benign as checking your e-mail several times a day), neuroplasticity will designate that action as the preferred one, regardless of the effect of that behavior on you and your life. In a very real way, the actions you perform now and how you focus your attention have downstream effects on how your brain is wired and how you will automatically respond to deceptive brain messages and events in the future. Thus, for better or for worse, focused attention creates the brain you will live with, which is why we constantly stress that *the power is in the focus*.

Finding Meaning in the Face of Adversity

Connie's ability to focus her attention constructively and reject her deceptive brain messages, sensations, and habitual responses was key to her recovery. As she and Levine both acknowledged, she was able to keep putting forth sustained effort in the face of significant adversity because she designed many of her goals around things that truly mattered to her.

For Connie, finding meaning and believing in her true self are what fueled her to keep going forward. For instance, Connie's first goal in therapy "was to tie a snake in a pillowcase. Of course, they laughed," she remembers, but it was a meaningful goal to her. She has a gift with snakes and greatly enjoys working with them. As she explains, "I put snakes to sleep!" and that talent meant the zoo staff always turned to her when they had a snake that was trying to bite or wiggle away. The trick with snakes, she says, is that you need two hands to properly handle and transport them. So, Connie's physical therapists put tennis shoes in a pillowcase and had her work on learning how to tie it with her right hand at the same time as she used her left hand to keep the snake in the bag and ensure it did not get caught up in the knot. Because of her continued effort and focus of attention, Connie was able to master this skill and within weeks was back at the zoo working with the animals.

As incredible as that progress was, at the end of those initial seven weeks she still could not use her left arm or grip with her left hand very well. Prior to the stroke, Connie enjoyed a full-time career as an outreach coordinator at the zoo, spent time cooking with family and friends, swam several days a week, and had many hobbies. Losing the use of her left arm severely curtailed Connie's ability to continue most of these activities, including her position at the zoo. But Connie did not let this dampen her spirits or pull her down.

In fact, finding ways to be of value and designing physical therapy goals around things that truly mattered to her inspired Connie and gave her the motivation to keep going forward, even when she had to face her very real limitations and changes in her roles. Rather than becoming demoralized or defeated, Connie found ways to make life meaningful by taking advantage of the opportunities available to her and by fulfilling new roles, such as fielding calls from the public about animals and teaching animal handling classes to the volunteers. "It's not what I wanted to do," she remembers, "but it was helping someone" and it signaled to her that she still "had something to contribute."

Psychiatrist Viktor E. Frankl knew a lot about finding meaning in one's life, especially when facing incredible adversity. Living through confinement in concentration camps during World War II, Frankl realized that those who survived the camps were the ones who found meaning in their lives and made the most of the opportunities presently in front of them. In his insightful and moving book *Man's Search for Meaning*, Frankl quotes Nietzsche: "He who has a *why* to live for can bear with almost any *how*."[1] That *why* could include anything, but Frankl specifically felt that having a purpose, role, or making an impact were key goals that provided people with meaning when they were facing difficult situations. He saw this play out with many of the prisoners and specifically remarked that any person

---

1. Viktor E. Frankl, *Man's Search for Meaning*, trans. Ilse Lasch (Boston: Beacon Press, 1962/1963), p. 76.

who "saw no more sense in his life, no aim, no purpose, and therefore no point in carrying on . . . was soon lost."[2] Having meaningful goals and looking forward to future events, Frankl believed, is crucial in maintaining your hope and resolve when times are tough.

In addition to defining meaningful goals, determining how you will view a situation can have a profound impact on your motivation. Frankl noted this when he said, "Everything can be taken from a man but one thing: the last of human freedoms—to choose one's attitude in any given set of circumstances, to choose one's own way."[3] When faced with uncertainty or significant difficulty, including the relentless onslaught of deceptive brain messages and uncomfortable sensations, realizing that you have a choice in how you respond to the situation is critical.

While the specifics of a circumstance may be out of your control, your response is firmly within your domain—something Connie knew and embodied. This includes how you see yourself and whether you believe you are worthy of overcoming your deceptive brain messages and changing your behaviors. One way to keep going toward your goals, even when you are being bombarded by false brain messages, is to infuse meaning into your life wherever you can. As Frankl noted and Connie's story proves, having future goals is one of the best ways to achieve this.

Defining Her Goals

Connie's ability to find meaning in her life and design goals that mattered to her is exactly what Frankl was talking about. Rather than giving up, Connie designed goals that held meaning for her and viewed each difficulty as a challenge that could be overcome rather than a roadblock.

Whether it was relearning activities she enjoyed doing before the stroke, such as sewing, playing her guitar, and swimming, or prioritizing things

---

2. Ibid.

3. Ibid., p. 66.

like being independent, living life to its fullest, spending time with family and friends, and being actively involved in her church as a commissioner to the national assembly, all of her goals were related to what mattered to her. Interestingly, what is clearly absent from her list is anything pertaining to social status or financial wealth—two things that Frankl did not identify as providing truly sustaining meaning in one's life.

If we were to place Connie's goals and values into categories, they would look something like this:

Goals			Values
ACCOMPLISHMENTS	RELATIONSHIPS	LEISURE	INTRINSIC QUALITIES
Teaching	Spending time with family members	Swimming	Being independent
Calming the animals and handling them safely	Thanksgiving dinner at my house	Playing guitar	Being loving and caring
Making crate covers for the animals' cages	Church community	Sewing	Having faith
Church commissioner	Monthly dinner with friends	Cooking	Being a good person, being ethical

GOALS

- **Accomplishments:** work/career, awards/accolades, giving to others, skills, knowledge, and legacy materials (things that will remain when you are gone, such as educational materials, videos, art, and so on).
- **Relationships:** family (including children, parents, partners, siblings), friends, pets—any connection that has an emotional component and involves caring about another being.

- **Leisure time/recreation/fun/self-care:** travel, hobbies, learning for the joy of it, sports, eating better, going to the gym, and other interests that engage/inspire you.

VALUES

- **Internal/intrinsic qualities:** personal characteristics that you are proud of, such as being loving, caring, giving, courageous, honest, smart, hardworking, industrious, a good provider, and more.

Now that you understand how important meaning is when setting goals, start defining your true goals and values in the categories listed below. As Frankl notes, prior achievements are important and give our lives meaning, but when facing uncertainty and adversity—such as beginning to tackle deceptive brain messages—looking toward the future is what provides meaning and motivation to persevere when times get tough. Therefore, in this table, focus on *future goals*, not past ones that you have already accomplished.

DEFINING YOUR MEANINGFUL GOALS— HOW DO YOU WANT TO ACT?

Accomplishments:
Relationships:
Leisure/Self-Care:

Intrinsic Qualities:

When times are difficult, you need to use meaningful goals as a foundation to help you persevere through adversity. At the same time, you must muster up the effort to keep going forward, even when your deceptive brain messages are at their worst. How can you generate and maintain a sufficient level of effort to achieve your goals? Let's review some interesting scientific findings that attempt to address this question.

Where Desire Was, Effort and Expectations Will Be

Why is it that some people seem to be able to change a habit quickly or bounce back from difficulties, whereas others remain depressed, anxious, or addicted? Part of the answer clearly lies in how deeply entrenched deceptive brain messages are and how strongly the patterns are wired into the brain. Once you know that your brain wiring is a large part of the problem and that you can do something about it, what causes some people to put forth the effort to make changes while others do not?

While no one knows all the answers, David D. Burns, M.D., a psychiatrist and author of the bestseller *Feeling Good*, has an idea about what separates out those who succeed. He has been studying who will improve from a depressed state by analyzing variables that scientists and therapists have assumed were key, such as motivation, character traits, and length of depressive episode. From his work, he found that *putting forth the effort* to learn specific ways to soothe oneself (known as emotion regulation skills) and examining thought patterns (i.e., identifying and Reframing deceptive brain messages) are among the best predictors of who will improve when they are feeling depressed. In essence, *the people who are willing to put forth the effort required of them to heal tend to do better.*

This is not that surprising a finding, but here's where it gets interesting. While effort was positively correlated with good responses (i.e., the more effort, the more improvement), *desire* to feel better was actually negatively correlated with positive outcomes. In other words, strong desire to feel better without the corresponding effort actually made things worse.

DESIRE

The experience of wanting to *avoid* something unpleasant or wanting to *achieve* a pleasant result.

At first, this finding may not make much sense. Most people assume that desire is a strong motivating factor in getting you closer to your goals. While that intuitively makes sense at some level, Donald D. Price, Ph.D., a distinguished placebo researcher at the University of Florida, knows this is not the case. He has been studying the placebo response for more than twenty years and has seen firsthand how desire can actually make a person feel worse.

Through his research, Price discovered that *expectation* of a positive result—for example, expecting pain relief when an inert cream is applied— is *more important than desire* in determining how much pain relief you experience. In his studies, if a person expected a placebo cream to work, his pain was much less than when he did not expect the cream to work. Even more intriguing, when people were told they were going to receive a drug known to cause pain relief in *most* people (it was really saline) before undergoing a painful experimental procedure, they reported that their pain relief was of a similar magnitude to what one would have with a therapeutic dose of novocaine. In related non-placebo studies, Price found the same thing: If a person had low expectations, coupled with a high desire to avoid an unpleasant outcome, he actually felt worse. The key finding from Price's work is that *desire—in many cases—works against you.*

From the findings of Dr. Burns and Dr. Price, it seems clear that what you think motivates and sustains your effort may not be what actually gets you closer to your goals. Expectations, it appears, are far more important than desire in achieving results. If you, like most of the world, made the assumption that desire was key, these beliefs may be part of the reason you have not made more progress in countering deceptive brain messages in the past.

Remember what Connie described when she got so frustrated and angry—feeling overwhelmed and having a *strong desire to rid herself of the uncomfortable sensations* that were caused by her deceptive brain messages? When she could not achieve what she wanted (e.g., completing a specific therapy exercise), Connie's deceptive brain message swooped in and told her she *should* be able to do it—thereby implying that something was wrong with her. This caused the uncomfortable sensations of anger and frustration to rise in Connie—negative sensations she wanted to be free from immediately. Her desire for relief was high and her expectation of achieving her goal, which had switched from completing the therapy exercise to feeling better immediately, was low. As long as she maintained the unrealistic expectation to get rid of those uncomfortable sensations and feel better, she was stuck and would feel worse—exactly what Price found in his research studies.

Instead, when she called the sensations what they were—anger and frustration—she was able to switch gears and focus her attention on a realistic expectation, such as completing the therapy exercise one more time for the day or switching to another exercise that was similar but easier for her to complete. It was only when she applied considerable effort to focus her attention on things that mattered to her (by creating a reasonable and achievable expectation based on her meaningful goals) that she was able to move forward and change her brain.

From our perspective, deceptive brain messages are harmful because they create unrealistic expectations coupled with strong desires that cause you to act in unhealthy ways to achieve momentary relief. By trying to achieve momentary pleasure or rid yourself of an uncomfortable sensation, you engage in actions that are not consistent with your long-term goals and values. This causes you to feel worse about yourself and the situation in the end.

What is desire and why is it not the best motivator when you are dealing with deceptive brain messages? Desire truly is a form of craving for an outcome, an event, or a specific feeling. As you will learn in chapter 4, craving originates in the brain's Drive and Reward centers—two regions that are focused on self-preservation and instant gratification. Why is this problematic? Remember that the brain is constantly receiving inputs and is heavily influenced by the environment, which means desire and craving are based on the *momentary, fluctuating* signals generated by your brain. In this way, desire emanates from basic brain drives that are designed to satisfy short-term goals, not the long-term goals related to your true self.

Responding to desire indiscriminately (i.e., without awareness) is like building a house of cards. Eventually, the whole thing is going to come crashing down because desire is not based on anything constant or stable. Rather, desire and craving ebb and flow based on what is happening in the world and in your brain. Desire can easily be derailed by competing priorities, lack of rapid results, or boredom. More to the point, any specific desire that is present right now can be overshadowed by another desire that is stronger or that pops up a few moments later.[4] That is why we want you to learn how to become aware of strong desire and craving as it arises and Relabel it with Step 1.

As Connie's story shows, putting forth the effort and setting realistic expectations based on meaningful goals are critical to succeeding. How do you strengthen your resolve to put forth the effort? The first step is *seeing*

---

4. This process of desires overshadowing one another leads to what is sometimes called "Monkey Mind" in Buddhism—an inability to stay focused on your goals and instead allowing your attention to wander (or be swayed), like a monkey swinging from tree to tree.

that there is a problem and that basing your level of effort on desire or craving is a losing proposition.

With these research findings in mind, think about the ways in which desire can fail you. Desire affects all aspects of our lives, from our eating habits to relationships to work. Some ways desire can wreak havoc in your life include the following:

- Causes you to want things you cannot have (leaving you feeling sad or depressed)
- Causes you to do things that are ultimately harmful to you
- Creates unrealistic expectations that do not come true
- Prioritizes based on brain-based craving, not on what is best for you in the long run (which can cause you to lose time or not complete important tasks)
- Fails to maintain the same level of effort when times get tough or the situation seems impossible (e.g., whatever you wanted to happen isn't occurring fast enough, so you give up—a good example of this is weight loss, changing your eating habits, or exercising more)
- Competes with and overtakes other cravings (such that new cravings arise that overshadow/replace the former desire)

EXERCISE: How has desire failed you? Take a moment to write down ways that being ruled by strong desire and craving has actually worked against you.

Why is it important to list the ways in which desire can hurt you? If you cannot see how detrimental desire is, you will not be able to reprioritize your life based on meaningful goals that help you put forth the effort needed to succeed.

Defining Your Meaningful Goals

Any goal-setting agenda begins with evaluating the current state of affairs. In the case of deceptive brain messages, you need to look at the costs to you of continuing on your current path. Let's start by considering how much your behaviors and thought patterns are interfering with your life and impeding you from reaching your goals. Answering the questions below, use the goals you generated earlier in the chapter and add new ones that may have come to mind.

WHAT ARE YOU DOING THAT YOU WANT TO STOP?

(e.g., eating carbs when I am stressed out; using alcohol to calm myself after I get into an argument with someone; calling my ex-boyfriend whenever I feel lonely)

_____

WHAT ARE YOU *NOT* DOING THAT YOU WOULD LIKE TO DO?

(e.g., eating healthfully; exercising more often; spending time with friends; meditating in order to notice my thoughts and soothe myself)

_____

Now that you understand how important *effort* is in achieving your goals and that competing priorities and desires can derail those efforts, rate how meaningful each of your goals is to you on a scale of 1 to 10, where 1 = not important at all, 5 = moderately important, and 10 = extremely important (a priority in my life). Also rate how much effort you are willing to put forth or which other opportunities you are willing to forgo to achieve each of your goals using a similar scale of 1 to 10, where 1 = will not expend any effort, 5 = would be willing to work hard/give up other things 50 percent of the time, and 10 = will work hard/prioritize this over everything else 100 percent of the time. We have provided a sample chart to help you get started. (Note: Use the categories only if they are helpful to you; otherwise simply list all of your goals on page 54—but make sure you do not include desires or cravings.) We have left intrinsic qualities, such as being honest, caring, or hardworking, out of this table because they represent values that tend to not include tangible goals. They certainly provide your life with meaning, but for the purposes of this exercise we want you to focus on accomplishments, relationships, and leisure/self-care.

DEFINING MEANINGFUL GOALS

Category	Goal	How Important Is This Goal? How Much Meaning Does It Provide?	How Much Effort Will You Put into Achieving This Goal?
Accomplishments	Get that promotion at work	10	10
Accomplishments	Stop eating carbs when I am stressed out	8	7
Accomplishments	Meditate thirty minutes a day	9	10
Relationships	Spend more time with my family	10	6 (other competing priorities like work)
Relationships	Go out socially with my friends at least twice a month	7	5
Leisure/Self-Care	Go to the gym four days a week	9	7
Leisure/Self-Care	Travel within next six months	6	3
Leisure/Self-Care	Eat healthier— more greens, protein, and fiber	8	4

DEFINING MEANINGFUL GOALS

Category	Goal	How Important Is This Goal? How Much Meaning Does It Provide?	How Much Effort Will You Put into Achieving This Goal?

Category	Goal	How Important Is This Goal? How Much Meaning Does It Provide?	How Much Effort Will You Put into Achieving This Goal?

Now that you have examined what you want to change and what provides you with meaning, determine what your true priorities are at this point in your life. Using the information in the table above, prioritize each of your goals based on how important it is to you *and* the effort you will expend to achieve it—do not rank them based on your desire.

If you honestly ranked how willing you were to achieve each goal, the priority list should begin with the things you ranked highest on the Effort scale. In our example, there was a tie in terms of Effort level—both "promotion at work" and "meditation" received scores of 10. Since "promotion" also received a score of 10 on Importance, it would be ranked #1 and "meditation" would receive the #2 spot. Look at the example we provided below to get a sense of how to rank your goals.

Meaningful Goal	Effort	Importance
1. Focus on promotion at work	10	10
2. Meditate for thirty minutes every day	10	9
3. Go to the gym four days a week	7	9
4. Stop eating carbs whenever I am stressed out	7	8
5. Spend more time with my family	6	10
6. Go out socially with my friends twice a month	5	7
7. Eat healthier	4	8
8. Travel within the next six months	3	6

List your priorities here:

Meaningful Goal	Effort	Importance
1.		
2.		
3.		
4.		
5.		
6.		
7.		
8.		
9.		
10.		

In the example above, the person ranked "stop eating carbs whenever I am stressed out" as #4 on his list. Obviously, if one of the person's problems is eating carbs whenever a deceptive brain message strikes, he may need to reevaluate how unhelpful that behavior truly is and figure out ways to make that goal more meaningful so that it ends up higher on the list.

How can you change your priorities? There are no easy answers, but our patients have mentioned one powerful motivator they've used: knowledge of the brain and what it is trying to do each time a deceptive brain message strikes. As they explain it, knowing that you are not the cause of the messages or urges, but that you can do something to make your brain work in helpful ways based on your goals and values, helps a lot. In chapter 4, we will introduce you to this powerful brain biology, which has inspired many people to increase their effort levels when dealing with deceptive brain messages. For now, the important point to realize is that the desire to feel better and the willingness to put forth the effort do not go hand in hand.

Even when you are ready to put forth the effort, finding ways to integrate these activities into your day can be daunting. In fact, not having enough time is one of the biggest challenges people face when beginning any kind of change. How do you work around this problem? Let's return to Connie's story and see how she fit her therapy into her daily life.

Finding the Time

Without the structure of her physical therapist telling her what to do and when, Connie had to be creative in finding ways to integrate her therapy into her day. "I'm not a person that can set aside a half hour a day to do certain exercises," she says. "That's just not my makeup." While the physical therapists recommended traditional exercises, Connie knew she would not do them. "Their thing was: Here's a Thera-Band. Go do so many pulls this way and that way. Regular therapy. I just don't have time for that."

Instead, Connie made progress because she was willing to continue working hard to achieve the goals that mattered to her. One of these areas was related to her fine motor skills, which have never completely come back to their original level. Grip strength is the most difficult for her and it's why she does not work with many of the animals she used to enjoy, including the larger birds. To continue strengthening her left hand, Connie would deliberately choose to use the hand even when it was not necessary. In the kitchen, she would hold a tomato rather than place it on specialty prongs on her cutting board. Similarly, if she was transporting items from the kitchen to the living room, she would "figure out ways to use the left hand to help support" whatever she was doing so she could make fewer trips. Her goal was to use her left side as much as possible while also devising ways to make her activities more efficient and easier. "I am good at coming up with alternate ways to do things, I always have been," she says. "If there was an easier way to do something, I'd find it. I enjoy that kind of challenge. Thinking things through . . . How can I use my hand to make this job simpler?" Similarly, Connie would exercise the fingers of her left hand while driving and would walk whenever possible.

A key to her success was that she made exercising the left side of her body a priority and used every opportunity that presented itself to her. However, this was not obvious or easy to do at first. In fact, for quite a while, Connie had to remind herself to use the left side of her body because the thought did not spontaneously occur to her. Like most people, this was not something she had to think about before the stroke, and her Habit Center had not yet been retrained to automatically use her left side.

What does that mean for you? Connie's struggle to find the time to integrate her treatment into her daily activities is *exactly* what you need to learn how to do—with your mind. The most encouraging fact about mindfulness and the Four Steps is that they can be practiced anywhere and at any time. So, just like Connie found opportunities to use her left hand when she didn't absolutely need to, you need to find times in your day to use your mind (i.e., by practicing the Four Steps) even when it might not be absolutely required for whatever you are doing. In short, you need to be on the lookout for deceptive brain messages all day long and use the Four Steps whenever deceptive brain messages arise. We will teach you how to do this in Part Two.

What's next for Connie? Continuing to find novel ways to use her left hand so that it strengthens even further. Currently, the zoo has two unruly inhabitants that sorely need her help and that require her to use both hands to work with them. As she explains: "I take the tough animals. We have two bearded dragons that are hell on wheels. I've been working with them—they are an accident waiting to happen. They just want to get away." As Connie works with them, her brain will continue to rewire and she will be that much closer to achieving her goals.

In the next chapter, we will explore the reasons why habits are so hard to break and learn about Free Won't and Veto Power—two powerful concepts that allow you to say no to deceptive brain messages and yes to your true self.

Why Habits Are
So Hard to Break

Have you ever found yourself doing something you didn't really want to be doing and wondered why you're still doing it? For Steve, a fifty-five-year-old executive in a high-powered job, this was a daily, if not hourly, question. As one of the most revered men in the office for his intellect and ability to resolve problems, Steve had people constantly coming to him for advice. He loved the attention and thanks, but it also stressed him out. Over the years, he began to believe he was the only person in the office who knew what he was doing and that no one was taking the initiative or responsibility to deal with their problems on their own. It was frustrating and he was sick of it.

When Steve would get home, he faced more of the same. His wife and two children were always asking his opinion and wanted to include him in their activities. He never had any time to himself—no matter where he was, he felt barraged by other people's needs, which led to anger and resentment. Wanting to escape all the responsibilities and pressures of the day, he would come home, have a glass of wine, and head to the den to watch TV. Once the wine began to take effect, those upsetting emotional and physical sensations would dissolve and Steve would feel better. Given how well it worked, one drink at night eventually became two, and so on.

Although drinking wine helped Steve relax, it cost him dearly in his relationships with his wife and children. They complained that he never talked to them, that he was distant and unapproachable. Steve felt conflicted about what he was doing. He loved his family and wanted to connect with them, but he just couldn't tolerate their needs after a long day at work. If only they could be more independent, then maybe he wouldn't have to drink so much.

He got to the point where he was drinking a bottle of wine every night and was having cravings to drink alcohol during the day. Whenever he had a stressful interaction, the urge to drink was strong. At work, this created huge problems for Steve. He couldn't throw back a shot in the office, but he could have a glass of wine at lunch. Drinking this much for several months reinforced the behaviors in his brain. He wound up having cravings for alcohol all the time and found that he would drink *even when he wasn't stressed out.*

What had started as a stress reliever had taken over his life. The urges to drink were present all the time and he could not stop thinking about the next time he could have one.

How Habits Form

What happened to Steve is essentially what happens in your brain whenever deceptive brain messages strike: Focusing on the deceptive brain messages and trying to make the uncomfortable, distressing sensations go away lead to automatic, unhelpful habitual responses. How does this happen? Whenever you repeatedly respond the same way to a deceptive brain message—by focusing on and engaging in an unhealthy behavior, such as drinking alcohol to calm your nerves—you essentially "teach" the brain to always respond in the same way (i.e., with the same unhealthy behavior) whenever a similar situation, thought, or impulse arises. So, every time

Steve felt stressed, took a drink, and felt relief, his brain linked these events together. After Steve had done this enough times, the response became hardwired into his brain and he would start drinking largely without any awareness of what he was doing. In essence, the repetitive behaviors became automatic and unconscious—Steve's mind was no longer involved in determining how he would respond to stress.

In addition to teaching his brain to automatically and habitually respond the same way to a deceptive brain message, the attention he focused on these behaviors caused something else to happen: *It strengthened the brain circuits associated with drinking wine, which meant that Steve's cravings for wine increased.* This is why he began to crave a glass of wine even when he was not stressed or under the grip of a deceptive brain message.

In fact, whenever you repeatedly engage in *any* behavior (not just those related to deceptive brain messages), the brain circuits supporting it strengthen and the behavior becomes a preferred routine. If it is a helpful activity, that's fine and being aware of what you are doing is not all that important. However, when you engage in a behavior as a result of your deceptive brain messages and feel temporary relief (or in this case, an urge that results in momentary pleasure), you are actually working against yourself. We cannot emphasize this point enough: *You are making things worse, not better.* So, not only do these actions waste your time, responding to a false brain message in this way actually amplifies the intensity of the uncomfortable sensations. We call this *feeding the monster.* We've coined this phrase to highlight how critically important it is to be aware of this process and how it can try to take over your life.

What, on a biological level, feeds the monster? *Hebb's law, the quantum Zeno effect,* and *attention density.* Let's review each of them now and apply them to Steve's situation.

HEBB'S LAW

Why is it that Steve's urges to drink got stronger the more he repeated the behaviors? The answer lies in Hebb's law, which states that when nerve cells are activated in the same pattern repeatedly, they eventually form a brain circuit. Once the circuit is established, the brain areas involved in the circuit automatically respond in the same way every time a similar situation arises. This causes the circuit to become stronger—and it is how habits, such as riding a bike, learning to drink when stressed, or relearning how to walk after a stroke, are created and maintained.

HEBB'S LAW

Neurons that "fire together wire together." This means that when groups of nerve cells (or brain regions) are repeatedly activated at the same time, they form a circuit and are essentially "locked in" together.

You can think of Hebb's law as being similar to forming a new and more scenic hiking trail. Suppose a hiker is dissatisfied with the views on the original path. He wants to get closer to the scenic points and sees that several little patches have been cleared already since they are the most frequently used sites. All he needs to do is align all the little patches together so that a cohesive trail is formed. The first few times he walks around the new path, it is difficult to see where to go. The path is overgrown and difficult to traverse. In some ways, it would be easier to just go back to the original path, but it is much less direct and includes many views that are not nearly as breathtaking. So, he perseveres and continues using the new path until one day it becomes well worn. Because it is easy to follow, other hikers start taking the path as well and soon the original path grows over from disuse. A new trail is formed and becomes the preferred route. We have demonstrated this process in figure 3.1.

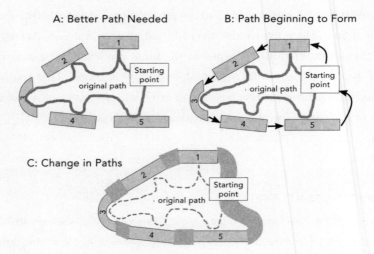

Figure 3.1. **A** represents the original path and the fledgling little patches, **B** represents the new path beginning to form, and **C** represents the new path becoming preferred while the original path withers. Note: Hebb's law is represented by the *linkages* or connections formed between the little patches, not the entire circuit (or path).

A very similar process happens in the brain. Using our hiking trail analogy, you can think of the little sections of the trail as the nerve cells or brain regions that have not been linked up yet. The more often these areas are recruited simultaneously ("fire together"), the more likely they will "wire together" and form a circuit. This is the essence of Hebb's law: *joining* brain areas together so that they work as one unit or circuit.

In Steve's case, when he combined wine with relaxation and social interactions, but did not engage in the behavior often, the circuits in his brain were weak and he did not crave wine on a regular basis. However, once he linked *wine and relief* together and repeated the behavior every night, the brain circuits began to strengthen. The more he engaged in the behavior, the stronger and more solidified that circuit became. As this happened, the Reward Center in his brain ramped up its activity and his cravings for alcohol became more intense.

How did Steve's brain learn to associate deceptive brain messages and urges with drinking? By focusing his attention repeatedly on the stress and urges to drink, Steve taught his brain that the preferred response to stress was drinking alcohol whenever he was at wit's end. This repeated focus of attention gave the quantum Zeno effect the power it needed to help stabilize brain areas so that they could wire together via Hebb's law. In doing so, the brain developed this automatic and unhealthy response to stress.

QUANTUM ZENO EFFECT

Hebb's law works only when the brain areas involved activate—and *stay activated*—at the same time. If this did not happen, the brain regions would not be able to "wire" together. What keeps the brain areas activated long enough for Hebb's law to work? The quantum Zeno effect. As originally explained by Dr. Henry Stapp of UC Berkeley's Lawrence Berkeley National Laboratory working together with coauthor Dr. Jeffrey M. Schwartz, the essence of the quantum Zeno effect is that it *stabilizes* activated brain areas and holds them in place long enough so that Hebb's law can take effect. How does it accomplish this? Via *focused attention*. This is why one of our favorite mottos is "The power is in the focus!" The cornerstone of our Four Step program is learning how to *focus your attention away* from deceptive brain messages and uncomfortable sensations and *toward* things in your life that are important to you. This is *how* the mind changes the brain and why learning how to recruit your mind to focus your attention is so critical.

In the brain, you can think of the quantum Zeno effect as being the glue that holds the brain areas in place in an activated state long enough so that Hebb's law can help form the connections needed to create new brain circuits. The main thing to remember at this point is that *attention* is the key ingredient.

Focused attention holds together and stabilizes brain circuits so that they can wire together by Hebb's law. Once they are wired together, the brain will respond to similar situations in a reliable "hardwired" way.

CREATING ENDURING BRAIN CIRCUITS WITH ATTENTION DENSITY

When acting in concert, Hebb's law, the quantum Zeno effect, and neuroplasticity explain why focusing your attention on something repeatedly causes brain circuits to form and strengthen. These brain principles explain how learning to ride a bike becomes automatic and why habits are so hard to break once they are formed. In the case of deceptive brain messages, following their false commands results in your strengthening the underlying brain circuits associated with those behaviors—circuits that cause you to act automatically and without awareness in ways that are harmful to you.

In Steve's case, focusing his attention on alcohol as a stress reliever caused his deceptive brain messages to drive responses in his brain that set up a strong, enduring brain circuit. This circuit got stronger each time he let his attention be grabbed by a destructive urge or thought. He fed the monster again and again. Eventually, with enough repeated acts of drinking to deal with stress, Steve's brain made alcohol the answer to many problems and wound up creating a huge new one in the process.

Attention Density

What gives deceptive brain messages, urges, and habits their strength? Repeatedly allowing your attention to be focused on them in a *passive* way (i.e., allowing deceptive brain messages to *control* your attention).

ATTENTION DENSITY

Repeatedly focusing your attention on something (a thought, sensation, event, response, action) over and over. The more you sustain your focus of attention on something (i.e., the denser your attention is), the more likely a specific habit will be wired into your brain.

In the brain, attention density is the first—and most important—step in creating strong, enduring brain circuits. Attention density makes the quantum Zeno effect "kick in" and causes focused attention to have powerful effects on the brain by activating Hebb's law.

Attention density is the key to stabilizing and strengthening brain circuits because attention is what drives the quantum Zeno effect. The main point is that the more you focus your attention on something, the "denser" your attention is. In Steve's case, this means that whenever he allowed his attention to be grabbed *repeatedly* by the urge to drink, his attention density increased and the corresponding brain circuits strengthened. Remember: The power is in the focus! When focus is passively applied in an unconstructive way, unhealthy habits get wired into the brain.

Why stress the concept of attention density? After the initial destructive brain message hits, you (via your mind) have the ability to determine whether you want to pay attention to it or to something else. This means that attention density can work for you or against you. When you let your attention *passively* be grabbed by deceptive brain messages, you will be stuck repeating the same unhealthy patterns and actions. However, if you *actively* choose where to focus your attention and repeatedly apply it to a wholesome, constructive activity, you will rewire your brain in healthy ways that are consistent with your true self. In this way, attention density is crucial for Self-Directed Neuroplasticity—that's why we have been spending so much time talking about turning your attention away from the deceptive brain messages and toward things that are helpful and meaningful to you.

Free Won't: Don't Believe Everything You Think (or Feel)

When Steve realized that his brain was being rewired because of his actions, he felt horrible. He believed that somehow he should have been able to control his deceptive brain messages and stop them from arising. If only he could find a way to beat the desires into submission or will them away, then he would be better and not feel the urge to drink. Sarah, the woman who became depressed and withdrew from her family when she was at her lowest point, also had these thoughts. She wanted to control the deceptive brain messages telling her she was a loser so that her depressive sensations (fatigue, lack of motivation, the urge to isolate and withdraw) and those upsetting thoughts would go away.

While this is an alluring and common thought process, it is a dangerous way to approach deceptive brain messages. The truth is you really are not in control of your deceptive brain messages or uncomfortable sensations—your brain is! This means that you cannot make your thoughts or urges disappear by using willpower alone. Trying to do so is a surefire prescription for discouragement, disappointment, and demoralization.

We see many people making this same error—much to their detriment. When Steve and Sarah believed they could control their unconscious thoughts and urges, they would mentally beat themselves up for not being stronger or better. The reality of the situation is that the brain generates these deceptive brain messages—not the mind—and none of us has a say in when or where those false messages will show up.

To help them understand that they are not to blame for their deceptive brain messages, we taught Steve and Sarah about Free Won't, a term popularized by the well-known neuroscientist Benjamin Libet. In a series of carefully executed scientific experiments completed in the 1980s, Libet studied how people decide whether and when to move their own bodies and what generated the *initial* desire to move. While the meaning of what he discovered is still the subject of passionate disagreement in academic circles, the bottom line for you is this: *Your brain—not your mind—generates the initial desires, impulses, thoughts, and sensations, but you can veto almost any action before it starts.* This means that while you are not responsible for the emergence of thoughts, desires, impulses, urges, or sensations, you *are* responsible for what you do with them once they arise.

Libet himself interpreted his results in this way and emphasized that you have a *choice* in whether or not to respond when your brain puts out the call—this is the essence of Free Won't. As he described it in one of his landmark papers:[1]

> *The role of conscious free will [aka Free Won't] would be, then, not to initiate a voluntary act but rather to control whether the act takes place. We may view the unconscious initiatives for voluntary actions as "bubbling up" in the brain. The conscious will then selects which of these initiatives may go forward to an action and which ones to veto and abort, with no act appearing.*

In other words, what Libet was saying is that you really can't decide or determine what will *initially* grab your attention—your brain does. However, his research also indicated that once your *initial* attention is grabbed, you can determine whether you keep your attention focused on that object (and act on it) or *veto it* based on the principle of Free Won't.

Free Won't turns out to be of the utmost importance because it tells us that we have, in essence, the power to *veto* almost any action, even though the desire to perform that action is generated by brain mechanisms entirely outside of our conscious attention and awareness. How might that Free Won't express itself? Through Veto Power.

---

1. Benjamin Libet, "Do We Have Free Will?" *Journal of Consciousness Studies* 6, no. 8–9 (1999): 54.

The ability to *not* act on a deceptive brain message, uncomfortable sensation, or intended habitual response.

Using Veto Power, *our minds can influence our actions* after the brain generates the initial signals and grabs our attention. For you, this means that the *brain* generates the deceptive thoughts, urges, cravings, impulses, and sensations below the level of your consciousness—and that these deceptive brain messages almost literally grab your focus. It's like when something shiny glints in the sun—you didn't cause the object to shine at that moment, but if your eye catches it, you look. It's natural and automatic—mediated by your brain—and not under your control. The same holds true for unwanted thoughts, urges, desires, and impulses: *deceptive brain messages grab your attention, and you are not responsible for that initial attention-grabbing moment.*

While that's true, Veto Power tells us you *can* and *must* veto detrimental actions generated by your brain (i.e., things that will make you feel better momentarily but that are harmful to you) if you want to sculpt a brain that works for you. This is why Step 3: Refocus aims to have you *consciously focus your attention* on wholesome, beneficial actions. Doing so not only helps rewire your brain in positive ways, it also ensures that you *do not act* on the deceptive brain messages that are harmful to you.

Veto Power, not surprisingly, is at the core of our Four Step program because it reassures you that when the brain puts out a false call, you have the power to withhold acting on that seeming command.

Armed with this knowledge, Steve began to take a hard look at his actions and his deceptive brain messages. He realized that his stress level got out of control because he could not see the deceptive brain messages—those telling him everyone else was helpless, that the only way he would be adored was if he gave people advice, and that he was drinking because everyone else was so needy—for what they were. The reality, of course, was far from what his brain was telling him. In fact, his coworkers and family could make decisions on their own and they did take responsibility for many things throughout the day—things that Steve never saw them doing. As for his drinking, he accepted that he alone was responsible for making the decision to escape reality in this way, rather than talking with people about how he was feeling or what his deceptive brain messages were falsely telling him.

Steve vowed to stop giving in to the urges and to find constructive ways of dealing with his frustration and anger. Rather than taking a drink, he would express when he was feeling stressed and would look at the situation from the more loving, rational perspective of his Wise Advocate. With time and considerable effort, Steve was able to stop drinking and stop taking on everyone's problems. Instead, he actively directed his attention toward things that mattered to him, such as going to the gym, expressing how he felt, and spending more quality time with his family.

In the next chapter, we'll revisit Kara, whom you met in chapter 1. Through her story, you will learn more about the powerful brain biology that generates the uncomfortable sensations and habitual responses associated with deceptive brain messages.

Summary

- Hebb's law: Neurons/brain regions that fire together wire together.
- Quantum Zeno effect is the glue that holds brain regions in activated states long enough for them to wire together.
- Attention density is the key ingredient to getting the quantum Zeno effect to work.
- When you repeatedly focus your attention on specific behaviors,

Hebb's law and the quantum Zeno effect create brain circuits associated with those actions.

- When you repeat the behavior numerous times, neuroplasticity helps it become the preferred action for similar situations.
- Combined, Hebb's law, the quantum Zeno effect, and neuroplasticity explain how habits get wired into your brain and why they are so difficult to change once they are established.
- How *often* (how repetitively) you focus on something determines which habits stay and which ones go.
- Cravings get stronger because these maladaptive brain circuits are being used more often.
- Free Won't tells you that you are not causing these thoughts, impulses, and urges—your brain is!
- Veto Power encourages you to resist the destructive messages and urges coming from your brain.
- When you focus your attention on constructive, healthy behaviors, your brain is rewired via Self-Directed Neuroplasticity to make those actions the preferred ones—this is how you change your brain!

CHAPTER 4

Why These Sensations Feel So Real

The Biology of Deceptive Brain Messages

In chapter 1, you met Kara, a twenty-five-year-old woman who held negative beliefs about her body image. From her story, you learned about the cycle of deceptive brain messages and began to identify how these negative communications are affecting you.

You also learned that your mind is your biggest ally. It gives you the capacity to choose where to focus your attention so that your actions align with your true self. As you've seen from the stories we've shared with you, recruiting and directing the mind is difficult, especially when you are dealing with anxiety, depression, addiction, or unhealthy habits. Why is it so hard to engage your mind and overcome the habits fueled by deceptive brain messages? The answer lies in your brain—in the way it is wired and how it functions. In this chapter, we will follow what happened inside Kara's brain whenever a deceptive message struck. Through her story, you will learn the brain areas involved and how the cycle of deceptive brain messages is maintained by some powerful brain biology.

To remind you, Kara had been dieting, bingeing, and purging since her teens. Her deceptive brain messages usually began with a negative thought about her appearance and an assertion that she was unlovable unless she was physically perfect. These thoughts caused uncomfortable emotional sensations in her—a feeling that she was "disgusting"—and she experienced a strong physical sensation to diet excessively or purge. Her distress rose until she could no longer tolerate the sensations. At that point, she gave in to the deceptive brain message by severely limiting her intake or purging. Once she did, her distress dissolved and all felt right in the world again—until another deceptive brain message struck.

Those moments of relief were few and far between because Kara's deceptive brain messages would strike often. As you now know, the more she gave in to the deceptive brain messages, the stronger the brain circuits supporting those uncomfortable sensations and habitual responses became. Kara's struggle really was about dealing with the incredibly intense and uncomfortable sensations she experienced and the habitual responses she engaged in whenever a deceptive brain message surfaced. We have referred to the process of doing almost anything to get rid of the uncomfortable sensations by automatically responding with detrimental actions as *feeding the monster* because this phrase perfectly encapsulates what is happening in the brain.

As you learned in chapter 3, the monster gets fed whenever Hebb's law and the quantum Zeno effect are working together. Learning how to make these laws work *for* you, and not *against* you, is a key to better functioning and better health. The question that remains is this: How does the monster generate these horrendously uncomfortable sensations and why do they cause you to act in ways that are detrimental to you?

Figure 4.1 depicts the process of how a deceptive brain message progresses to unhealthy behaviors and habits. After a deceptive brain message arises, you experience intensely uncomfortable sensations that can be physical (such as rapid heartbeat, shallow breathing, sweating, or cravings) or emotional (such as fear, anger, anxiety, or sadness). Because of how unpleasant and powerful the sensations are, you feel an urgent desire to make these sensations go away. As a result, you respond in an *automatic* (habitual) way that is ultimately unhelpful or unhealthy for you.

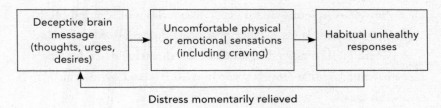

Figure 4.1. Cycle of Deceptive Brain Messages

Biology Underlying Deceptive Brain Messages and Habits

Kara described experiencing a deceptive brain message followed by an intensely uncomfortable sensation that she desperately wanted to go away. Her response to this sensation was to engage in purging, bingeing, or excessive dieting to alleviate her distress. What caused Kara's deceptive brain messages? While it is not clear exactly how deceptive messages originate in the brain, they likely have some roots in these brain areas:

- *Frontal cortex*—the part of the brain involved in strategy, organization, detecting errors, and more, also known as the *Executive Center*
- *Hypothalamus*—the part of the brain involved in hunger, thirst, sex, and other basic bodily drives, also called the *Drive Center*

Note: It is *much* less important that you know the names of where the deceptive brain messages emanate from and more important to realize why you feel the way you do once the thought emerges. We simply want to stress that the brain has a lot to do with causing these upsetting sensations—and that these sensations are not the real you.

As the deceptive brain message arose, Kara's feeling of distress intensified because one or both of the following brain areas were activated:

- *Amygdala*—responsible for generating feelings of fear and physical sensations, such as rapid heartbeat, shortness of breath, and sweating.[1] The amygdala also assesses threats and sends signals that indicate that "this is something to fear and/or to avoid" or "this is safe."
- *Insula*—responsible for generating "gut-level responses," such as dread or what many would describe as a "pit in my stomach," "gut-wrenching pain," and similar sensations.

Along with either the amygdala or insula, an adjacent area in Kara's brain was activated: the *anterior cingulate*. When the anterior cingulate is active, you can get a rapid sense that something is wrong (one famous brain researcher calls this the "Oh Shit!" area of the brain), because this brain region is intimately involved with detecting errors and assessing risks and rewards.[2]

Collectively, you can think of the amygdala, insula, and anterior cingulate as the warning center of the brain, or what we like to call the *Uh Oh Center*. When these areas are active, you can get an overwhelming sensation that something is wrong or off. As that overpowering sensation of "uh oh!" arises, you experience an incredibly uncomfortable state in which you will do almost anything, including following your old ways—your habits, avoidance, whatever it is that you normally do when confronted with a situation similar to the one presently in front of you—to rid yourself of the distress. This is when the *basal ganglia* kick into action.

The basal ganglia are responsible for your *automatic* thoughts and actions—your habits, both physical and mental. In reality, the basal gan-

---

1. The amygdala's connection to the autonomic nervous system (responsible for the fight-or-flight response) causes these physical manifestations of anxiety.

2. The *orbitofrontal cortex* is also very important in estimating risks and rewards. It works alongside and regulates the Uh Oh Center to some extent. We will discuss the orbitofrontal cortex briefly in chapter 5 when we talk about the relationship between the deceptive brain messages and your sense of self.

glia are composed of two major structures: the *caudate* (responsible for automatic thoughts) and the *putamen* (responsible for automatic actions/ movements). For the purposes of this book, we have chosen to talk about the basal ganglia as one unit because it is responsible for your habitual ways of thinking *and* your habitual actions. You can think of this as the *Habit Center* of the brain. In the case of deceptive brain messages, this means that every time you have an uncomfortable sensation that you want to get rid of, the basal ganglia are going play a significant role in determining what you do next.

Note: As we mentioned in chapter 1, we consider the repetitive, automatic thoughts generated by the basal ganglia to be habitual responses. Therefore, when we talk about the Habit Center and habitual responses, we are referring to repetitive thoughts, actions, or inaction—anything that you do repeatedly that is caused by a deceptive brain message and takes you away from focusing on something that is beneficial to you.

Once Kara's Habit Center responded in an *automatic* way to her distress, the uncomfortable sensation very briefly resolved. This created a vicious feedback loop in her brain between the Habit Center and the *frontal cortex* (*Executive Center*). The frontal cortex *passively* assembled the useless information provided by this feedback loop (i.e., the information was not sent to the attentive mind) and created a repetitive association between the uncomfortable sensation, action, and relief. The result was that the circuit supporting those actions was further strengthened and became even more automatic.

Obviously, the brain is quite complex and the intricacies of its functioning can be confusing. Distilling it down to the most important parts, figure 4.2 outlines how deceptive brain messages result in unhealthy habits (including inaction and repetitive thoughts). This figure illustrates the pattern Kara described in which deceptive brain messages result in harmful actions that bring momentary relief and strengthen harmful brain circuits. Below the descriptions are the centers involved and their associated brain regions. The arrow at the bottom of the figure demonstrates how the repeating circuit is activated over and over when the attentive mind is not engaged or recruited to make new choices.

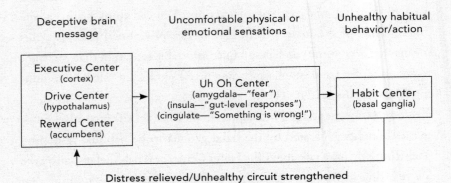

Figure 4.2. Brain Regions Involved in the Cycle of Deceptive Brain Messages

The Executive Center is composed of many brain areas that are involved in strategy, planning, organization, and detecting errors. The Drive Center is where many of our instinctual (life-preserving) drives are generated, whereas the Reward Center is involved in pleasure and obtaining rewards. The Uh Oh Center includes the amygdala (fear, including the related physical sensations of rapid heartbeat, shortness of breath, and so on), insula (gut-level responses, like the sensation of gut churning or a "pit in my stomach"), and cingulate ("Something is wrong!"—assigns emotional significance to events). The Habit Center is where the basal ganglia are located; they are responsible for automatic thoughts and actions.

ACTIONS THAT BRING US MOMENTARY PLEASURE

In this chapter, you learned how Kara's deceptive brain messages caused her to experience incredibly upsetting emotional and physical sensations that led to unhealthy habits. Her actions were mostly driven *by a desire to rid herself* of these horrible sensations. She was trying to get away from how she was feeling—to avoid feeling so bad.

What about the opposite—when you are craving something that will make you feel good (momentarily), such as candy, fried foods, alcohol, cigarettes, drugs, video games, sex, or shopping? The pattern shown in figure 4.2 is the same regardless of whether you are trying to approach something to satisfy a desire or avoid something upsetting.

Remember, we defined craving as an uncomfortable sensation and acknowledged that it is difficult for people to see how craving something that brings pleasure and feels good also is an uncomfortable sensation or experience. When people are so focused on the reward, they don't recognize the pain that precedes it. However, if you really stop and experience it, the actual craving *is* painful—your body feels off, your emotional sensations are unpleasant, and you want those sensations to go away, so you do something that makes you feel better. Once you act, you experience a rush or flood of satisfaction. It's the same process that happened in Kara's brain, but the associated relief is far more pleasurable and gratifying—which makes it all the harder to stop the behavior. This means that you truly have to see how detrimental the behavior is for you to change your ways.

The biology generating pleasure is strong for a reason—nature wants us to take care of ourselves, so it developed a region of the brain (the accumbens, also known as the *Reward Center*) to make sure you kept engaging in important survival-based activities, like eating, by making them pleasurable. The problem is many of the things we do, while pleasurable, are not good for us in the long term. Since the Reward Center is intimately connected with the Habit Center, this can mean trouble if the Habit Center is left to its own devices and we do not manage our responses in helpful ways. This is precisely how addictions and other unhealthy behaviors can spiral out of control.

Refusing to Feed the Monster

One of the most upsetting and distressing parts of deceptive brain messages is that the physical and emotional sensations feel so real and overwhelming. When your sense of self is tied to these sensations, you believe that you are the problem and that you are causing these sensations to exist because of who you are or what you crave. As you now know from learning about Free Won't, that simply is not the case. Your brain is responsible for generating these uncomfortable sensations, not you. Even more to the point, these *emotional and physical sensations are not true.* Rather, they are generated as a result of deceptive brain messages. Knowing that these sensations are false and that acting on them with habitual responses makes you worse—by strengthening the underlying brain circuitry supporting those actions—empowers you to dismiss these false sensations and urges whenever they strike. You now have a compelling reason to refuse to feed the monster each time it appears.

In the next chapter, we will introduce you to John, a man whose sense of self had fused with his deceptive brain messages to the point that he was constantly looking for reassurance that his girlfriend loved him and was committed to their relationship. Through his story, you will learn how he applied the Four Steps to overcome his deceptive brain messages, uncomfortable sensations, and habitual responses.

Summary

- Each time a deceptive brain message arises, it triggers uncomfortable sensations (physical and/or emotional) and a strong urge to engage in a habitual response.
- Acting in a habitual way in response to a deceptive brain message causes the uncomfortable sensations to subside and generates a sense of relief, but almost always causes worsening problems to develop.

- Each time that cycle of deceptive brain message → uncomfortable sensation → habit → momentary relief occurs, the underlying brain circuits are strengthened.
- As the brain circuits strengthen:
  - The deceptive brain messages occur more frequently
  - The uncomfortable sensations become more intense
  - The habits become more entrenched and harder to resist
- The brain centers supporting this cycle include:
  - Uh Oh Center, which sends out a false alarm that "something is wrong!" and generates the uncomfortable physical and emotional sensations
  - Habit Center, which is responsible for generating all automatic thoughts and actions
  - Executive Center, which organizes information, plans, and detects errors
  - Drive Center, which generates basic bodily drives
  - Reward Center, which generates pleasure and facilitates urges to seek out pleasurable activities
- When you are able to see that the uncomfortable sensations are generated by the brain, and not by you, you are empowered to make new choices and refuse to give in to the deceptive brain messages.

CHAPTER 5

A New Sense of Self

Overcoming Your Deceptive Brain
Messages with the Four Steps

In chapter 4, you learned how the cycle of deceptive brain messages plays out on a biological level. You saw that most deceptive brain messages originate in the Drive, Reward, and Executive centers and that these false messages cause the Uh Oh Center to sound the alarm—generating the uncomfortable physical and emotional sensations you experience. You also learned how those overpowering sensations lead your Habit Center to respond in automatic, repetitive ways that are detrimental to you. The end result is that the brain circuits supporting these thoughts, sensations, and habits are strengthened, making it much harder for you to resist them when they strike again.

John, a thirty-eight-year-old English teacher, knows this cycle all too well. For him, the deceptive brain messages relate to his relationship with his girlfriend, Alicia, whom he has been dating for the past two years. By all standards, they have a loving relationship and each of them is fully committed and faithful to the other. John plans to ask Alicia to marry him soon, but he has nagging—and unfounded—doubts that she might leave him at any moment.

Throughout their relationship, John's deceptive brain messages kept telling him that Alicia is "too good" for him and it is only a matter of time before she figures this out. The false messages told him that to keep her love, he needs to put her first and take care of her above all else (including himself). If he can do whatever will make her happy, maybe then she will stay. His brain has also told him that he cannot be himself, that he is not worthy of Alicia's love the way he is, and that anytime she is upset, it always is his fault.

Because of these incessant deceptive brain messages, John would experience a surge of nervous energy in his body—a heightened awareness of feeling shaky, anxious (like butterflies in his stomach), and slightly nauseated. When those physical and emotional sensations struck, John would immediately go check his e-mail or call Alicia. Why? He was looking for any evidence he could find that would prove or dispute the deceptive brain messages. Since he believed she was going to leave at any minute, checking e-mail and seeing that she sent him a message would make him feel calmer. He would relax for a few minutes and could go back to focusing on his work—at least until another round of deceptive thoughts would strike.

However, if Alicia did not respond to his most recent e-mail, John would engage in a series of mental rituals to determine if the lack of a response signified anything of importance. He would try to remember what she was doing that day in an attempt to come up with reasons for why she was not getting back to him. If he came up with a plausible reason, he would calm down. If that did not work, he would keep worrying about whether this was a sign that Alicia was about to end their relationship. These concerns would prompt him to check his e-mail again or go down the intellectual path of finding excuses for why she was not communicating with him at that moment.

John was locked in a series of habitual responses that got him nowhere and tormented him. He would keep checking e-mail or compulsively try to come up with reasons for why Alicia was busy—all the while experiencing extremely upsetting physical and emotional sensations. No matter what he did, he was never at peace and never felt reassured that Alicia was committed to the relationship. In short, John had fused his sense of self with the deceptive brain messages so that those false messages became his reality and his truth. In this chapter, we will review how this happens biologically and show you how John overcame his bad brain wiring with the Four Steps.

A (False) Sense of Self

We have been telling you that part of the reason you cannot stop engaging in unhealthy behaviors is that you have bought into your deceptive brain messages and assimilated them into your sense of who you are. Although it may be surprising, integrating your sense of self with deceptive brain messages actually has roots in your brain. Remember the Executive Center we talked about in chapter 4—the part of your brain that is involved in planning, strategy, organization, detecting errors, and making assessments? It turns out that the Executive Center has specialized regions that focus on information pertaining to "self" versus "non-self."

The middle part of your Executive Center, called the *medial prefrontal cortex*, is involved in many functions related to thinking about yourself, including your "inner monologue," envisioning your future, remembering your past, and inferring other people's states of mind. Nearby is the closely related brain structure called the *orbitofrontal cortex*, which is particularly involved in error messages and obsessions. We call this whole area the *Self-Referencing Center*, because it is focused on internal processes related to you. A key point is that the Self-Referencing Center can act in helpful or unhelpful ways. For example, when the unhelpful aspects of the Self-Referencing Center are active, you might react in an *automatic*, unhealthy way to emotional information, such as Steve drinking to dissolve stress, Ed avoiding auditions, or John repeatedly checking e-mail. You may also take things too personally.

In contrast, the helpful aspects of the Self-Referencing Center are crucial in choosing how to respond in a voluntary way to situations. This part of the brain is intimately involved in social interactions and relating to others—we use the helpful aspects of the Self-Referencing Center to grasp the inner life of both ourselves and others. Thus, there are times when we really need to use the helpful aspects of the Self-Referencing Center to relate to and understand where other people are coming from.

Compare this with the outer part of your Executive Center, known as the *lateral prefrontal cortex*, which is involved in *voluntarily* modulating the responses coming from your Uh Oh Center and overriding actions that your Habit Center wants to initiate. A key job of this part of the brain, which we call the *Assessment Center*, is to help the Self-Referencing Center not take information too personally. The Assessment Center is able to do this because it has the capacity to regulate and calm other areas of the brain, such as the Uh Oh Center, on the basis of information external to yourself and your sensations. In essence, the Assessment Center is distanced from thoughts about yourself, which makes it a very important ally of the Self-Referencing Center. In fact, when the Assessment Center combines with the helpful aspects of the Self-Referencing Center, you are better able to evaluate your deceptive brain messages from a clear perspective, which enables you not to take them too personally.

An analogy that might help put these two areas into perspective comes from the business world. Imagine a junior executive who has never worked anywhere else and who only focuses on what he knows from his experiences at this company—this is the Self-Referencing Center. Compare this with an experienced senior partner who has worked extensively in the outside world and can rationally evaluate the entire organization because of her wide array of knowledge and experience. This is the Assessment Center. When they combine and balance their perspective and knowledge, they can powerfully shape the company in beneficial ways.

Figure 5.1 reviews these two brain areas in more detail.

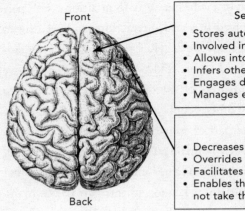

Front

Self-Referencing Center

- Stores autobiographical information
- Involved in daydreaming about the future
- Allows intospection about self
- Infers others' states of mind
- Engages during social interactions
- Manages emotions automatically

Assessment Center

- Decreases emotional responses
- Overrides the Habit Center
- Facilitates voluntary emotion management
- Enables the Self-Referencing Center to not take things too personally

Back

Figure 5.1. Self-Referencing and Assessment Centers

These Emotional Sensations Are Not You!

How is it that your sense of self has been linked so tightly with your deceptive brain messages? One likely reason is that the brain wiring for the Self-Referencing Center is *strongly tied* to the Uh Oh Center. Although this relationship between the Self-Referencing Center and the Uh Oh Center is beneficial in many respects, when these two areas are too tightly connected, you have trouble seeing yourself as distinct from your deceptive brain messages and emotional sensations. Remember what Ed and Sarah talked about—that inability to see life and what is happening as it truly is? The intense connection between the Self-Referencing Center and the Uh Oh Center likely is responsible for that sensation or belief.

When the brain wiring for the Self-Referencing Center and Uh Oh Center becomes too tightly locked together *in an unhelpful way*, it becomes difficult to evaluate reality from an outside perspective (like the Assessment Center can do with the Wise Advocate's help and direction). This means that when the Uh Oh Center's alarm goes off, telling you something is terribly wrong, the unhelpful aspects of the Self-Referencing

Center cause you to conclude that the problem is with or about you. (Note: This includes threats in your environment, both emotional and physical.) This happens because the Self-Referencing Center is constantly referring back to you and acts automatically. When it is acting in unhelpful ways, it is not taking in all the information from the environment or processing things in a purely rational way; consider, for example, when John's brain incorrectly assumed that Alicia was leaving him.

The intense connection between the unhelpful aspects of the Self-Referencing Center and Uh Oh Center causes you to believe that your physical and emotional sensations are true. As this happens, you begin to think, "These thoughts and feelings *are me . . .* this is *who I am*." The problem with this approach is that you are unable to incorporate other relevant information, consider alternative explanations, or conclude that the situation has nothing to do with you—ultimately limiting your options and responses.

For example, when Sarah was at work, she would often find herself thinking, "Wow, I really didn't like how that person talked to me," or "That was inconsiderate." When supervisors were "abrupt, abrasive, or a little blunt" in offering her feedback, Sarah would feel attacked. She'd leave the interactions feeling confused and shaken up, thinking that people were being cruel for no reason. In most cases, she would then replay the botched interaction over and over in her head, hoping to come to some sort of resolution. She never did. Instead, she would become anxious and conclude that something was wrong with her.

In those moments, Sarah was not considering the possibility that her boss was having a bad day and that his reaction had nothing to do with her at all. Why did she ignore this possibility? The unhelpful aspects of her Self-Referencing Center were filtering out any information that could have helped her reach an alternate conclusion about why he was acting that way. At the same time, her Uh Oh Center was pumping out strong sensations that something was terribly wrong. In reality, nothing was wrong with her. The Uh Oh Center was generating a *false alarm* based on deceptive brain messages. However, because Sarah's deceptive brain messages were making her take things too personally, she concluded that the overpowering sensations coming from her Uh Oh Center had to be real and correct and that the problem must be with her.

With the unhelpful aspects of the Self-Referencing Center in charge, Sarah's Assessment Center could not help her see the larger picture and take in other pieces of information that would have been relevant to her, such as the fact that her boss had just finished having an argument with his girlfriend on the phone and was upset about that interaction. With the mind-set that she was the problem and that the deceptive brain messages and sensations defined her reality, Sarah was not using her Wise Advocate and therefore was not able to use her Assessment Center to its fullest potential. Rather than acting in a voluntary way and choosing the best course of action, Sarah's natural instinct was to alleviate her discomfort. This caused her Habit Center to kick in. As a result, she repetitively thought about ways to make things better (an automatic and habitual response), when in reality there was nothing she could do because she was not the problem.

This same process occurred in John, too. Rather than being able to remember all the ways Alicia had demonstrated her love and commitment to him and believe what he knew in his heart to be true—that she loved him and wasn't going anywhere—John constantly checked e-mail and doubted reality. The unhelpful aspects of his Self-Referencing Center took over and his Uh Oh Center made him feel horrendously anxious and scared most of the time. As a result, he responded in automatic and harmful ways.

We've depicted the process of the unhelpful aspects of the Self-Referencing Center taking over in figure 5.2. Here you can see that when the deceptive brain messages are in full force, the unhelpful aspects of the Self-Referencing Center are active, whereas the Assessment Center is relatively passive or dormant (shown as dashed boxes and dashed arrows).[1] When this happens, it is difficult to use your Assessment Center to calm the Uh Oh Center or to stop the Habit Center from engaging in a behavior that is unhelpful to you. Instead, you respond to the deceptive brain messages because you perceive that these sensations are a part of you, who you are. Your Uh Oh Center's alarm goes off and your Habit Center acts in its usual, unhealthy automatic ways.

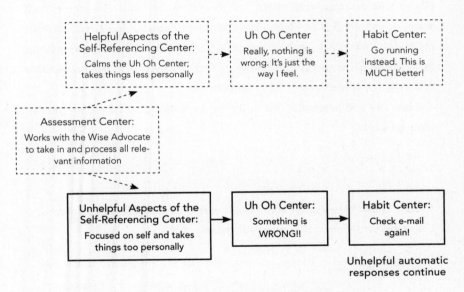

Figure 5.2. Unhelpful Aspects of the Self-Referencing Center in Charge

Figure 5.2 demonstrates how the unhelpful aspects of the Self-Referencing Center can drive the Uh Oh Center and Habit Center to perform unhealthy actions in an *automatic way* when the Assessment Center is quiet. In John's case, the deceptive brain messages made him con-

1. When we talk about either the Self-Referencing Center or Assessment Center being "active," we are referring to relative levels of activation as seen in brain imaging scans. In reality, the Self-Referencing and Assessment centers are working all the time. The key distinction is which one is *more* active at one time—this strongly influences which function the brain is performing.

stantly check his e-mail. Once his Habit Center responded in this way, the brain circuit supporting these deceptive brain messages, sensations, and habitual responses strengthened and checking e-mail whenever he thought Alicia was leaving became his brain's preferred, automatic response.

As figure 5.2 indicates, as long as you rely on the automatic responses coming from your Self-Referencing and Habit centers, this cycle will repeat over and over, resulting in the same unhealthy behaviors. Worst of all, because of underlying principles governing the brain that you learned about in chapter 3 (i.e., Hebb's law and the quantum Zeno effect), repeating the behaviors causes the circuits associated with those deceptive brain messages to get stronger and stronger. This is why it is so hard to break a habit once it gains a foothold in your brain.

How can you overcome this problem? Let's return to John and find out what he did.

THE FOUR STEPS

Step 1: Relabel—Identify your deceptive brain messages and the uncomfortable sensations; call them what they really are.

Step 2: Reframe—Change your perception of the importance of the deceptive brain messages; say why these thoughts, urges, and impulses keep bothering you: They are *false brain messages* (It's not ME, it's just my BRAIN!).

Step 3: Refocus—Direct your attention toward an activity or mental process that is wholesome and productive—even while the false and deceptive urges, thoughts, impulses, and sensations are still present and bothering you.

Step 4: Revalue—Clearly see the thoughts, urges, and impulses for what they are, simply sensations caused by deceptive brain messages that are not true and that have little to no value (they are something to dismiss, not focus on).

Not Taking Your Deceptive Brain Messages at Face Value

Although John was not aware of the processes occurring inside his brain, he knew he was miserable, felt powerless, and wanted to find a solution. He was often in a state of fear and was spending most of his time thinking about and taking care of Alicia, even though she did not want him doing this. He never spent time or energy on himself and led a very unbalanced life. John's problem, as you now know, is that he had no idea how to engage his Wise Advocate to recruit his Assessment Center so that it could make decisions that were in his overall best interest.

Then, as luck would have it, John was introduced to the Four Steps. He learned how to identify his deceptive brain messages (Step 1: Relabel) and became more curious about and open to whatever thoughts passed through his head. By becoming more aware, John was able to be increasingly attentive to the thoughts and began to notice the deceptive brain messages when they emerged. With time, he could see the links between the negative messages telling him Alicia was about to leave, the distress these thoughts caused, and his response of constantly checking e-mail as a way to reassure himself.

As he continued using the Four Steps, he began to change his relationship with the deceptive brain messages and was able to see these false messages for what they were—"useless chatter, not reality" (Step 2: Reframe). When those uncomfortable feelings would emerge and instigate an urge to check his e-mail, John would remind himself that these physical and mental sensations were the result of deceptive brain messages and were not a reflection of his true self, reality, or the kind of relationship he wanted to have with Alicia.

How did he accomplish this? John's ability to step outside what his deceptive brain messages were telling him and believe in himself so that he could make better decisions was due to believing ever more strongly in his Wise Advocate. You can think of the Wise Advocate as an inner guide and friend that you can use to help determine which information to pay attention to and which information to disregard—especially when doubt or other strong sensations are overwhelming you. In many ways, the Wise Advocate is supported by the Assessment Center. Indeed, you can think of the Assessment Center as the Wise Advocate's executive arm. The major difference between them is that the Assessment Center is a physical brain region that processes information, whereas the Wise Advocate is a cognitive construct and mental aide to help you determine what information is truly relevant and important. In these ways, the Wise Advocate and Assessment Center support decision-making processes by first ensuring that all possible explanations are considered and erroneous messages are discarded.

What happened in John's brain when he used his Wise Advocate? John started recruiting his Assessment Center and quieting the unhelpful aspects of his Self-Referencing Center, the area that was generating all the "useless chatter" and was so strongly linked to his Uh Oh and Habit centers. As the Assessment Center lessens the Uh Oh Center's alarm system, the activity in the unhelpful aspects of the Self-Referencing Center and Uh Oh Center decrease. This means that John does not take things so personally. As this happens, the Habit Center's automatic response to engage in an unhealthy behavior is partially blocked. The result is that the brain circuit supporting those automatic responses is weakened and John is more frequently able to veto the urge to check his e-mail.

Overcoming Your Deceptive Brain Messages: Making Choices and Rewiring Your Brain

At the beginning, John's Wise Advocate was weak and not fully formed. After all, John had been paying attention to the content of his deceptive brain messages and the false alarm coming from his Uh Oh Center for years. It was only when he became adept at recognizing the deceptive brain messages and learned how to pay less attention to the Uh Oh Center when it set off that false alarm that things began to change. Although it was difficult, John learned not to fight the uncomfortable sensations and he did not try to make them go away. Instead, he let those sensations exist, paying as little attention to them as possible, while he continued with his day.

His final breakthrough occurred when he realized that checking e-mail often fueled the thoughts and escalated his behaviors, rather than decreasing them. With this insight, he finally understood why Step 3: Refocus emphasizes engaging in another behavior that *requires you to focus your attention* while the uncomfortable sensations are present. He could not do anything about the fact that the anxiety was there, but he could choose how he responded by not giving in. That's when he made a commitment to quit engaging in these behaviors altogether. He replaced those unhealthy habits with constructive actions, such as meditating, taking walks, and focusing on things that were important to him. As he learned to focus his attention in new, healthy ways, his brain rewired accordingly. He was able to focus on his work or spending time with Alicia, rather than worrying about what her intentions were. In short, he wired new healthy responses into his Habit Center.

Now, John's brain responds more like what is shown in figure 5.3 on page 94.

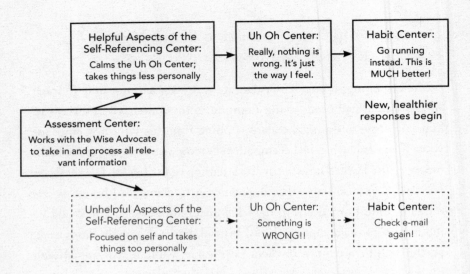

Figure 5.3. Wise Advocate Strengthened and in Control

As shown in the figure, the Assessment Center is now ordering new healthy behavioral responses—based on decisions made by the mind with the help of the Wise Advocate. The unhelpful aspects of the Self-Referencing Center and the Uh Oh Center have quieted down, which means the frequency and intensity of the alarms coming from the Uh Oh Center have decreased.

John's commitment to himself paid off. Now, whenever that old message comes along telling him that Alicia is leaving and that he must check his e-mail immediately, with Step 4: Revalue, John rapidly identifies it as nothing but a deceptive brain message, and he moves on. As he explains, once he is able to see what's happening, he uses Step 4 to remind himself that he does not have to let the deceptive brain messages "run my life or take over anymore." So now even if he has an uncomfortable feeling or urge to act on a deceptive brain message, John uses his mind to direct his attention elsewhere and deflate the importance of the nagging thoughts and urges. With the help of his Wise Advocate and the Assessment Center, John's mind is in charge, not his brain. He has begun to act in ways that make his Habit Center work *for* him, not *against* him.

Self-Directed Neuroplasticity: A Basis for Hope and Motivation

John's triumph over his deceptive brain messages is amazing because it actually rewired his brain in the process. By choosing different responses and learning how not to take his deceptive brain messages at face value, John utilized *Self-Directed Neuroplasticity,* just as Connie did, to heal himself.

How can you apply Self-Directed Neuroplasticity to your situation? Let's review what you have learned about the brain and identify what approaches work from a biological perspective.

The goal of Self-Directed Neuroplasticity is to weaken brain circuits associated with unhealthy habits and strengthen those that support healthy actions. To lead a healthier life and weaken those unhealthy brain circuits, you need to break the cycle Kara described in chapter 1 and that hopefully you now easily recognize:

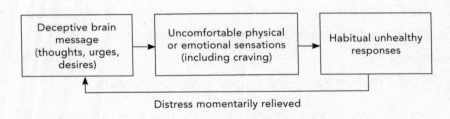

Figure 5.4. Cycle of Deceptive Brain Messages

Of course, you could attempt to break the chain anywhere along the line—at the level of deceptive brain messages or uncomfortable sensations or behaviors. However, as you have already learned, it is virtually impossible to stop your thoughts from coming or not experience a physical or emotional sensation once they arise because your brain is generating them. In fact, one of the central tenets of our Four Step program is this: *You should not try to stop the thoughts or sensations from arising—instead you should learn how to work around them.*

How do you work around the thoughts and sensations? By concentrating on the one thing you have the most control over: your actions and your ability to focus your attention on things that matter to you. As you have seen, paying attention to or responding to the deceptive brain messages makes them occur more frequently and results in your experiencing more intense physical and emotional sensations. If instead of responding to the negative messages you learn how to dismiss and not act on them, as John did, you will weaken the strength of those brain circuits and build healthier circuits in their place. That is the goal of the Four Steps—to teach you how to disregard the erroneous messages coming from your brain and instead *focus your attention on things that are genuinely important to you.*

Easier said than done—we know that from a vast amount of real-life experience with people who have successfully worked to conquer their own "bad brains." When the deceptive brain messages and sensations are strong, as they usually are at the beginning of using the Four Steps, it is extremely difficult to change the meaning and significance of these messages. That's why focusing your attention on adaptive alternative behaviors, and not the messages or sensations, is so important.

The Four Steps and Emerging Research

John succeeded because he was able to use the Four Steps to become aware of his deceptive brain messages and consistently change his behaviors. John healed himself using the Four Steps and so will you. In this way, John's story is yours and his journey is the same one you will be embarking on.

Let's review the keys to John's success:

- He used awareness (mindfulness) to *identify* (Step 1: Relabel) and *reevaluate* (Step 2: Reframe) the content of his deceptive brain messages as "useless chatter."
- He chose to stop engaging in unhelpful behaviors that were hurting him and replaced them with healthy ones (Step 3: Refocus).

- He learned to *focus his attention away* from the erroneous content of his deceptive brain messages (Step 3: Refocus) and deflate their meaning (Step 4: Revalue).

Most important, John did all of this while experiencing significant distress: At first and for quite a while, his Uh Oh Center was wildly firing, trying to tell him something was terribly wrong. That is, until he was able to use his Wise Advocate to reliably recruit his Assessment Center and diminish the importance he placed on the Uh Oh Center's alarm and its corresponding unsettling sensations. His perseverance and commitment to change worked. With time, his deceptive brain messages decreased in intensity and frequency because he had weakened the brain circuits associated with them and had learned how to see the deceptive brain messages as a nuisance, rather than a harbinger of the truth.

Let's review what John learned:

WHAT DOESN'T WORK
- You cannot control the initial thoughts or stop them from coming.
- You cannot block the physical or emotional sensations or stop them from arising.
- The more you pay attention to the deceptive thoughts and uncomfortable sensations (and try to make them go away—which is the primary way you inadvertently focus attention on them), the worse they get:
  - The frequency of the deceptive brain messages increases.
  - The intensity of the uncomfortable sensations increases.
- The more you engage in an unhealthy behavior, the stronger the brain circuits supporting that behavior become. This makes it much harder to break the habit once it forms.

- You can choose how you respond to a deceptive brain message or uncomfortable sensation.
- You can learn to change the meaning of deceptive brain messages and sensations.
- You can learn various techniques to manage your emotions and decrease the intensity of the sensations.
- You can focus your attention on what is important to you, not solely the messages coming from your brain.

Encouragingly, an explosion of scientific research in the past ten years substantiates what John did, how it changed his brain, and why our Four Step program works so well. We will discuss some of these findings in Part Two, when we explain the Four Steps and the skills needed to master them. For now, we simply want you to be familiar with these findings:

- Labeling an emotion (as in Step 1: Relabel) increases the activity of the Assessment Center and quiets the unhelpful aspects of the Self-Referencing Center and the Uh Oh Center's false alarm.
- Reframing a situation (as in Step 2: Reframe)—seeing it from another perspective or in a different context—activates the Assessment Center and further calms down the Uh Oh Center's false alarm.
- Mindfulness—using the Four Steps as you focus your attention on moment-to-moment experiences (staying focused on what is really happening right now, rather than focusing on the dialogue of the Self-Referencing Center)—activates the Assessment Center and the helpful aspects of the Self-Referencing Center.

We will begin Part Two, "The Skills," with chapter 6, where we will explore where many of our most deeply held deceptive brain messages come from: our experiences in life and especially our childhood.

Summary

- The Self-Referencing Center can be helpful or unhelpful, depending on how it is activated.
- The Assessment Center works with the Wise Advocate to take in and process all relevant information.
- The Assessment Center supports the Wise Advocate and acts as its executive arm.
- The Wise Advocate is a guide that helps you see the larger picture. It recruits your Assessment Center so that you can learn to dismiss the deceptive brain messages, not take things too personally, and ignore the false alarm coming from your Uh Oh Center.
- Together, the Wise Advocate and the Assessment Center empower you so that you can make decisions that are rational, in your best interest, and aligned with your true self.
- The Four Steps are scientifically grounded, rooted in mindfulness, and teach you how to:
  - Accurately identify your deceptive brain messages, sensations, and habits
  - Reframe the meanings of deceptive brain messages and the alarms coming from the Uh Oh Center
  - Focus your attention on healthy, constructive behaviors
  - Strengthen your Wise Advocate
- When you use the Four Steps on a consistent basis, you literally rewire your brain based on your actions: The brain circuits associated with unhealthy behaviors wither while the circuits supporting healthy habits are strengthened. This occurs as a result of Self-Directed Neuroplasticity, Hebb's law, and the quantum Zeno effect.

PART TWO

The Skills

CHAPTER 6

Ignoring, Minimizing, and Neglecting

How Deceptive Brain Messages Distort Your View of Yourself

At the beginning of her work with the Four Steps, Sarah, the bright young public relations specialist, came to us in a very frustrated state and launched into a story about an interaction she had with her boss that she could not get out of her head. They had been working on an important press release and Sarah had done everything right. Her boss had told her the release looked amazing and that she had done a great job. He assured her that the client would be "quite happy" and then mentioned that next time she should try to get the job done earlier so that they did not have to scramble at the last minute to get everything done.

Devastated by his one corrective comment, Sarah felt "deflated," like all the energy had drained from her body, and she could not hold the positive comments he made about her efforts in her mind. She had worked very hard and even stayed late the day before to make sure everything was done perfectly. Although she did not say anything to him, she knew the reason they were running around at the eleventh hour was that her boss kept making changes up to the very last minute. It wasn't her fault the press release was going out so late; it was his inability to be clear about what he wanted in the first place that caused the delay.

Despite knowing this, Sarah kept doubting herself, running the events of the day through her head and wondering what she could have done differently. She blamed herself and felt horrible about her work. Rather than giving herself credit for what she did right and accepting that unpredictability can throw a wrench in the best-laid plans, she berated herself and said, sadly, "I felt like a loser yet again."

When she finished, we asked Sarah why she didn't thank her boss for the advice and realize that the reason the project was late was because of him. In other words, why did she take his comments so personally? She seemed startled by this question, almost as if it was coming from left field. "But he's my boss," she replied. "I have to do whatever he asks in the way he asks for it. In fact, on the way over here, I realized I should have been able to figure out what he wanted or that I should have picked up on the clues better. Maybe I just wasn't paying attention well enough; maybe he did tell me what he wanted and I just missed it. Either way, I was the problem—it must be my fault."

When we pointed out to Sarah that her belief that she needed to be perfect was a deceptive brain message and that she was minimizing her abilities and contributions by wholeheartedly buying into his version of events, she became visibly upset. She said in all seriousness, "I know what my brain is doing, but what I really want to know is *why* do I overanalyze and overthink every interaction I have? Why can't I just drop it and move on with my life?"

Throughout the years, many patients have asked us this same question: If the deceptive brain messages are false and not me, then where did they come from? Why are they there? All too often, people want to know: Are the deceptive brain messages and unhealthy habits the result of my biology, childhood, environment, bad luck, or something else?

Our response always begins in the same way: Humans are incredibly complicated beings and there is no one-size-fits-all answer. Biology and environment interact in complex ways to shape how we think and what we do. That said, we tell people that most deceptive brain messages arise from our incredible ability to absorb information—how we learn and adapt in healthy *and* unhealthy ways—especially in childhood.

To Sarah, this intuitively made sense, but she still couldn't help wondering where some of her most entrenched deceptive brain messages came from. She knew she often felt like a "loser," especially when her boss corrected her, but believed she had a good childhood and that her parents were great. "No one yelled at me or beat me, they were around, we lived a comfortable life . . . what is there to complain about?" she asked. She had a good group of friends and did not remember having problems at school. She was active and engaged in life as a child, so "there was no reason I should think like this," she said.

When we encouraged Sarah to pay attention to the negative comments in her head and put a name, voice, or face to them whenever they arose, a surprising thing happened. She started to remember an incident with her older brother when she was six years old. It was a hot summer day and the family had gone out to get ice cream. Sarah loved mint chocolate chip in a sugar cone and could not wait to have one—it was always a special treat. Once everyone had their ice cream, the family sat at a picnic bench and dug in. Unfortunately, Sarah dropped her cone on the ground by accident. She immediately became embarrassed when her brother started laughing at her and mocking her. He loudly announced what she had done and told her she was a "useless, pathetic loser." Not helping matters, her mother responded by telling Sarah that the consequence of not paying attention was that she would have to go without any ice cream that night. Perhaps, her mother mused aloud, this would be a lesson to Sarah that she needs to be more careful—otherwise, she will miss out on things in life and people will not trust her to be responsible or worthy of important tasks.

When Sarah was able to see how something that seemed so inconsequential actually had a significant impact on her, she could properly place her deceptive brain messages in context. With that insight, she was able to understand that the negative thoughts about being a loser likely stemmed from *repeated* seemingly insignificant interactions like those when she was a child and that her reactions to her boss emanated from the same place. Realizing that the way she was treated as a child was still affecting her helped her separate those deceptive and false messages of the past from who she really was—a bright, young professional who was absolutely capable and reliable.

We All Have Genuine Needs and True Emotions

Why would inaccurate messages from the past leave such an impression on Sarah? How did she learn to incorporate these deceptive brain messages into her psyche and adopt them as markers of who she was? The answer, we told her, lies in the fact that we are powerfully shaped and affected by our sincere desire and need to connect with people on an emotional level. Especially as children, we want and need the important people in our lives—the ones who are caring for and protecting us—to genuinely hear, see, understand, and accept us. This is what makes us feel safe and allows us to explore our world from a secure position. This sense of safety and security is what also enables us to share our true emotions and needs as we travel through our lives.[1]

Our first—and most important—bonding relationship was with our caregivers,[2] those people whom we relied upon to provide virtually everything to us when we could not provide it to ourselves, including comfort, safety, food, shelter, love, and affection. In essence, we sought them out for all of our fundamental physical *and* emotional needs and looked to

---

1. The importance of attachment and the ability to develop close, healthy bonds with others was first emphasized by John Bowlby, M.D., and later refined by Mary Ainsworth, Ph.D., and many others.

2. For simplicity, we refer to all the important people in your childhood as *caregivers*, because in some way they represented people who you expected to keep you safe and comforted as a child. We recognize that the important people in your life could have included grandparents, aunts/uncles, siblings, cousins, teachers, coaches, friends, troop masters, and so on.

them to provide us with an emotional safe zone, a place where we felt protected from the dangers of the world. With this supportive environment in place, we could learn how to express our deepest true emotions and spend the majority of our time learning, growing, and exploring our environment in ways that allowed us to become independent adults capable of navigating the world in healthy, adaptive ways.

In addition to providing us the security to explore and grow (i.e., what children are supposed to be encouraged to do), our caregivers were our first models for how we should treat ourselves and the people around us. From them we learned how love is expressed, what we should and should not do, how we should think about and view ourselves, what we deserve in life, and so on. These messages are what we carry into adulthood and use to define our sense of self—our concept of who we are.

Safe Zones Help Us Process True Emotions Constructively

That emotional safe zone in childhood was critical because it provided you with the necessary training ground to learn how to deal with your true emotions, such as anger, sadness, grief, fear, happiness, and anxiety, in a constructive, loving way. It is in this space that you would have been taught that allowing and expressing (rather than suppressing) your true needs and emotions was a caring, healthy act.

How would you have learned this? From how your caregivers treated you and others in your life (including themselves). If your caregivers were relatively emotionally available and responded to your needs and emotions most of the time, you felt soothed and safe, understood and loved. For example, if you cried when you fell and your mom[3] showed concern and caring for your scared, sad feelings while also not becoming overly dra-

---

3. In this case, we are using Mom as the example, but as we have said previously, the caregiver can be anyone whom the child cares about and wants to seek safety and comfort from.

matic, upset, or alarmed by the event, you would have walked away from that experience calm and comforted—and your Uh Oh Center would have been soothed by your mom's interest, love, caring, and affection.

This loving action by your mom would have taught you that your true needs and emotions were important and would have provided you with examples of how to choose healthy responses to soothe yourself when you are upset or dealing with difficulties. If you had many such experiences, you would have grown up firmly knowing that your true emotions, needs, and interests mattered and that it was safe and acceptable to express them with the important people in your life. This ability to acknowledge your true emotions and needs—and to interact with people in genuine, honest, and loving ways—would have kept your Uh Oh Center relatively quiet most of the time, unless of course you were in real danger.

"GOOD ENOUGH" CARETAKING— THE 50 PERCENT MARK

Our caregivers did not have to be perfect, but we did need them to respond to our needs, emotions, and interests in a genuine, interested way most of the time—or acknowledge and apologize for the times when they failed to meet our true needs.

Conversely, if our caregivers did not respond to our legitimate cries, overreacted whenever something happened, disregarded or minimized our true fears, smothered us, catastrophized about what might happen, used our needs to control us, or did not show interest in our activities, lives, or emotions, these actions would have led us and our brain to conclude that our genuine thoughts, emotions, interests, and feelings did not matter. It also would have signaled that we were not safe, which would have caused our Uh Oh Center to fire often. This repetitive firing of our Uh Oh Center would have led to chronic distress and anxiety that the brain would have tried to calm with unhealthy habits.

In short, we needed our caregivers to do their best, to be "good enough," by responding to our needs, concerns, and fears with love, attention, and affection at least about 50 percent of the time. If they were able to do this, we felt safe, our Uh Oh Centers were calm most of the time, and we took away from our childhood healthy ways of coping and responding to stress. If they could not, we left childhood with many deceptive brain messages, a chronically firing Uh Oh Center, and many unhealthy ways of behaving and coping in the world.

Most Deceptive Brain Messages Are Learned

What if the opposite happened when you fell? What if your mom, who was completely overwhelmed and stressed herself, became annoyed with your tears, told you to "suck it up," dismissingly said it was "no big deal . . . stop being a crybaby," or devalued, ignored, minimized, or neglected your genuine reaction in some way? What would your kid brain take away from that reaction if it happened once? Would you feel calm, safe, and soothed, or would you begin to equate expressing true emotions and needs with danger? How would you make sense of her reaction? What if this occurred many times throughout your childhood?

This is exactly what happened for Sarah. At key moments, when she needed people to understand and attune to her needs and emotions, she unfortunately received a very different message—that she would be loved and accepted only when she was "perfect" and did not bother anyone with her true emotions or needs. These repeated interactions left Sarah seeing herself as a "burden," someone who was not worthy of unconditional love, acceptance, and affection.

If you are like Sarah and had many such interactions as a child, you would have become chronically anxious and concluded that the problem was somehow related to you, not the important caregivers in your life. Although Sarah's mom and brother loved her and truly did want the best for her, they had their own limitations that Sarah's growing brain simply could not incorporate into her thinking process. She could not see that their inability to be emotionally available, respond to her true needs adequately, or acknowledge or apologize when they had made a misstep had nothing to do with her.

Instead of being able to see that it was not her fault that she was not receiving the care, love, attention, affection, and interest she—and every child—deserved, she received the message that her true emotions and needs did not matter. Her directive in life, so her young brain thought, was to devalue or neglect her true emotions and needs, just as her caregivers did. This is how her deceptive brain messages were born and how Sarah learned to second-guess and demean herself whenever her needs and true emotions emerged or when she thought she was disappointing someone important to her, like her boss.

Habitually Ignoring, Minimizing, and Dismissing Your True Needs and Emotions Is Painful

Another consequence of being chronically ignored, minimized, dismissed, neglected, and devalued, as Sarah knows all too well, is that it causes deep pain and sadness to develop. In response to such treatment and a perceived threat to her safety (i.e., that her caregiver might not be available to her), Sarah's young brain learned to suppress these hurt, sad, and angry feelings related to not having her true needs met. To deal with this dilemma and keep herself "safe," Sarah's brain learned to mask and replace those deeply painful feelings with deceptive brain messages, anxiety, depression, panic attacks, and overthinking. This was ostensibly done to ensure that her caregivers did not abandon her.

Although the deceptive brain messages and unhealthy responses kept her from having to deal with that genuinely deep sadness and pain, they also caused her Uh Oh Center to fire often and resulted in her spending most of her time anxious, depressed, or filled with self-doubt. No matter the response, she was stuck, living under the thumb of deceptive brain messages, unable to approach life, and especially her true emotions and needs, from the loving, caring perspective of her Wise Advocate. Instead, she went through life assuming that she was the problem, unable to see herself as a person deserving of love, compassion, understanding, and caring, and firmly believing that her deceptive brain messages were true.

If you are like Sarah, this stifling and unhealthy approach to your true emotions and needs also was fueled and maintained by the deceptive brain messages you learned in childhood. Like everyone, you have a sincere need to be seen, heard, understood, and loved for who you are and you wanted to be able to connect with the important people in your life by being able to express your true emotions and needs to them. Unfortunately, the deceptive brain messages kept you from believing you were worthy of such genuine connections, which led to considerable pain, sadness, and grief that you continue to carry with you to this day.

This means that the more you squelch your true needs and emotions, the more the deceptive brain messages are fueled and the more entrenched they—and their associated responses of anxiety, depression, excessive anger, addictions, unhealthy habits, and miscommunication—will become. That is, unless you do something to change your perspective on those deceptive brain messages, allow your true self, emotions, and needs to arise, and begin to see yourself from the loving, caring view of your Wise Advocate.

Your Brain Was Sculpted by How You Learned to Deal with True Emotions and Needs

In chapter 3, we taught you that the power is in the focus and that repeatedly focusing your attention is what stabilizes brain circuits so that they can wire together. This means that if your caregivers repeatedly focused their attention in loving, caring ways on your genuine needs and emotions, you would have learned to do the same thing. In that scenario, your brain would have learned that tending to and caring about yourself was a priority, which would have caused your brain to wire in ways that would allow you to automatically notice and value your true emotions, needs, and interests from a balanced and loving perspective.

Conversely, if your true needs and emotions were ignored, dismissed, or neglected often, you were given the covert message that you were a problem and that your emotional needs and reactions did not matter. In those cases, you would have learned that you should not tend to your own distress in a balanced way, but rather should either endure it or overvalue it,[4] since this is how your caregivers approached your genuine distress. In essence, you would have been taught that your emotions were either inconsequential or something to be hysterical about. Both of these approaches would have led to feelings of helplessness, anxiety, and depression. What's worse, you would have learned that you were *supposed to* live with these sensations of anxiety or depression—that such uncomfortable physical and emotional sensations were *normal and to be expected*. From these lessons, you would have adopted the same unhealthy, maladaptive approaches to your distress (i.e., ignoring, minimizing, and dismissing it), which would have led to fear and insecurity, anxiety and depression, and an endless cycle of attempting to avoid pain and pursue pleasure.[5]

In Sarah's case those intermittent but significant missteps by the impor-

---

4. Learning to overvalue your emotional responses arises from your caregivers repeatedly responding to your genuine emotions in excessive, almost hysterical ways.

5. Much of the pioneering work in understanding and emphasizing how people ignore, neglect, dismiss, devalue, and minimize their feelings as a result of their early life experiences comes from clinicians focusing on attachment relationships in experiential psychotherapy. Although little has been written on the subject for general audiences, Josette ten Have-de Labije, Psy.D., Robert Neborsky, M.D., and Robin L. Kay, Ph.D., among others, have been teaching and writing about these patterns of behavior for years for professional audiences.

tant people in her life taught her that she would miss out on opportunities down the road—and possibly be ridiculed for making honest mistakes. As that message took hold, somewhere in her brain, she vowed never to make mistakes again, which resulted in her developing chronic anxiety and the unhelpful habit of always trying to be perfect. Rather than adopting the perspective of her Wise Advocate and concluding that sometimes people will disagree with you, are disappointed in you, or act inappropriately (and it has nothing to do with you), Sarah took the emotional overreactions of her mother and brother literally—as young brains will do—and she began a lifelong quest to never disappoint people or be made fun of again.

Although it was an unhealthy and unrealistic way of dealing with her distress in the long term, in Sarah's still growing and very literal brain, it made perfect sense. Moreover, there seemed to be evidence that it worked: The more often Sarah was "perfect," the more she was rewarded and accepted. The problem is that Sarah's perfectionism came at a steep price: Being perfect and overthinking situations became Sarah's way of calming and soothing her Uh Oh Center's alarm and dealing with life's stresses.

As you know from the cycle of deceptive brain messages, once her brain associated those actions with momentarily calming the Uh Oh Center, those unhelpful responses got wired into her brain as automatic habits. This meant that in the future her brain would automatically select those same responses (e.g., being "perfect") whenever a similar situation arose. To Sarah's brain, the repeated attention and focus on overanalyzing and monitoring her caregivers calmed her body on a short-term basis, but unfortunately reinforced the idea that these were responses that should be repeated and relied upon.

While this approach of striving to be perfect seemed adaptive when she was young and unable to independently care for herself, it often required Sarah to neglect her own true emotions and not to say what she needed or what she thought. Rather than learning to value herself (and her opinions) and use healthy methods to alleviate her distress, Sarah adopted her caregivers' approach to her, which included often minimizing her own true needs and emotions and viewing herself as a burden.

Sadly, this pattern of suppressing her true emotions and not saying how she felt with important people became Sarah's automatic response. Her brain learned to associate a feeling of danger and anxiety with any situations that were reminiscent of her interactions with her mom and brother or that left her feeling as though she was disappointing someone. This meant that any event or interaction that her brain perceived to be similar (even when it was not) triggered the same uncomfortable physical and emotional sensations inside her body and caused her to act in unhealthy ways, such as overanalyzing, assuming that she was a "loser," or trying to come up with ways to "fix" her behavior in the future.

As Sarah now realizes, this same scenario plays out to this day whenever her boss appears to disapprove of her or correct her actions. Her brain perceives the situation to be as emotionally and socially dangerous as things were when she was a child, which sparks a twinge of that old pain, followed by sharp spikes of anxiety. Her brain responds to that pain and anxiety in its same ways—it ignores, dismisses, and minimizes the pain and instead automatically acts in an unhealthy way (e.g., overthinking or becoming instantly fatigued and exhausted) in an attempt to alleviate Sarah's distress in the short term.

In the end, these unhealthy coping strategies, based on her deceptive brain messages, caused her chronic distress and made her blind to the fact that she was creating more problems for herself, not fewer. As long as she bought into, and thus paid attention to, the deceptive brain messages—and ignored her true self—she would keep engaging in the same unhealthy patterns repetitively in a hardwired and habitual way. Sadly, as long as she remained unaware of the triggers or associations between her childhood distress and current life situations, nothing would change and her unhealthy strategy of trying to attain perfection would continue to cause problems in all of her relationships.

As discussed above, deceptive brain messages and uncomfortable sensations block you from accessing your true self or expressing your true emotions and needs. When this happens, you ignore, minimize, neglect, dismiss, or devalue your true self and experience uncomfortable sensations that can lead to unhelpful responses, including depression, chronic stress, anxiety, excessive anger, communication problems, stress eating, substance abuse, unhealthy habits, and more.

With the Four Steps, you learn how to break down the associations between unhealthy thoughts and habits so that your loving side, which is aligned with your true self and Wise Advocate, shines through and allows you to respond in beneficial, healthy ways.

Deceptive Brain Messages Get Stronger the More You Ignore, Deny, and Neglect Your True Self

Clearly, habitually dismissing and devaluing your true emotions and needs causes your brain to adopt unhealthy responses and to strongly discount much of the positive information about you that is coming in. As Sarah's story demonstrates, once your deceptive brain messages formed in childhood and took hold in your brain, you began to see yourself from a distorted perspective that did not reflect who you are or your goals and values in life. These inaccurate views of yourself and the desperate attempts to calm your Uh Oh Center caused you to act in ways that resulted in short-term relief but ultimately wired your brain in unhealthy ways. These strategies, while effective in the short run (such as Sarah overanalyzing important interactions to remain as "perfect" as possible), most often are likely to be detrimental in the long run.

What Triggers Your Deceptive Brain Messages?

How do you begin to change these patterns and teach your brain new ways of seeing you and the world around you? By learning how to become aware of those deceptive brain messages and what triggers them. Only then can you choose to act differently.

To begin to make changes in your life, you need to be able to recognize when a deceptive brain message might get triggered. In chapter 1 you made a list of your deceptive brain messages, uncomfortable sensations, and unhealthy habits. Go back and review them now. Then think of situations that might trigger those—or similar—deceptive brain messages.

To help get you started, we included some situations that triggered our patients' deceptive brain messages. For example, Ed and Sarah were often triggered by how people perceived and treated them, whereas Abby often was triggered by having to say no or when she stood her ground. Use these examples as a guide to figure out what situations trigger your deceptive brain messages. If you are having trouble, you can start by writing down your list of deceptive brain messages in the table below and then think about and specify what kinds of situations would cause those deceptive brain messages to arise.

Situation (e.g., Person, Place, Event)	Associated Deceptive Brain Messages
Someone is rude or insensitive, or acts entitled	You are not important or deserving of equal treatment.
Saying no to someone/asserting what is best for you	You are harming the other person. You are a bad person/a selfish person.
Communication gone awry/you *perceive* someone is hurt or upset by what you said	You are the problem. You must take care of others and make them the priority/put them first.
Someone gives you a compliment/you perceive someone likes you	You must do what they ask. You must sacrifice what you want/need to satisfy or please them.

Situation (e.g., Person, Place, Event)	Associated Deceptive Brain Messages

Now that you have identified situations associated with specific deceptive brain messages, add a person or event to that message, as Sarah did with the ice cream incident. Why is this important? It's not to make you feel like a victim or to place blame on anyone—in fact, this is the opposite of what we want you to do. The reality is that you will be destined to repeat what happened in childhood with the current people in your life if you cannot see how false and inaccurate those messages from childhood were. In essence, you will conflate your reactions to people in your present life with the upsetting actions and messages of people who hurt or upset you in the past. This means that you will not be able to see the person in front of you for who he or she is. Rather, you will distort your perception of that person, much like Sarah did with her boss. You will not be basing your responses or actions on what is true, but on deceptive brain messages that were formed in your past.

For example, John's near-constant e-mail checking and focus on whether Alicia was going to leave him was based on a series of experiences he had as a boy. Growing up in a cash-strapped family, John watched as his parents took on second and sometimes third jobs to make ends meet. This meant they had little time for him and that he had to figure out ways to take care of himself. Although they loved him dearly and he seemed to be doing fine, he did not have an emotional safe zone and frequently felt lonely. To deal with his distress, John joined a soccer team and formed a positive relationship with his coach. As John explains, he was a star player on the team, which caught his coach's attention and garnered him praise and many accolades. He became the favorite, which was demonstrated by Coach regularly inviting him over to his house for dinner with his family. This made John feel special and led him to believe that he found a place where he truly belonged and was safe.

John excelled in school and on the soccer field until a new boy—who was a far better soccer player—moved into town. Immediately, the new boy took over John's exalted position on the team and in Coach's heart. John felt rejected, like he had lost his "home," and he became consumed with Coach. He wanted desperately to have his old life and sense of security back. The problem was that the only way he could get Coach's attention or affection was to do things *for* Coach. So John started managing the team, picking up Coach's dry cleaning, bringing him his favorite foods, and so on. Whenever he did, Coach praised him and things felt right in John's world. He was calm and relaxed in those moments and could focus on school, soccer, or something else of his choosing.

However, those moments of reprieve never lasted long because John's influence on Coach was only as good as his last effort or act. From these experiences, John's brain concluded that he had to continually monitor what Coach wanted or needed—that was how he felt safe and avoided anxiety. Although he did not realize it, John became preoccupied with

Coach and his brain took away from these interactions that to receive attention and approval from Coach, John had to give up his life, focus on Coach, and do whatever he could to make Coach happy. This is how John's deceptive brain message that he must care for others at all costs was born.

Sound familiar? This is exactly how John describes acting with Alicia, only Alicia does not want John to act this way and wishes he would take better care of himself. The truth—that she supports and loves him as he is—is completely lost on John, because he can only see Alicia through the eyes of his deceptive brain messages. In his brain, if he does not cater to her at all times and focus solely on her, she will leave him—and no facts or words will be able to shake that message until he can clearly understand that these damaging messages are not true.

Knowing that his preoccupation with the important people in his life came from a place in the distant past—his coach—helped John see why he acted the way he did with Alicia and others he was emotionally close to. Even more significantly, seeing that deceptive brain messages were ruining his life—and that there was another way—helped him vow to use the Four Steps to make important changes.

Similarly, Ed realized that his deceptive brain message telling him he was of no value came from how his mother acted toward him when he was a child. "She never treated me like I was important, unless I did something that made her look good—and the bar was high," he said. For example, excelling artistically meant nothing to her, only his academic grades did. As he remembers, "Unless they were A pluses across the board, she would reprimand me and ask why I had not done better." She never accepted Ed or praised him for his artistic accomplishments, no matter how many parents remarked at how talented Ed was or how they wished they had a son like him. "Nothing was ever good enough to her," he sadly recalled, "which left me perpetually feeling like a second-class citizen."

As soon as Ed accepted and internalized that message from his mother—the one telling him he had no inherent value—one of his most deceptive and devastating brain messages was formed. This message plagued him and caused him to avoid many things in life, including auditions and asking women out on dates. He lived a limited life because, at some level, he kept believing that he had no value. That is, until he was able to see, as he explains it, "that this was my mom's message, not mine. This is not who I am." Once he realized that for all these years he had been under the thumb of her deceptive message—one that he had incorporated into his sense of self—he felt significant grief for the lost time, but he also experienced incredible relief. Seeing the truth, he was liberated and no longer believed that he was mandated to follow his brain's erroneous messages. He was able to start "putting myself out there," as he thinks of it, and create a new life for himself.

Take a moment to review your deceptive brain messages and assign a person or persons to those messages. If you have trouble coming up with messages or assigning a source to them, try to recall situations in your life where your needs and emotions were ignored or where you could not express how you felt to the people who mattered most to you. Also try to think about times when you were dismissed, neglected, or devalued in some way—when you were not accepted for who you were.

Deceptive Brain Message	Original Source of the Message	Current People Who Unknowingly Stir Up That Message
You have no value or worth.	Ed's mom	Anyone who treats Ed poorly or with disrespect
You are the problem.	Sarah's brother (and parents)	Anyone who gets upset with Sarah or questions her
You need to put me first.	John's coach	Alicia and anyone John sincerely cares about and is afraid of losing

Keep these original sources of your deceptive brain messages in mind as you begin your work with the Four Steps. While it is absolutely not necessary to attribute each deceptive brain message to a specific person or pattern of events, doing so helps you see that *you were not the source of these initial negative thoughts* and helps you create a separation between your true self and the inaccurate, false messages coming from your brain. By seeing them for what they are—false messages that your child brain took as literal and real—you will be able to start countering them whenever they arise.

The Antidote to Minimizing and Neglecting Healthy Needs: The 5 A's

From their stories, what seems clear is that Sarah, Ed, and John learned to minimize and neglect their healthy needs as children. As they incorporated unhealthy coping strategies into their lives, they lost touch with their meaningful goals and values and put themselves and their genuine interests and emotions on the back burner indefinitely.

What they needed to learn instead—and still hadn't in their adult years—was that they should be valued and loved for who they are. How could they develop those beliefs now and what would that look like?

The antidote to those deceptive brain messages, they learned, was using the Four Steps to truly see that those negative brain messages were absolutely false. In truth, they were good people who strove for what we all want—to be loved, valued, and appreciated for who we are and to form healthy, wholesome relationships with other people. Psychologist and mindfulness expert David Richo, Ph.D., has focused on how these healthy connections are formed and what is needed to keep them alive. He describes the "5 A's" as the qualities and gifts we all naturally seek out from the important people in our lives, including family, friends, and especially partners. What are these 5 A's?

- *Attention*—genuine interest in you, what you like and dislike, what inspires and motivates you without being overbearing or intrusive. You experience being heard and noticed.
- *Acceptance*—genuinely embracing your interests, desires, activities, and preferences as they are without trying to alter or change them in any way.
- *Affection*—physical comforting as well as compassion.

- *Appreciation*—encouragement and gratitude for who you are, as you are.
- *Allowing*—it is safe to be yourself and express all that you feel, even if it is not entirely polite or socially acceptable.

What Richo is describing, in essence, are those genuine needs we have that form the basis of secure, healthy relationships. The 5 A's are what we all should have received most of the time from our caregivers when we were growing up. They are also what we want in our adult relationships today. In his book *How to Be an Adult in Relationships*, Richo compares and contrasts the 5 A's with what happens in unhealthy or unequal relationships. We have expanded his examples to emphasize the fact that the 5 A's are what we needed when we were young to form secure bonds and that what we received instead was often the antithesis of the 5 A's, which are all forms of minimizing or devaluing you and your healthy needs.

The 5 A's: What You Deserved to Receive, but Likely Didn't	Opposite of the 5 A's— What You Likely Experienced
Attention	You were ignored or not listened to; caregivers were unavailable or not willing to hear/see the truth.
Acceptance	You were shamed or otherwise made to believe that you had to conform to what they wanted you to be—you were not loved for who you are or want to be.
Affection	They put themselves first or were abusive; they withheld love and/or comforting gestures.
Appreciation	You were criticized.
Allowing	They controlled or manipulated you; they were demanding.

Adapted from David Richo, *How to Be an Adult in Relationships: The Five Keys to Mindful Loving* (Boston: Shambhala, 2002), pp. 1, 26-40, 50, 65.

Obviously, Richo's work points out that most people have been lacking the 5 A's in some way in their lives. Most important, Richo emphasizes that you should only expect to have approximately 25 percent of your needs met by any one other person, especially in romantic relationships. Therefore, *the goal in life is not to seek out validation or acceptance from others, but to cultivate your sense of worth and value from within*—to learn how to provide yourself with the 5 A's most of the time. In fact, dealing with obstacles and learning how to respond constructively to problems and setbacks (i.e., healthy emotion management) allows you to grow and learn healthy ways of caring for yourself. It teaches you how to take a balanced approach to life in which you do not act entitled, but you do not deprive yourself, either. Rather, you keep an open attitude toward what life brings your way and are able to deal with it. In doing so, you develop deepening insight into yourself and the world around you.

It's no easy task to accomplish this, especially when you've spent most of your life agreeing with the content of your deceptive brain messages. This is why it's so important to use the 5 A's as a guide to remind yourself of what you deserve from the people in your life (and from yourself). The more you allow yourself to believe that you can care for yourself in healthy ways, the easier it will be to dismiss the deceptive brain messages and follow the Four Steps. We will discuss ways to incorporate a version of the 5 A's with gratitude lists in chapter 11, but for now start noticing which of the 5 A's are missing in your life and how you can start providing them to yourself. Doing this will help you reevaluate the content and veracity of your deceptive brain messages so that you can rewire your brain in healthy, adaptive ways.

In the next chapter, we will provide you with many tips and recommendations our patients found helpful as they started using the Four Steps. With this background, you will then learn what each of the Four Steps is and how you can apply them to your particular deceptive brain messages.

CHAPTER 7

Moving Forward with the Four Steps

Tips and Recommendations

With a solid understanding of how deceptive brain messages are generated, both biologically and through events in your childhood, you are now ready to start learning the Four Steps. To help you prepare for your journey, we have filled this chapter with tips and recommendations based on the collective wisdom and experiences of our patients. They have gone through the program and know many of the obstacles you may face, especially in learning mindfulness and staying with the uncomfortable physical and emotional sensations whenever they arise.

Let's begin with a quotation from mindfulness expert and teacher Bhante Henepola Gunaratana. It beautifully encapsulates what deceptive brain messages are, what they do to you, and how they keep you from following the path of your true self:

> We see life through a screen of thoughts and concepts, and we mistake those [thoughts] for reality. We get so caught up in this endless thought-stream that reality flows by unnoticed. We spend our time engrossed in activity, caught up in an eternal pursuit of

pleasure and gratification and eternal flight from pain and un-pleasantness. We spend all our energies trying to make ourselves feel better, trying to bury our fears, endlessly seeking security.[1]

To phrase it another way: We spend a considerable amount of our time engrossed in following deceptive brain messages until we begin to see them for what they are and value our true emotions and needs.

Learning to See How Harmful Your Deceptive Brain Messages Can Be

The biggest challenge you will face as you start using the Four Steps is in believing that you are worth the time and effort required to challenge the deceptive brain messages and not give in to their commands. This is why we spent so much time teaching you about how your brain automatically ignores, minimizes, dismisses, neglects, and devalues your true needs and emotions and why we taught you about the 5 A's. Up to now, that healthy side of you—the part that believes you are worthy and a good person—has been relatively dormant or severely suppressed by the deceptive brain messages. That's why you have not been able to change your perspective of yourself or your actions: The unhealthy parts of your brain have been in charge.

Many times our patients have asked us, "Well, if the healthy side is what I want to recruit, can't I just think positive and everything will be okay?" Unfortunately, the answer to that question is no, but not for the reasons you might be thinking. The truth is if you really *believed* in those positive parts of you—that you were worth the time and effort—you *could* simply "think positively" and make changes relatively easily. The problem is that you believe more strongly in the deceptive brain messages

---

1. Bhante Henepola Gunaratana, *Mindfulness in Plain English* (Boston: Wisdom Publications, 1992), p. 33.

than you do in your positive qualities. This is because your sense of self is so tightly fused with the deceptive brain messages and it explains why your habits are so hard to break.

That's one of the main reasons we developed the Four Steps: to help you break that unhealthy allegiance to the deceptive brain messages. In fact, once you can see how *false* and destructive the deceptive brain messages are, you naturally will believe more strongly in yourself and your right to follow your true goals and values in life. You will take a firm stand against those false messages and make an enduring commitment to your true self.

Our patients began to change their perspective and believe what their Wise Advocate was telling them by using the Four Steps to increase their awareness of the deceptive brain messages. As they learned how to use the Four Steps, they were able to witness how often the deceptive brain messages surfaced and how much time, effort, and energy they were expending to follow those false messages. The experience of learning how to Relabel, Reframe, Refocus, and Revalue was eye-opening for them because it allowed them to see that their time could be better spent on other pursuits and in healthier ways. Let's turn to their stories now and hear how they took the first step to change their perspective on the deceptive brain messages.

Abby, who avoids confrontation at home and has trouble making decisions, was constantly worrying about her family and questioning herself. "Literally, it took hours of each day out of my life," she laments. "It was exhausting, but I didn't know any other way of being." As she recalls, "I finally realized that it takes so much effort to think things through over and over—it takes so much time and causes so much pain." And it led to no positive results or forward progress. Instead, giving in to her deceptive brain messages only fueled them. "I realized the deceptive brain messages stay alive inside of me because I give in to the habits, the repetitive thoughts, and the 'what-ifs.' I told myself, if I give in, I am feeding into this monster inside of me. I'm making it stronger each time I do it and making myself weaker." Conceptualizing the deceptive brain messages as a monster—as something that was trying to thwart her and take her away from her true self—is what finally inspired Abby to start making changes. With her resolve to use the Four Steps daily, she was able to "choose to use my energy to do something productive and healthy."

Similarly, John realized that his constant e-mail checking and worrying about Alicia's whereabouts were draining him and taking him away from work, his interests, and a real life. "It used to be terrifying to think of getting rid of the symptoms. This is how I've always lived." With time, he became frustrated by how the thoughts and checking were taking over. Despite that justifiable and healthy annoyance with the deceptive brain messages, he just couldn't muster up the effort to change. Deep down, he wanted to act differently and have quality interactions with Alicia, but he felt considerable resistance. His deceptive brain messages were making him doubt himself and believe that he had to continue his unhelpful behaviors, such as checking e-mail and putting Alicia first, to receive love. "It's kind of scary to do things differently," he said, "but I was so tired of the same behaviors resulting in the same results." Once he saw the choice—to be overrun by deceptive brain messages or take a stand against them for a healthier life—he made a commitment to himself to use the Four Steps every day.

In addition to being exhausting, living under the domination of deceptive brain messages causes you to lose out on other opportunities and time, as Steve realized when he began to look at what his drinking was doing to his life. "I had this moment," he recalls, "where I said, 'Okay, I am willing to change, I cannot live this way anymore.' The deceptive brain messages and drinking were running my life. I was depressed because I wasn't manifesting anything I wanted in my life. I wasn't moving forward and saw everyone else as a problem. I was jumping from one thought to another." His relationship with his wife was on the rocks and his daughters were angry with him. It took a terrible toll on him, as he describes, "The drinking and deceptive brain messages really tried to uproot my relationships. I can never get that time back, but I can change how I act moving forward." Remembering what happens when he drinks or ignores his true feelings helps Steve continue forward with the Four Steps whenever he is tired or wants to give up.

Ed had a similar realization to Steve's. He, too, avoided important things, such as auditions and interacting with anyone he thought might reject him (e.g., a potential employer or date). As he recalls, "I would avoid doing a lot of different things. In other words, when the deceptive brain messages became very intense, I became very afraid, almost paralyzed. I remember times when I wouldn't even want to come out of the house because I knew I would be running into all these things in a minute's time that would cause me anxiety. It only takes a second to get triggered." So he would avoid people, places, and opportunities in a desperate attempt to ensure that his Uh Oh Center did not fire and that he would remain calm. Over time, these unhealthy habits got hardwired into his brain.

This avoidant behavior came at the steep price of loneliness and lost opportunities until Ed began to realize just how limited his life had become. Somewhere along the way, he says, "I made the decision not to dwell in it, not to fall for the trick. If I were to obey the deceptive brain messages, then I would really be sad and I would really be down. I told myself I can't afford to do that." He realized that he had the ability to help himself by not letting the deceptive brain messages take over. As he explains, "I just started to look at reality in the way that it is. I have the control to let me down or not." Seeing that he had this power helped Ed persevere and overcome his unhealthy habits.

This idea of having the power to make choices was critical to many of our patients, especially Abby who often was plagued by indecision. As she struggled with overthinking and repetitive worrying, she came to this conclusion: "I want to make choices in life and be able to live with those choices. Accept that I made choices. Refusing to make choices is making a choice. And, if I don't make any choices in life, I will let the monster win." Although it was initially scary to do so, Abby now makes decisions quickly and does not waste time second-guessing herself, thanks to her work with the Four Steps.

Learning to see clearly the damaging effects of following deceptive brain messages was crucial in our patients' evolutions. When they finally saw what their deceptive brain messages were doing to them, they were able to make a commitment to themselves and to put forth a sustained effort to use the Four Steps every day. This commitment was based on their sincere striving to be free from the negative effects of these deceptive brain messages and a burgeoning belief that they were the people their Wise Advocate told them they were.

THE TOLL OF DECEPTIVE BRAIN MESSAGES

Whenever our patients were in doubt or felt defeated by their deceptive brain messages, they would remind themselves of the true facts about deceptive brain messages. Armed with this knowledge, they could strengthen their resolve to see the deceptive brain messages for what they were, dismiss their faulty logic, and instead act in healthy ways on their behalf. Some of those insights are listed below. When you're feeling tired or want to give in, remind yourself that deceptive brain messages can:

- Suck up your time
- Take over your life
- Exhaust you
- Cause you to lose time or other opportunities
- Restrict your life and activities
- Cause you to avoid people, places, or events you enjoy
- Cause discord in your relationships
- Make you miss out on important relationships
- Obscure your reality so that you think the negative messages are true

- Keep you from following the path of your true self
- Keep you trapped and serving others
- Cause you to indulge cravings/urges/desires that lead to unhealthy habits

Assessing the Impact of Deceptive Brain Messages on Your Life

In chapter 2, you defined your meaningful goals and made a list of the things you currently are avoiding (but want to do) and the things you do not want to do (but are). Your next step is to do what our patients did— clearly see how deceptive brain messages and their associated unhealthy habits are hurting you. What happens to you when you follow your brain's false messages? Take a few moments to think of opportunities you've missed, people/places/events you've avoided, relationships that have been negatively impacted, and other consequences of paying allegiance to deceptive brain messages. Write them down below. We've included a few examples from our patients to help you get started.

Deceptive Brain Messages Tell Me X, So I think . . .	This Makes Me Miss Out on . . .
That she is leaving, so I look for reassurance, including overchecking e-mail	Getting my work done, hanging out with my friends, exercising
Everyone else is right, so I repeatedly analyze conversations with people and try to guess how I should act/what I should do	Actually living in the moment and having a conversation with the person in front of me. I am not enjoying it—I am in my head the whole time!
I am not worthy of love—I likely will be rejected, so I do not ask women out on dates or go to auditions	Opportunities to meet new people, network, build my career

Deceptive Brain Messages Tell Me X, So I Think . . .	This Makes Me Miss Out on . . .
That everyone is needy and pathetic, so I get annoyed and drink to escape	Spending time with my family, seeing the positive parts of the people in my life and that they are capable, taking care of myself properly without using drugs or alcohol
That nobody cares about me, so I become exhausted and hide from the world	Going out with friends (dinners, parties), going hiking, being social, feeling connected
That he doesn't care about me or my feelings, so I start fights and argue with him even though I want him to care	Discord in our friendship—not the supportive and loving relationship I want with him

With this awareness of how deceptive brain messages impact you and your life, you're ready to move forward. The only thing left to do is think of ways to empower and inspire yourself when the deceptive brain messages strike. As you saw above, our patients took the first step when they decided that *no matter how true the deceptive brain messages felt, they were false.* The truth, they realized, is that they were worth the time, effort, and investment—and so are you.

You will learn more about their journeys and how to use the Four Steps to your advantage in the pages that follow. To help you along the way, our patients shared these catchphrases they used that inspired or motivated them when they were feeling down or defeated. Use one of theirs or come up with some of your own.

- Only I have the power to let myself down.[2]
- I don't have unlimited time to flail around in the universe.
- I don't really want to give up ever . . . if I give up, what else do I have?
- Reality is better than the fiction in my head.
- I'd rather feel the uncomfortable sensations for a while (by not giving in to the false messages) and have my sanity.
- What am I doing today to improve my life?
- These thoughts and sensations are not real—do not give in to them.
- Do not feed the monster.
- Remember what it is like to give in—you lose time, energy, and relationships.
- With respect to deceptive brain messages, it's not what you think or feel, it's what you do that counts.[3]
- These deceptive brain messages have no power—they are false.

---

2. Or, as Eleanor Roosevelt famously proclaimed, "No one can make you feel inferior without your consent."

3. This is an important clarification: With deceptive brain messages, what you *do* matters far more than the false, inaccurate, and destructive thoughts and feelings created by your brain. Of course, when you are dealing with your true emotions, beliefs, and needs (i.e., based on and reflecting your true self), those thoughts and feelings matter *as much* as your actions and should be appropriately and constructively dealt with and tended to.

EXERCISE: Write down what you will say to inspire and motivate you to keep going when you feel like giving up or believe the deceptive brain messages are true:

THE FOUR STEPS

Step 1: Relabel—Identify your deceptive brain messages and the uncomfortable sensations; call them what they really are.

Step 2: Reframe—Change your perception of the importance of the deceptive brain messages; say why these thoughts, urges, and impulses keep bothering you: They are *false brain messages* (It's not ME, it's just my BRAIN!).

Step 3: Refocus—Direct your attention toward an activity or mental process that is wholesome and productive—even while the false and deceptive urges, thoughts, impulses, and sensations are still present and bothering you.

Step 4: Revalue—Clearly see the thoughts, urges, and impulses for what they are, simply sensations caused by deceptive brain messages that are not true and that have little to no value (they are something to dismiss, not focus on).

Tips for Beginning Your Journey
with the Four Steps

Through their work with the Four Steps, our patients made many pivotal insights—ones we think are important to share with you. The first and most critical is that the thoughts and sensations are overwhelming and difficult to confront, especially at the beginning. What our patients stress over and over is that living with the uncertainty—the doubt of whether following the Four Steps will help you—and refusing to act in your previous ways is scary, but not a reason to quit or give up hope. Here are their tips, insights, and words of encouragement as you start using the Four Steps.

ALLOW THE SENSATIONS TO BE PRESENT,
BUT DO *NOT* ACT ON THEM

This is probably the hardest thing to do when you start using the Four Steps. When you refuse to give in to the content of your deceptive brain messages by not performing the action your brain is telling you to do, your Uh Oh Center fires even more intensely, which makes you feel extremely uncomfortable. You want to do virtually anything to get rid of those sensations, both physical and emotional, and know that simply following your deceptive brain messages will accomplish that task in the short term. The problem, as we all must learn the hard way over time, is that doing so will only fuel the negative messages and further entrench the maladaptive circuits ever more powerfully into your brain. Said another way, short-term relief rapidly causes more pain and suffering, not less.

Although it was difficult to live with the uncertainty of whether or not following the Four Steps would help her, Abby vowed to allow the emotional and physical sensations associated with deceptive brain messages to be present but *not to act on them*. Doing so was difficult. As she remembers, "It was intense and painful when I did not give in. I felt like I was going to jump out of my skin at times. But I sat with it and did not act on those false sensations." Abby knew there was no other way. She says she "had to endure the pain of these uncomfortable sensations to get to the other side." What she saw with time was that she *did* improve. "The relief comes in small packages," she says. "It doesn't happen all at once. It's not a light switch. It happens gradually over time—you may not even notice all of the changes until much later when you reflect back, but it does happen."

Similarly, Steve explains the way his deceptive brain messages assailed him: "It's a sensation that is very bad and you really want to get rid of it—that's why you do those [unhealthy actions] again and again. It's an unending cycle. So, the first thing would be to live with the uncertainty, the fear, and the pain that the deceptive brain messages and uncomfortable sensations leave you with." Rather than fighting them or denying their existence, he recommends that you "stay with the intense feelings until you are able to look at them more objectively, from another perspective—then the deceptive brain messages and sensations are less damaging or upsetting."

We will talk more about how to deal with the uncomfortable sensations in the next chapter, where we discuss Step 1: Relabel.

PRACTICE, PRACTICE, PRACTICE

A key to success, all of our patients agree, is wholesome *repetition*—literally just continuing to complete the Four Steps over and over while not acting on the deceptive brain messages. Over time, it becomes second nature because the "habit" of turning to the Four Steps to effectively deal with erroneous messages becomes ingrained in your brain. In essence, using the Four Steps to deal with stress or upsetting situations *becomes* your new, healthy response and replaces the unhealthy habits you have been using.

Kara agrees: "Practice makes perfect. Just follow the steps, follow the four R's, and you will notice results. It worked for me—you notice some kind of result pretty much right away. Once you've done your first Refocus, there's a sense of achievement, and if you just keep at it, it will become gradually easier. Be patient—feeling like you've had a success spurs you on to keep going."

Although it seems straightforward, Steve makes this important point: "I think a lot of people think the Four Steps are simplistic—they think, 'Hey, if I just do these four things, I'll be cured.' It's effective and it's a great treatment, but it's not easy. It takes practice." Steve likens the Four Steps to the Twelve Steps in Alcoholics Anonymous. "You have to keep going through them, working them. It's a continuous program. You're going to have to apply and work through the Four Steps over and over." As you do this, he says, "you can apply the Four Steps to many situations. The more you do it, the better and better you'll get at it. To think it's going to be easy and that you're magically going to be able to do it without putting in the work is setting yourself up for failure and disappointment because it's challenging." That said, he encourages people to make the commitment to themselves and the Four Steps: "The more I just opened myself up and tried it, I saw that it worked."

JOURNAL YOUR SUCCESSES

To help you realize you truly are making progress, Steve gives this advice to people who are new to the Four Steps: "Write down the successes that you have early on because it encourages you to keep going. It's not always easy, but over the long haul, it does make a big difference and you will see how much progress you've made." The main point to keep in mind is that you want to focus on the things you have accomplished, no matter how small or inconsequential they seem to you. Do not minimize, ignore, or neglect even the most seemingly minuscule achievement. Rather, use the 5 A's and celebrate your successes.

DO NOT TACKLE ALL DECEPTIVE BRAIN MESSAGES OR HABITS AT ONCE

One point Kara often makes is that you should not try to be a "superhero" and take on too many changes at once. "It can be overwhelming and make you feel like you are failing, even when you are making progress." Abby agrees with this and says she found great comfort and relief in knowing that she did not have to change all of her habits at once or go cold turkey. Knowing that she could, for a while, keep going with some of her habits, as long as she did so mindfully, helped. As she explains, "It's way too much pressure if you think you have to change everything at the same time. Telling me I could keep doing some of the behaviors was almost like a relief." She offers this advice if you maintain a few of your habits at first: "You have to do it mindfully. If you're engaging in an unhealthy habit, the least you can do is tell yourself you are doing it and admit to yourself, 'That's what I am doing.' That's helped me a lot." This is using Step 1: Relabel to its fullest, meaning that you're mindful and aware of your actions all the time—something we will discuss in depth in the next chapter.

FOCUS ON PAYING ATTENTION

When Ed started working with the Four Steps, he says one of the biggest difficulties he faced was learning how to pay attention. As he explains, "At [the beginning], the deceptive brain messages are very strong and dominate a lot of your attention. It's very real to you." He and most of our patients recommend simply beginning the journey by learning how to pay attention to your deceptive thoughts, impulses, sensations, and actions— and to Relabel them as such. At the same time, they strongly suggest that you be gentle with yourself and not beat yourself up for any thought or desire that runs through your brain. As Sarah knows all too well, "You have so much shame for having these symptoms. It's important to be kind toward yourself. It's about moving forward. It's about forgiving yourself and knowing that you are a good person despite whatever your brain is throwing at you."

DON'T PROCRASTINATE! IT'S WHAT YOU *DO* THAT COUNTS

A problem that many of our patients face is using procrastination as a way to avoid using the Four Steps. For example, their brains come up with reasons *not* to follow the Four Steps, such as being too busy or too tired. Alternatively, their brains flood them with the distracting thoughts that they aimlessly follow. Similarly, many people's deceptive brain messages tell them they have to do the Four Steps *perfectly* or not do them at all. This is a cardinal example of the "perfect" being the enemy, even the assassin, of the good. All you really want is to put forth a *serious effort* to use the Four Steps every day. You are never trying to achieve perfection; rather, a serious effort not to act on the negative messages truly is good enough.

Remember, you cannot control the initial thoughts that come into your head or the uncomfortable sensations you experience. That's why we strongly emphasize and repeat as often as possible: *When dealing with deceptive brain messages, it's not what you think or feel that matters, it's what you DO that counts!* As Abby explains, "You just can't control them and there's no use in trying—it's like a hamster on its wheel . . . you go nowhere." Ed agrees and often tells people, "Just do the darn thing! Don't focus on the negative consequences your brain is trying to tell you [are inevitable]. Those messages are false and must be discredited whenever they arise."

While it sounds easy enough, John acknowledges that it's hard work and that inertia and habit can be big obstacles. He found that when he started to use the Four Steps, his brain would come up with some other thing that he had to do *before* he did the Four Steps. "I would follow the deceptive thoughts wherever they wanted to take me. I was so caught up in how I felt [i.e., the emotional and physical sensations] that I could not see anything else. I had to just assume for a while that *everything* that made me feel uneasy or question myself was a deceptive brain message." When he did this, he was able to "take a breath and think for a minute." This space between the thought/urge/impulse/uncomfortable sensation and action allowed John to consult his Wise Advocate to make informed decisions based on his true goals in life.

Of course, as we mentioned before, when you are dealing with your true emotions, goals, and interests, your thoughts, feelings, and actions *all* matter. It's only when you are dealing with deceptive brain messages that your false, unhelpful thoughts and feelings—which are not representative of you or how you want to be in the world—do not matter.

WHEN IN DOUBT, USE RATIONAL FAITH

Another tip all our patients agreed on is this: A key to overcoming deceptive brain messages is to use the Four Steps even when you experience considerable doubt and to believe that you will get better the more you use the Four Steps. With this ability to believe in yourself and to persevere when you are feeling overwhelmed, you will be using rational faith:

RATIONAL FAITH

Believing in what you know to be true when doubt enters your mind.

Rational faith helped many of our patients keep moving forward when their deceptive brain messages made them feel like they were about to do the wrong thing. As Abby explains, *"Don't have blind faith, have rational faith."* The difference between them is this: Blind faith gives the power (and credit) for making changes in your life to some other entity, not the real you. Rational faith, in contrast, encourages you to believe that by trusting in the process, focusing on your true goals, and expending effort by following the Four Steps, you will achieve positive results that get you closer to those true goals.

Steve agrees that rational faith is important, especially at the beginning of using the Four Steps when the deceptive thoughts, impulses, cravings, and uncomfortable sensations are the strongest. When he started using the Four Steps, he recalls, "it was hard for me to believe that just by following the Four Steps I could get another perspective and not believe the deceptive brain messages as strongly." He describes it as being "like a leap of faith" because the more significant results and changes do not come until later in the process. As he remembers, "I think it takes a little bit of patience because of the very intense feelings. I think [really knowing that the Four Steps work] is only learned by experience." In this way, rational faith is a leap, but it is a leap that takes you *toward* your true goals and values.

The Four Steps Work

What is it that you will learn from experience? That the Four Steps really do help you separate your sense of self from the deceptive brain messages and that by doing the hard work required, you will see results. As Steve stresses repeatedly, "The whole point is that you begin doing the work before you make the separation. The separation [between your true self and the deceptive brain messages] is made with time—the Four Steps are brilliant for that. The Four Steps are a wedge you can put between your brain's [false] reality and the more clearheaded or mindful view of your Wise Advocate."

He uses this analogy to describe the process of how the Four Steps make a difference in your brain and life:

In the old days there were the Fuller Brush men. They used to come sell brushes at your door and they were there every month. They'd give free samples and they'd almost literally get their foot in the door that way—no one could really close the door on a Fuller Brush man. The same thing happens with the Four Steps—the principle of getting a little room in there, getting my toe in the door between the automatic, thoughtless reaction [and the] deceptive brain message. To try to work on expanding more and more time in between, to not start automatically reacting. Over time, and it does take some time, you begin to get this sense that you indeed are not your emotions and you are not your feelings and you are not even your thoughts. And then you have to practice these things. You have to practice having a different reaction to something. You have to change the way you react to these feelings instead of automatically assuming they are true and doing something with them.

John agrees, saying, "It won't happen immediately. I would say it's normal not to see results at first. For anybody who is just barely beginning to understand the Four Steps, the separation can be really hard—to see the false reality of deceptive brain messages, to separate from them and look at them objectively."

Abby also found it difficult at first to make the separation: "It takes some time because first you have to understand what you are going through; you've got to be educated about what the deceptive brain messages are all about and then you start experiencing them and looking at that problem." That struggle to see the false reality, which the deceptive brain messages have created in you, is hard. With time, she says, "you realize that the deceptive brain messages have no power." And the more you apply the Four Steps and begin to see the deceptive brain messages from that more educated and empowered perspective, she says, "they diminish in importance completely."

When you refuse to give in to those deceptive brain messages and instead use the Four Steps, miraculous things begin to happen. As John remembers, "I was losing five hours a day to checking e-mail and thinking about Alicia. I had no life. When I started working with the Four Steps, I immediately got life back. By using the Four Steps, instead of spending five hours on those activities, I was spending thirty minutes checking e-mail or worrying about my relationship. I got four and a half hours back right away when I refused to give in to the deceptive brain messages and Refocus on something healthy instead."

We hope these words of wisdom will help as you start using the Four Steps and that you will come back to this section whenever you are feeling frustrated or defeated. As our patients repeatedly emphasize, there is hope and things do get better.

Summary

To review, here are a few things to remind yourself of as you begin tackling your deceptive brain messages:

- At the beginning, you may feel overwhelmed, but try as hard as you can not to give in to the deceptive brain messages or unhealthy habits.
- Live with the uncertainty and stay with the sensations—do not try to change them.
- Repetition and practice further your progress the most.
- Just do it—don't let your brain procrastinate or make excuses.
- Journal your successes—it encourages you and shows you the progress you've made.
- Be gentle with yourself.
- Do things gradually—do not try to change all your habits or behaviors at once.
- If you engage in an unhealthy habit, at least be aware of it and acknowledge what you are doing.
- If all else fails, work on increasing your awareness of your deceptive brain messages and habits—pay attention to what is happening in your brain and body.
- Be patient—feeling like you've had a success spurs you on to keep going.

CHAPTER 8

You Can't Change What
You Can't See

The Power of Awareness and Step 1: Relabel

Ed had always thought of himself as a pretty observant guy. After all, he was a performer. He was in touch with his feelings and had an exceptional ability to study people, know what they were thinking, and surmise what they were feeling. He could see life from many angles and had a broad perspective on the world and how it works. Why, then, would he need to learn mindfulness? Isn't mindfulness what he was already doing—observing and looking, knowing things as they are?

Ed continued to think this way, despite his paralyzing fear of rejection, until we pointed out to him that for years he never "saw" his deceptive brain messages. Sure, he could look outward and see what was happening in others, but he could not apply those powers of observation to himself. Instead, he let the deceptive brain messages pass by unnoticed. Eventually, with an education on what deceptive brain messages are and how the Four Steps work, Ed learned how to survey his internal monologue, bodily sensations, and habits with precision guided by mindfulness. It was then that he realized that this inability to see his thoughts as deceptive and false was holding him back in innumerable ways.

Ed describes the process of learning how to be mindful:

> I spent a long time paying attention to deceptive brain messages, living with those feelings and those beliefs of myself as being a certain way. That was all I knew. It's just so habitual to ignore what is happening inside you. To believe what your brain is telling you. When that's your reality, how the hell are you going to know it's a new day? It's almost as if you have to struggle to realize that you *can* recognize a different flower in the bunch of bushes you've been walking by every day. When you finally are mindful, you realize you have never seen the yellow flower in there. And you don't just walk by it assuming it's a red one anymore. You look, you observe. When awareness starts to pop its head up, you have to be able to recognize it and let it happen. That's what mindfulness is—being aware and seeing things as they truly are.

In this analogy, Ed compares his belief that all the flowers are red with assuming that all the deceptive thoughts, urges, and impulses he's had throughout his life are true. When he finally stopped and looked, rather than blindly following what his brain was telling him, he was able to realize that he had been viewing life through a harmful and inaccurate filter that caused him to see life from this one very skewed perspective—that of the deceptive brain messages. The way to deal with this blind spot, he learned, was to increase his awareness so that he could see his experiences with a new pair of eyes—his own. What Ed described so elegantly is the process of becoming aware of what your brain is doing as it is doing it and of truly learning how to see the deceptive brain messages for what they are.

MINDFULNESS OR MINDFUL AWARENESS (AS APPLIED TO DECEPTIVE BRAIN MESSAGES)

THE ABILITY TO SEE WITH FRESH EYES, FROM THE PERSPECTIVE OF THE WISE ADVOCATE AND YOUR TRUE SELF

1. What the deceptive brain messages are and what they cause you to do.
2. How they are blinding you to all kinds of important information.
3. How they are causing you to experience only one version of life: *a false one.*

In this chapter, we will begin by teaching you about mindfulness, the foundation of the Four Steps. In fact, the core of Step 1: Relabel is designed to teach you how to become more mindful of your deceptive brain messages and habitual actions. When you are able to Relabel effectively, you can instantly see the deceptive brain messages arise in real time and call them what they are. That's the whole goal of Step 1 and it is critical because this ability sets you up to follow the rest of the Four Steps. Obviously, you cannot Reframe the meaning of something (Step 2), Refocus on another activity (Step 3), or Revalue the entire experience as nothing more than the feeling of deceptive brain messages (Step 4) unless you can clearly see what is happening as it is happening and call it what it is. Mindfulness is your gateway to seeing the fallacy of the deceptive brain messages and to making new, healthy choices based on your true self.

So, what is mindfulness? You've probably heard the term before and might even have an idea of what it encompasses. Although it's helpful to have some familiarity with the concept, we want you to keep an open mind as we describe what mindfulness is *as applied to deceptive brain messages.* Why? Depending on the context and tradition, mindfulness can mean different things to different people. This leads to many common misunderstandings about mindfulness that need to be dispelled so that you can understand the Four Steps correctly.

What is absolutely true, no matter the context, is that mindfulness is an *experiential* process. One of the best ways to think of learning mindfulness is that it is a lot like learning how to walk, drive, or play a new sport. Someone can teach you the basics and tell you what to do in a step-by-step fashion, but you will not really "get it" until you try it yourself. That said, you can learn a lot by understanding the principles underlying mindfulness and by following the exercises we have included in the remaining chapters of this book. So, let's look at what mindfulness is and what it isn't so you can start learning how to apply the Four Steps to your particular deceptive brain messages.

Mindfulness Is an Activity, Not Merely a State of Mind

Most people think of mindfulness as a state of mind, as being analogous to being "in the zone." This is a common misunderstanding that can lead to frustration because mindfulness isn't something you can just switch on like a TV and expect that it will remain in that state indefinitely. A more accurate way of thinking about mindfulness would be tuning in to a specific TV station because this analogy implies *actively* doing something and it requires you to pay attention.

In fact, the best way to conceptualize mindfulness is as an *activity*, not a state of mind or way of being. Unlike being tired, anxious, or excited, you can't simply be mindful without effort. You don't just fall into mindfulness or suddenly say to yourself, "Oh, I've been being mindful and didn't realize it," in the same way that you can passively be listening to music.

Mindfulness, like any activity, requires effort, vigilance, and willingness, because in each moment of your life you are choosing whether to be mindful or not. And, like most activities where focus and skill are involved, the more you practice, the better your abilities become. In this way, mindfulness literally is a training ground for your mind—a mental gym where you strengthen your powers of observation and awareness so that you become more proficient at seeing what is happening in each moment of your life.

Mindfulness Is Awareness

At its core, mindfulness is about awareness—being fully knowledgeable that something is happening right now, in this very moment. In this way, mindfulness is not concerned with the act itself, but with the awareness that something is transpiring. For example, if you are being mindful right now, as you read these words, you are *aware* that you are reading. You are not engrossed in the details of each word, but you are aware of the process of reading as it happens.

Similarly, if you are experiencing a deceptive brain message right now but you are focusing only on the content, then you are thinking, not being mindful. However, if you are aware that you are thinking or that you are experiencing a deceptive brain message, then that's mindfulness. A wonderful example Henepola Gunaratana provides is the following:

> If you are remembering your second-grade teacher, that is memory. When you become aware that you are remembering your second-grade teacher, that is mindfulness. If you then conceptualize the process and say to yourself, "Oh, I am remembering," that is thinking.[1]

When properly understood, mindfulness teaches you how to be in contact with your actual experience. For example, if you are sitting in the sun and you feel the warmth touching your skin and are clearly aware of that sensation, then you are being mindful. Similarly, if while you are eating something you take the time to really notice what the food tastes like, how

---

1. Bhante Henepola Gunaratana, *Mindfulness in Plain English* (Boston: Wisdom Publications, 1992), p. 140.

it feels in your mouth, whether it is sweet or salty, how the taste changes over time, and so on, you also are being mindful.

Your goal as you learn how to Relabel is to be aware of the *process*—of what your brain and body are doing in each moment of time. Do not concern yourself with the content or reasons right now, just the process of what is happening. To help you with this endeavor, we developed the following exercises to help you become aware of what your body is doing without your knowledge or conscious consent.[2]

INCREASING AWARENESS OF YOUR BODY

EXERCISE #1: AWARENESS OF MOVEMENT

While you are engaged in another activity (such as reading, working, watching TV), try to pay attention to every movement you make for five to ten minutes. Try to notice everything you do. Here are examples of activities or movements you may not be aware of but do habitually:

- Crossing/uncrossing your legs
- Scratching your skin
- Moving your clothing around
- Changing your body position
- Tapping repetitively
- Moving things around in your environment
- Stretching
- Sniffling
- Clearing your throat

---

2. Although there are many different places you could begin when learning and practicing mindfulness, starting with bodily sensations and movements tends to be much easier for most people because there is less content involved (i.e., we are not asking you to focus on anything in particular, just whatever sensations come up in your body over a certain period of time).

EXERCISE #2: AWARENESS OF SENSATIONS

Sit somewhere quietly for five minutes—make sure there are no distractions. Turn off your cell phone, shut down your computer, put any reading materials away. Literally sequester yourself in a place where no one will disturb you and nothing is likely to grab your attention. It's often easier to do this with your eyes closed, but eyes open are fine, too.

With no goals or objectives, simply sit somewhere and notice what *bodily sensations* come up. Do not focus on thoughts, emotional sensations, or other phenomena, such as what you are hearing. Focus only on the sensations you experience in your body, such as tingling, itching, pressure, pain, discomfort, lightness, energy, warmth, cold, fullness, and dryness. Do not try to influence the sensations in any way.

Most important, *do not try to change the sensations or ascribe meaning to them.* Simply let them bubble up with an attitude of curiosity and acceptance. Be open to whatever arises.

When you are done, try to remember what physical sensations arose in that time period and whether you were able to simply notice them or if you got caught up in them. For example, did you ascribe meaning to them? If your stomach was gurgling, did you think to yourself, "Oh, I must be hungry," or did you simply notice the gurgling itself? If you felt an itch, did you scratch it? If you experienced pain, did you say to yourself, "I wonder if something's wrong" and think further about it?

Becoming aware of your movements, sensations, impulses, and automatic tendencies to think about and to ascribe meaning to your sensations with exercises like these is the first step in increasing your awareness. As we have mentioned before, you cannot change what you are not aware of and you cannot make choices about things you do not know exist. Until you are aware of your impulses, you simply act. So, your goal is to become more aware in each moment of your day. From our experience, noticing what happens in your body is a great place to start.

For the next day or two, try to notice whenever you move or have a physical sensation. Just notice what pops up and do not try to change it or give it meaning. Remember, the goal of mindfulness is not super awareness of everything, but the *ability* to be increasingly more aware of what is happening as it happens. It's about being "awake" to your experiences and capable of noticing life as it transpires.

Awareness and Focus Are Not the Same Thing, but They Are Related

Another common misconception is that *awareness* is just another word for *focusing*. From the exercises you just completed, you might have a sense that awareness is different from focusing, though they are related. Focusing is an activity in which you consciously direct your attention. Awareness, on the other hand, is being fully knowledgeable of whatever is happening right now, in this very moment. Both are important and necessary for mindfulness and rewiring your brain.

With deceptive brain messages, focusing on them without awareness of what they really are is what has gotten you into trouble. Whenever you focus on and give in to deceptive brain messages, without simultaneously realizing what they are, you are allowing your attention to be grabbed. You are not being mindful and are not aware of what is happening. For example, if someone just rejected your idea, you might be thinking, "Well, it was a good idea. I have no clue what's wrong with him. Why can't he see that this would really work? I bet if I showed him the other spreadsheet, the one with the detailed breakdown, then he'd get it and want to know more . . ." and so on. When you are in this "mode," you are absorbed in and focused on the content. However, if you are able to take a step back and say, "Wow, I am lost in thought; I'm following these deceptive brain messages," then you are aware of what is happening and are being mindful.

Although they are both rooted in mindfulness, this difference between awareness and focus when you are dealing with deceptive brain messages is so important that we made them two distinct steps. When you closely look at them and understand what they each are trying to achieve, you see that Step 1: Relabel is centered on increasing *awareness* of your deceptive brain messages—in other words, knowing when one is present. In contrast, Step 3: Refocus is concerned with how you *direct* and *focus* your attention (and thereby change your brain).

To help you experience this firsthand, try exercise #3. This exercise teaches you how to focus on your breath as an object of meditation. Of all the mindfulness exercises available, this is the most common and popular for people to try. It is a great way to train your mind to remain in the present moment and is a great entry point into traditional meditation.

ENHANCING YOUR FOCUS AND AWARENESS

EXERCISE #3: AWARENESS OF BREATH

To help you see how focus and awareness are related, we are going to ask you to make your breathing the object of your attention in this exercise. Learning how to focus on your breath is beneficial because it gives you an *anchor*, something to come back to, whenever your mind wanders.

Similar to the bodily sensations exercise, sit somewhere quietly for at least five minutes—make sure there are no distractions. Turn off your cell phone, shut down your computer, and go somewhere no one will disturb you and nothing is likely to grab your attention. It's easiest to complete this exercise with your eyes closed.

With no goals or objectives, simply notice your breath as it goes in and out of your body. Place your attention on the inner rim of your nostrils, where you can feel the subtle movement of air as you breathe in and out. As with the other exercises, do not focus on thoughts, emotional sensations, or other phenomena. Focus only on your breath and do not try to influence your breathing patterns in any way.

If you notice that your attention is wandering away from your breath, note what is happening and then go back to your anchor, your breath. For example, if you start thinking about what you are going to have for dinner, how you are going to fit in exercising today, or running through a list of things to do before the day is done, note this by saying to yourself "thinking," "planning," or just "wandering," and then go back to your breath.

Many people find this exercise is easier with counting. One of the most effective ways is to count each in-breath and out-breath separately up to 10. For example, count the in-breath (inhalation) as "1," the out-breath (exhalation) as "2," the next in-breath as "3," and so on up to the out-breath of "10." Then repeat this exercise until you are able to maintain awareness of your breath without counting.

If you are able to be aware of your breath the entire time, you will be able to count up to 10 in one pass. Don't be surprised or disheartened if this is not the case. When you are just starting out, this ability to count up to 10 (and only up to 10) in one fell swoop is a rare event. In many cases, especially early on, you likely will find that you forgot what number you were on or find that you are on 14 (i.e., you forgot to stop at 10) before you notice that your attention has wandered.

Obviously, the longer you are able to sit with this exercise, the more adept your mind will be at noticing when your attention has wandered. If possible, make a plan to notice your breathing for up to thirty minutes each day—doing so will definitely hone your ability to recognize when your attention has wandered and enhance your powers of observation.

Mindfulness Includes Seeing That the Deceptive Brain Messages Are False

Throughout our description of mindfulness, we have deliberately kept one word out: reality. Why? It can be a loaded term, depending on the context,[3] and it implies that the thoughts, impulses, urges, desires, sensations, and habits you experience are not real in some way. The truth is, they are real—you *are* experiencing them. The problem is that those deceptive brain messages, sensations, and habits are *false* and they take you away from following your true goals and values in life. We want you to see with clear eyes that:

- The content of the deceptive thoughts is not valid or true
- The urges, impulses, and desires do not need to be satisfied
- You have choices beyond the narrow options your deceptive brain messages are presenting to you

Learning how to see that those three statements are correct is the whole point of the Four Steps. Therefore, when we talk about mindfulness as applied to deceptive brain messages, we want you to start seeing that the negative messages, sensations, and habitual patterns are false and that they are not representative of your true self.

We will talk more about this in chapter 9 when we teach you how to Reframe the content of your deceptive brain messages. For now, simply keep in mind that while the experience of deceptive brain messages is real, their content and directives are false.

---

3. For example, in traditional Eastern practices, the goal of mindfulness is to see certain "truths" about existence. When used in that way, mindfulness has very specific goals and aims that are far beyond the scope of this book.

Mindfulness Is Nonjudgmental *and* Judgmental at the Same Time

When most people think of mindfulness, the word *nonjudgmental* almost universally comes to mind. When applied in a global way, this is a serious mistake and it is one that we need to make sure you do not make. Why is this so important? When you conceptualize mindfulness as nonjudgmental, it gives the impression that anything goes, that no matter what you do, mindfulness will simply accept whatever happens as perfectly fine and appropriate.

While it is true that some parts of mindfulness require you to suspend judgment so that you can see what is happening, including the ugly and unpleasant aspects of life (e.g., your darker thoughts), there are places where judgment is absolutely necessary. The distinction lies in whether you are looking at and observing your thoughts or whether you are evaluating your choices and actions. Remember what we said before: You cannot control the initial thoughts, impulses, desires, or cravings you have—it is impossible to do so. However, you can and must choose how you will respond if you want to change your life and how your brain works.

Therefore, when you are trying to be aware of your thoughts and impulses (i.e., your deceptive brain messages), you must not judge them. You need to let them bubble up so you can see what is there. Berating or shaming yourself for the deceptive brain messages that arise is counterproductive and takes you away from being mindful. If you see that you are heading in that direction, remind yourself of what Sarah says to herself: "You have so much shame for having these symptoms. It's important to be gentle with yourself. It's about moving forward. It doesn't matter what your deceptive thoughts or feelings are in the end, it's how you act. You have to have a certain amount of gentleness and acceptance." This is when nonjudgmental mindfulness comes in and is so important.

The other side of the coin, as we've said, is your actions. Here, you want to judge things in a rather aggressive way. Why? Think about what *non-*

judgmental means when taken to its extreme—it implies that it would be okay to hurt someone or to act in a reckless manner purposely. Applied in this way, mindfulness would simply look at your actions, note them, and accept them as perfectly legitimate. Clearly, this is taking things too far and could be used as an excuse to act in a way that is devoid of values or morals. That's why we spent time explaining that deceptive brain messages are anything that takes you away from your true self—from your sincere striving to achieve things in your life based on your values and goals. Mindfulness, when appropriately understood, does not dispassionately recognize all actions as equally acceptable, and nor should you.

The bottom line is this:

- Do *not* judge your initial thoughts, impulses, cravings, or desires (i.e., your deceptive brain messages and uncomfortable sensations). You have no control over their presence and it is not your fault that they are there. Let them be present and notice them *without* acting on them.
- *Do* judge your actions, including mental ones, such as overanalyzing or "perfectionism." You have control over your actions, including overthinking, and mindfulness does not give you a free pass to act recklessly or in a manner that would hurt you or others. You are responsible for what you do once the deceptive brain messages arise.

Objects of Mindfulness

As you can see from this brief overview, mindfulness is a complex topic because it encompasses your entire life—everything you think, experience, and do. Realizing this can be overwhelming: How can you be mindful of everything? Although the possibilities are endless, the point is to be aware of *some aspect* of your current experience, not everything at once. To help you conceptualize common objects of awareness, we have divided the following table into three parts based on broad categories of experiences you can have and be aware of. Later, we will outline the kinds of experiences frequently related to deceptive brain messages. For now, simply allow yourself time to understand the various kinds of phenomena you can notice if you start looking. As Yogi Berra was known for saying, you can learn a lot just by watching.

SOME OBJECTS OF MINDFULNESS

Physical Sensations	Mental Phenomena/ Emotional Sensations	Activities
Warmth, cold	Happiness	Talking, breathing
Pressure, pain	Empathy	Touching
Light-headedness, dizziness	Love, affection, caring	Feeling
Itching, irritation	Anxiety, fear	Listening, hearing
Dryness, sweatiness	Anger, rage, hatred	Thinking, analyzing, planning
Fullness, emptiness	Shame, guilt	Smelling, tasting
Craving, desire, impulses	Craving, desire, impulses	Exercising, moving
Energy coursing through the body, jitteriness	Sadness, depression	Seeing, watching

From the table above, it's clear that anything your mind can perceive, sense, feel, or think can be an object of mindfulness. This means that all your deceptive brain messages, sensations, and activities can be objects of mindfulness, too. In fact, if you look closely, the categories in the table above are ones frequently found in the cycle of deceptive brain messages we described in figure 1.1 in chapter 1. However, as we mentioned, the goal right now is not to analyze or focus on any particular thought, impulse, or activity, but to learn how to increase your *awareness* of experiences with Step 1: Relabel.

<hr>

STEP 1: RELABEL

Identify your deceptive brain messages and the uncomfortable sensations: Call them what they really are.

<hr>

For example, we want you to use your increasing powers of awareness to notice whenever the following arise—without getting lost or engrossed in thoughts about them:

- Deceptive brain messages, including your thoughts, impulses, desires
- Physical and emotional sensations, including cravings
- Habitual patterns of action or inaction

Once you become adept at the process of Relabeling, you will delve into the content and find ways to counteract and refute the deceptive brain messages with Step 2: Reframe. But first you need to learn how to become aware of your thoughts without becoming ensnared in them. Let's turn to a universal problem we all face—being lost in the activity of repeatedly thinking.

Lost in Thought

As you completed the awareness exercises focusing on your bodily sensations, movements, and breath, you likely noticed the running commentary going on in your head. If you really noticed it, you were probably amazed by the fact that your brain is going nonstop and that you are thinking about something almost all of the time. When you become more aware of your constant thinking, you realize that this experience is your default mode—run by your Self-Referencing Center. Although it has become the "norm," constantly thinking takes you away from being aware of other parts of your experience and from being mindful.

Why is being lost in thought a problem? It keeps you from doing what you want and need to do in life. As Gunaratana explains:

> Our *habit* of getting stuck in thought is years old, and that habit will hang on in the most tenacious manner . . . conscious thought pastes things over our experience, loads us down with concepts and ideas, immerses us in a churning vortex of plans and worries, fears and fantasies.[4]

Our patients agree that being unable to step outside of your thoughts is a huge obstacle when you are trying to be mindful and use Step 1: Relabel. They describe the process in different ways, but they all agree on what happens: They end up losing time and have trouble harnessing the power of their attention when their thoughts are running rampant. Many of them refer to this process of overthinking and overanalyzing as "spinning" and use that word to Relabel what is happening. For example, Liz, a sixty-five-year-old woman who had a successful career as a human rights activist and who began to worry whether she, as she says, "would end up in a nursing home at eighty-five with no one to care for me," often got stuck in repetitive thoughts about her future and asked herself all kinds of questions for which there was no answer, such as: Would she be alone? Where would she live? How would she support herself? What would she do all day? Would she have her memory? It got to the point, Liz says, where "I would just sit there spinning in a circle, going over and over it. I would get caught up in the spinning and there was no way out until I

---

4. Gunaratana, *Mindfulness in Plain English*, p. 143.

was able to start Relabeling it as 'spinning.' That's when I was able to break the cycle and move on."

John, who often gets stuck in repeating cycles of thoughts, describes the process in a similar way: "Your mind is going a million miles an hour when you indulge the deceptive brain messages and it's hard to switch gears. That's why Relabel is so helpful. For example, sometimes I start thinking about something other than work, like Alicia. I get a bit sidetracked—I think over and over about it. Then, I realize what I am doing. That's when I Relabel it. I say to myself, 'You're ruminating, you're mind-wandering.' Then I try to Refocus by going back to work, but if that isn't effective, I just concentrate on my breathing for a minute or two. It centers me and helps me regain the ability to focus my mind. It seems to help."

Abby, who worries a lot, knows all too well what they are talking about. She often would get caught in loops in which "my brain would go to the worst-case scenario over and over. Then, it would find another scenario to worry about. No matter how I tried to solve the problem, my brain would just find something else to worry about. For example, I know I do a lot of *thinking through*. . . . I will go over and over the same material. I will think to myself, 'Well if I do this, X will happen. But maybe if I do that, then Y will happen.' I go through all the pros and cons of this, the pros and cons of that. I'll just go over them and over and over. There was no end in sight!"

Sarah, who replays conversations with people in her head, overanalyzes her actions, and often wonders if she's upset or angered anyone, experiences similar thoughts. As she recalls, "I mull things over. Lots of 'what-ifs' go through my mind. I just keep asking myself, 'What if I do this? What if I do that?' I think of all these far-reaching scenarios that are so unlikely to happen, but if there's even a remote possibility it might happen, I worry about it." Both Sarah and Abby have found that if they simply Relabel the whole process as "what-ifs," "thinking," or "worrying," the cycle is broken and they can bring their attention back to what *they* want to focus on.

From their stories, it may seem like it's a piece of cake to notice when you are lost in thought. Not so, says Steve. Learning how to notice the endless stream of thoughts was very difficult for him because "instead of doing a behavior where an observer could watch me check and say, 'Oh, he's checking, he's coming back to check again and again,' this was all happening inside my brain. No one can point it out to me and no one knows what I am thinking. Even worse, these kinds of thoughts obviously can be hidden from one's own self. You just don't see it as an activity, like checking or drinking. You keep thinking it's a valid and necessary process you are going through. And why wouldn't you? You've been doing it your whole life. It's like you have a blind spot there because you think it's natural, normal, and helpful." As Steve was able to start seeing the process of being lost in thought as an *activity*, one that was clearly not helping him, he was able to Relabel it and move on.

Now that you understand what being lost in thought is all about, try the following exercise, designed simply to help you notice what your brain is doing all day long.

EXERCISE #4: INCREASING AWARENESS OF YOUR THOUGHTS

Sit somewhere quietly for five minutes—make sure there are no distractions. Turn off your cell phone, shut down your computer, put any reading materials away. Just like with the other exercises, find a place where you can be alone and not bothered. This is a time for you to notice your thoughts and not force any particular topic or issue to come up. It's often easier to do this exercise with your eyes closed.

Using the breath awareness exercise to guide you, focus on your breath while simultaneously noticing *when* thoughts come up. Do not focus on bodily sensations, pain, emotional sensations, or other phenomena. Focus only on the fact that thoughts arise. When they do, quietly (in your mind, not aloud) say to yourself, "Thinking," then go back to your breathing anchor (e.g., air coming in and out of your nostrils).

As with the other exercises, do not try to control or change the thoughts, simply notice them. Most important, *do not judge the thoughts*. Simply let them bubble up with an attitude of curiosity and acceptance. Be open to whatever arises.

A variation on this exercise is to write down one or two words related to each thought that arises in those five minutes or to simply journal for five minutes about whatever comes up—again, without judging or trying to direct the content. You are not trying to solve a problem or figure anything out—you are simply *allowing and providing the space* for the thoughts to present themselves.

The goal of this exercise is for you to see how many thoughts you have in a very short period of time and how disconnected, repetitive, inconsequential, or even inappropriate many of them are. The more times you do this exercise, the more you will see that it is relatively easy to start noticing your thoughts if you pay attention to noticing them.

As you are able, extend the length of time you sit and notice your thoughts—this will help train your mind to naturally increase your awareness of thoughts as they arise throughout your day (and not just when you are deliberately trying to pay attention to them).

This exercise is an important one because it sets the stage for you to start noticing your deceptive brain messages whenever they arise. As we've mentioned before, you can't change what you can't see. Therefore, after you have become more adept at noticing your bodily sensations from the previous exercises, take a few days to try to notice when you are lost in thought. The best way to do this is to continue using exercise #3 or #4, which are both forms of meditation, for up to thirty minutes a day. This is the ultimate way to increase your awareness—it is that mental gym we were talking about before.

As you become more proficient at being aware of when you are thinking, then you can start noticing the content of your thoughts. For now, we want you to notice the *process* of thinking and leave the *content* to Step 2: Reframe.

Overpowered by Sensations—Craving, Impulses, Pain, Anxiety, and So On

Becoming aware of your thoughts is vital, but they are not the whole story. Remember, deceptive brain messages are not only defined as thoughts, but also as *impulses, and desires* that take you away from your true self. Now that you have an idea of what thoughts can arise, you need to be as familiar with your physical and emotional sensations because they can be as distracting and overpowering as the thoughts.

The easiest sensation to start with is anxiety because it is something we all experience at some point in our lives. When people think about anxiety, they usually conjure up images of someone having a panic attack, such as the heart beating faster, sweating, and becoming short of breath. While those absolutely are symptoms of anxiety, the range of physical symptoms is much broader, and we think it's important for you to be able to recognize the different ways anxiety can manifest beyond the traditional symptoms.

Why is this important? As we mentioned in chapter 6, you likely have been ignoring, minimizing, or neglecting your true emotions. When you do this, anxiety rises in your body and acts as a signal, alerting you to the fact that you are somehow dismissing your true self. If you are not aware of how anxiety can express itself in your body, then you will not be able to recognize all the times when you are ignoring, neglecting, or minimizing your true emotions and needs. This will lead you to continue using the same unhelpful, automatic responses and coping strategies that have become deeply ingrained in your brain.

To break those patterns, you need to know the range of anxiety symptoms you can experience and how to start recognizing them. One way to think about and categorize anxiety is based on how your brain reacts to perceived stress and threats in your environment. For example, if you are stressed but are not in any real danger, your muscles likely will tense up in some way, but your body will not respond further. However, if your brain perceives a threat and concludes that you might be in danger, it will initiate the fight-or-flight response. Conversely, if the perceived danger is very high or your system is overloaded, your body may prepare to shut down physically and your thoughts may become clouded to the point that you are confused and unable to think straight. The symptoms of each of these brain-body responses vary, as we have indicated in the table below, and sometimes more than one type of anxiety reaction can be present (e.g., muscle tension *plus* fight-or-flight, thinking problems *plus* shutdown, and so on).

TYPES OF ANXIETY REACTIONS RELATED TO DECEPTIVE BRAIN MESSAGES

Muscle Tension in Your:	Fight-or-Flight	Shutdown	Thinking/ Perceptual Problems
Face, jaw	Shortness of	Slower breathing	Difficulty thinking
Throat, including	breath/rapid	Slower heart rate	Slowed thinking
voice cracking or	breathing	Light-headedness	Losing track of
weakness	Wheezing	Dizziness	thoughts
Neck	Increased heart	Fainting	Confusion
Shoulders	rate	Nausea/vomiting	Disorientation
Arms, hands	Heart pounding	Diarrhea or	Changes in clarity
Chest, including	Heart racing	constipation	of vision or
sighing	Dry mouth	Need to urinate	hearing
respirations	Cold hands/skin	Fatigue	Tunnel vision
Back	Shivering	Tearing eyes	Ear ringing
Legs	Shaking	Heartburn	
Feet	Sweating	Stomach pain	
	Dilated pupils	(increased acid)	

Understanding the range of anxiety symptoms—and that you can experience symptoms from different categories at the same time—is critical when you are trying to Relabel your uncomfortable sensations. For example, Abby told us that when she is really anxious, her body reacts in the following ways: "I become very tense, my brain is foggy, and I can't see the other person clearly. Sometimes I am dizzy and disoriented, too. When this happens, I Relabel the entire thing as 'brain fog.'" Similarly, when Liz was at her worst, worrying often about whether she would end up in a nursing home alone with no one to care for her, she described the following: "Every morning I was waking up with a gut-wrenching anxiety. I was really scared about the future and I could tell in my body that I was waking up with a knot in my stomach. I recognized these as the uncomfortable sensations related to deceptive brain messages that I was afraid I would be alone. I knew it was irrational, so I Relabeled it as such. I said to myself, 'Irrational' and 'Stomach churning,' which helped a lot."

Sarah also deals with anxiety, usually panic attacks. When she has the symptoms of panic, such as a rapid heartbeat or sweating, her brain "felt like it was screaming, telling me, 'Oh my God, there's a huge emergency!' And I would perpetuate the false message by thinking, 'Help, help, I'm gonna die!' It's a horrible feeling," she says, "but eventually I realized it wasn't true." As she learned the Four Steps, she began to Relabel those experiences as "anxiety" or "panic." Often, she would simply note the sensation she was having, such as saying to herself, "Rapid heartbeat." As she became more adept at using the Four Steps, she would become more precise and tell herself, "Hey, this is my anxiety that's making my heart beat faster and making my palms sweat, but it is not something I have to act on or believe is signaling a real emergency."

Likewise, when John was feeling anxious and was on the verge of checking e-mail, he says, "I would get panicky." His response? "I would Relabel those sensations as a 'false body message' and say to myself, 'The body is sending you this ridiculously unnecessary, excessive response. Notice that, but don't give in to it.'"

Anxiety is not the only way the body can respond. As Sarah knows all too well, the body can also shut down from depression. For instance, whenever she was depressed her physical sensations included feeling "de-energized, lethargic or weak—of being deflated. That's when I would want to go hide in bed or fall asleep," she says. "When I got that feeling, which is physical and mental, I'd Relabel it as 'This is my de-energizing depression' or 'The depression is why I don't have any energy or my muscles are weak.'"

Similarly, when Steve was drinking and emotionally distant from his family, he would feel guilty and ashamed. Rather than empowering him to quit drinking, all these sensations did was ensure that he would stay further away from his family and not talk with them about how he felt. As he realized this, he says, "I would feel hopeless and overwhelmed. With the Four Steps, I recognized that those experiences were coming from my deceptive brain messages and bad habits. I would say to myself, 'This is an emotional sensation that is outside of me, it's not me, but I can do something about it.' Then, I would Relabel it as depression or guilt or shame and Refocus on another activity, like playing a game with my daughter or working out."

John also dealt with depression at times. "It was like walking a path in the darkness," he says. "I would have this depressive dialogue with myself and feel exhausted. I would start craving starches, like pasta, and sweets. When I was unaware, I would eat everything in sight and it made me feel better [for a few minutes], but I gained weight." His solution was to start calling these cravings for sweets and starches deceptive brain messages and to Relabel them as "craving" or "false message."

Other symptoms of depression, both physical and emotional, include the following:

- Headaches
- Pain, including back pain, joint pain, and muscle pain
- Muscle aches

- Exhaustion and fatigue
- Difficulty sleeping (falling asleep, staying asleep, waking frequently, waking up too early in the morning)
- Digestive problems (nausea, diarrhea, constipation)
- Change in appetite or weight
- Increased craving for carbohydrates or other "comfort" foods
- Hopelessness, helplessness
- Sadness, feeling down, depressed, low mood
- Feeling like life isn't worth living or the world would be better if you were not here

Two important notes:

1. If you have any suicidal thoughts, see a mental health professional immediately. If you have any plans to harm yourself, do not hesitate to call your doctor or go to the nearest emergency room. You can also call the National Suicide Prevention Hotline: 1-800-273-TALK (1-800-273-8255).
2. If you have new, worsening, or severe physical symptoms, see your doctor to rule out an underlying medical problem. Although we are trying to show you the links between emotional states and physical symptoms, sometimes there is a real medical problem. Since many medical problems start out with some of these same physical sensations, if you are at all concerned or have new, worsening, or severe symptoms, have them evaluated by your doctor before calling them physical sensations or using the Four Steps with them.

Finally, no discussion of physical or emotional sensations would be complete without mentioning cravings, desires, longings, and impulses. Obviously, craving comes up most clearly in the case of addictions, but it can also occur with anxiety (such as stress eating) or with depression (such as craving carbohydrates). Therefore, you need to be on the lookout for cravings, desires, and longings, such as the highs you feel when you use alcohol or drugs, play video games, eat, or start new relationships. While they make you feel better in the short term, engaging in these actions and seeking the pleasure they bring can cause you long-term problems and continued bad brain wiring.

EXERCISE: Take a moment now to assess your deceptive brain messages and how they affect you. In the space below, write down all the different ways your body and brain respond when you are stressed out, anxious, depressed, feel hopeless, or are craving something.

Making Mental Notes

Becoming aware of what their bodies were doing and ascribing those sensations to their deceptive brain messages helped our patients properly Relabel their experiences. The best way to do this, they agree, was by making mental notes.

What are mental notes? They are a shorthand way of Relabeling something quickly that ensures you will not get ensnared in the process of thinking. In essence, they are one- or two-word statements that encapsulate what is going on in that moment. For example, when you completed the thought awareness exercise #4 and said to yourself "thinking" whenever a thought arose, that was making a mental note. Similarly, when Liz used the word *spinning*, and Abby and Sarah said to themselves "thinking," "what-ifs," and "worrying," they were making mental notes.

Obviously, there are endless possibilities and options for making mental notes. The key is that they need to be short and simple. Most important, and this bears repeating, the word chosen does not have to be the *perfect* word, just one that sums up the experience so that you can pull yourself out of the repetitive process of being lost in thought or obsessively focused on your uncomfortable physical and emotional sensations. As always, with mental notes (and Relabeling), don't worry too much about the words you use. *It's the process of observing that counts.*

What are other examples of mental notes? We asked our patients how they use mental notes to Relabel when deceptive brain messages strike. Here's a list of their favorite phrases, divided up loosely into the following three categories:

EXAMPLES OF MENTAL NOTES

Thoughts and Actions	Physical Sensations	Emotional Sensations
Deceptive brain message	Sweaty palms	Depression
Ruminating	Anxiety	Anxiety
Thinking	Heart racing	Helplessness
Worrying	Stomach churning	Nervousness
Mind wandering	Upset stomach	Scared
Procrastination	Feeling sick	Anger
Something is wrong	Ears ringing	Feeling down
Trigger	Dizziness	Pain
Sabotaging	Fatigue	Low mood
Mental cloud	Light-headedness	Shame
Irrational	De-energized	Guilt
Learning experience	Lethargy	Fear
Perfection	Urge	
Avoidance	Impulse	
Uncertainty	Craving	

Clearly, the list could go on and on. The point is that you need to find some way to make a fast mental note of what is happening inside your body and brain so that you can then choose what to do about it.

Take a moment to write down some mental notes that might be helpful for you to use when a deceptive brain message strikes. Remember, the goal is for it to be short and sweet. It does not have to accurately describe the situation, but it needs to be somewhere in the ballpark. Therefore, pick a few labels now that you can use to help you notice the thoughts, impulses, sensations, and actions but that will ensure you do not get caught up in the content of those erroneous and deceptive messages.

EXERCISE: Mental notes I can use when I encounter a deceptive brain message, uncomfortable sensation, or maladaptive habit include the following:

THE BIOLOGICAL POWER OF RELABELING

In chapter 5, we mentioned that Step 1 was capable of recruiting the Assessment Center to help calm the Uh Oh Center and activate the helpful aspects of the Self-Referencing Center. How do we know this is true? From the very intriguing work done at UCLA by Matthew Lieberman, Ph.D., and his colleagues. In their experiments, they placed people in a brain scanner and asked them to look at pictures of people's faces.

What Lieberman and colleagues found was that *labeling* the observed emotion with a word—basically what you do when you make mental notes and Relabel—resulted in increased brain activity in the Assessment Center while simultaneously decreasing activity in the Uh Oh Center. In a follow-up study, they found that people who were more mindful were more effective at recruiting the Assessment Center and enhancing its ability to calm the Uh Oh Center.

This means that something special happens in your brain when you actively Relabel your emotional (and physical) sensations—when you call them what they are. The very act of putting a label on those emotional sensations activates your Assessment Center, which then quiets down its noisy, easily upset neighbor, the Uh Oh Center. That's why, from a biological perspective, learning how to Relabel your experiences and use mental notes is so important. It actually helps you manage your emotional sensations to some extent. We will discuss this more in chapter 11 when we discuss Step 3: Refocus and how to use mental notes in a special way to calm your Uh Oh Center.

For now, the thing to remember is that Lieberman's research and that of other mindfulness investigators shows that very act of Relabeling and becoming aware of your deceptive thoughts, sensations, and actions *helps you create distance* between the false messages and your true self. With repeated practice, you get to the point where you Revalue the entire experience and can easily say, "Oh, that's a deceptive brain message. It's not me and I am not going to give it the time of day. It has no value or meaning, so I am not going to listen to it, but instead will move on and do something that matters to me."

From these descriptions, the process of Relabeling probably seems rather clear and simple. In one way it is, but in other ways, noticing your deceptive brain messages can create new challenges. Our patients know this well and highlighted several things you should be aware of as you start turning your attention toward noticing your deceptive brain messages.

The Deceptive Brain Messages Can Seem to Get Worse When You Start Relabeling

One of the problems with becoming more aware of your experiences is that you start noticing things that were not even on your radar before. For example, if you were never aware of how popular white minivans are and then your friend points it out to you, you will start seeing white minivans everywhere. It's as if a screen has been lifted or a new door has been opened and now you can see something that you previously overlooked. The same thing happens when you start learning how to notice your deceptive brain messages, uncomfortable sensations, and habits. What had seemed like intermittent or sparse events in the past become hard to ignore.

For example, Abby describes feeling "like once I started looking, everything seemed like it was a deceptive brain message or unhealthy habit. It was like an octopus with all of its tentacles tangled together. I could not make heads or tails of anything. It became very frustrating and depressing—it was almost paralyzing. I wasn't sure what was true and what was false." To deal with this, she says, "I just assumed everything was a deceptive brain message and labeled my actions. When I was thinking, analyzing, feeling anxious, and so on, I noted it and moved on." That was how she started the process until she was able to strengthen her Wise Advocate enough to help her sort out what was a deceptive brain message and what was based on her true interests and goals.

Sarah agrees, especially when you are dealing with panic attacks or depression. As she explains, "The whole thing—these thoughts, sensations, and habits—is a package. The body and the brain thing are going on all at once. The scared and terrified thoughts that you're having in your brain are very much tied up into the reaction your body is having. And which one is leading which is a little hard to tell. But it's all the same process: Relabel it, then you can move on." When you do this, you pull your brain out of the endless loop of thoughts and can begin to make different choices. As Steve said, it's about putting a wedge between the deceptive brain messages and your responses—giving yourself time to fully evaluate what is happening with the Four Steps so you can act differently.

Steve's recommendation is to use an Alcoholics Anonymous Twelve Step adage to help you out when the thoughts, impulses, or sensations feel like they are getting out of hand. As he explains, "Just like alcoholics learn to say, 'Don't take that first drink,' I learned to say, 'Don't take that first thought' because it spirals from there, gains a hold, and makes it difficult to stop and realize what your brain is doing."

The sensations can also seem to get more uncomfortable when you do not give in to them. As Abby knows, you need to endure the distress "to get to the other side. Even when they are really bad," she says, "you have to sit with the pain and distress, that's what I learned with the Four Steps and it works." When Steve tried to allow the uncomfortable cravings for alcohol to be there, but not drink, he would "just stay with it and tell myself it's natural to have these cravings, my body has been getting them fulfilled for years. But that doesn't mean I have to act on it. I can choose not to give in to those cravings or anxiety or whatever arises and place my attention somewhere else instead."

If You Can't Identify the Thoughts, Then Start with the Physical Sensations

Several of our patients told us it was hard in the beginning to be aware of their thoughts and pick out which ones were deceptive brain messages. To help them, we recommended they start by noticing their physical and emotional sensations because those tend to remain consistent. Over the years, we have found that deceptive brain messages tend to evoke the same physical and emotional sensations in any one person, such as always getting an upset stomach, having headaches, or feeling fatigued. For example, when Sarah experienced deceptive brain messages, she almost always experienced a "de-energizing depression" or panic-like symptoms. Liz, on the other hand, would wake up with "gut-wrenching anxiety" and Abby often had "brain fog."

The point is that most people have a specific pattern of sensations they experience whenever their brains are telling them to do something that is not in accordance with their true self. Therefore, if you are having trouble identifying which thoughts are false messages at the beginning or your Wise Advocate is not yet strong enough to help you out, make an effort to identify those specific physical and emotional sensations you experience whenever something feels wrong. To remember them, write down your pattern of responses in the space below.

When I experience deceptive brain messages, my specific pattern of physical and emotional sensations includes:

Being able to realize what those sensations are will be one of your biggest allies as you work with the Four Steps. Why? Often, you are not aware of what situations or people trigger your deceptive brain messages because you have been blind to them for some reason, just as with the white minivan example. When you let your physical sensations (and emotional ones, to some extent) guide you, you will identify more places where deceptive brain messages are present—places you never knew existed.

Kara agrees: "The hardest step is the Relabeling because you have to be able to see it in yourself before you can address it. Rather than try to parse out the thoughts, the sensations in my body are an obvious clue. I just have to notice them because when a deceptive brain message strikes, eventually it will be in my body."

Dealing with Avoidance

In many ways, anxiety and cravings are easier to identify than avoidance because they cause you to *act* in some way in an attempt to relieve your distress or cause you to feel better momentarily. You can literally see when you are grabbing the bottle, heading to the fridge, or opening your Web browser. Similarly, if you engage in repetitive acts to decrease anxiety, you can more easily see them as well, or others can point them out to you. What makes avoidance much harder to identify is that you are now looking for the *absence of action*, which often is difficult to pick out.

How do you deal with this? Look at what you are giving up or what you are not doing because you are trying to avoid the uncomfortable sensations or negative thoughts. In fact, using the inventory you developed in chapter 2 of what things you are doing now (but wish you weren't) and what things you wish you were doing (but are not) should help a lot. This is the most effective way we've found to help people identify when they are avoiding important aspects of their lives. Making lists and checking them from time to time, or asking someone to remind you, is the best way to recognize when you are avoiding something.

Ed knows this all too well: His career was on hold for many years because he would not pick up a phone to call his agent or go to auditions. "One huge avoidance," he says, "was not putting myself out there where I might get rejected in the office of some casting person or agent. It was a big problem for me. I put all kinds of things off and said, 'Well, later. Later I can do that when I am feeling better or stronger.' The problem was, I kept waiting for a feeling that never came because I kept listening to those darn deceptive brain messages."

Wanting a specific feeling to come around or wishing that certain ones would go away is a common scenario we see. The problem with this approach is that emotional and physical sensations, like desire, change all the time—that's the nature of the brain and how it responds to the environment. This means that basing your actions on how you feel will result in lots of starts and stops, missed opportunities and frustration. This is why we repeatedly tell people, *with respect to deceptive brain messages, it's not what you think or feel, it's what you* do *that counts.*

Another problem we often see is people getting caught in the "if only" syndrome—*if only* I had a better place to live, a partner, a good job, more money . . . then I'd be happy. When people use this kind of reasoning, they put their lives on hold while they wait around for that unrealistic event to take place.[5] For example, Ed often thought to himself, "If only I can get the right agent to represent me, then my career will take off." Staying in this thought process—which was the result of a deceptive brain message—and waiting for his "feelings" to change only ensured that he would keep avoiding auditions indefinitely.

We will tackle the issue of how to deal with avoidance when we discuss Refocus in chapter 11. The point for now is to start becoming aware of the situations, events, and people you avoid and Relabeling them "avoidance" or another mental note that works for you. Once you are able to see what you avoid, you can start changing your behaviors.

If in Doubt, Ask Yourself: What Am I Doing and Why?

The goal of this chapter was to give you a good sense of what Relabeling is and how you can use mental notes to your advantage. As we mentioned

---

5. We say it is unrealistic because the house, career, partner, and so on are not going to show up at your door. Therefore, as long as you avoid certain people, places, or events, you will be stuck in the same situation you currently are in.

before, the Relabel step was designed to help you increase your *awareness* of your deceptive brain messages, uncomfortable sensations, and habitual actions. Your goal is to be aware of the *process and actions* related to deceptive brain messages, such as thinking, remembering, planning, moving, and avoiding, not the *content*. In the next chapter, we will help you learn how to Reframe your deceptive brain messages and begin to see more clearly that they are false.

Although we have endeavored to make deceptive brain messages clear, we know that the process of deciding whether something is false or not is extremely difficult, especially when you are lost in thought or your brain is spinning. Therefore, if you are in doubt, we recommend you ask yourself this question: Why am I about to do X? If the answer is because that action is aligned with your true goals and interests, then it is a helpful action and you should proceed. However, if the answer includes some variation of "because I should" (or "should not," in the case of avoidance), has any element of guilt, shame, anxiety, depression, or irrational fear, or is designed to alleviate distress coming from your Uh Oh Center, then you likely are dealing with a deceptive brain message and need to use Step 2: Reframe, along with the Wise Advocate, to determine what to do next.

SAMPLE QUESTIONS TO ASK YOURSELF BEFORE ACTING OR AVOIDING

1. Is this action I am about to do helping or hurting me?
2. Is it aligned with my true goals and values?
3. Am I avoiding something right now?
4. Am I about to go do something based on craving?
5. What is motivating me to do this?
6. Why am I about to do this?

Summary

- Mindfulness is an activity, not merely a state of mind, and must be practiced.
- Awareness and focus both are important aspects of mindfulness, but they are not synonymous.
- When dealing with deceptive brain messages, it's not how you think or what you feel that matters, it's what you do that counts— therefore, judge your actions, not your initial thoughts, impulses, desires, or sensations.
- Relabel means identifying your deceptive brain messages, uncomfortable sensations, and habitual actions as they arise in real time—call them what they are.
- It is easy to get lost in thought—use your increasing powers of awareness and mental notes to bring you back into the present moment.
- Learn your pattern of physical and emotional sensations and be on the lookout for them as a way to identify your deceptive brain messages and triggers.
- Don't be discouraged if the deceptive brain message or sensations become more apparent or overwhelming once you start Relabeling them—this is natural and to be expected.
- Don't wait around for a specific feeling or event to occur—start using the Four Steps now.
- When in doubt, make mental notes and ask yourself: What am I doing and why?

CHAPTER 9

Changing Your Relationship to Deceptive Brain Messages with Step 2: Reframe

For Liz, the sixty-five-year-old human rights activist, retiring was difficult and not what she imagined. Throughout her life, she had been a leader, traveling the world and making friends everywhere she went. As she explained to us, "I thought retirement would be grand and fun, but once I retired, I started worrying about my future." Although she could rationalize away her repetitive thinking and worrying as "a normal part of the process of getting older," she could not shake the gut-wrenching anxiety she woke up with every morning.

While it was upsetting to wake up this way, she assumed that focusing on her worrisome thoughts was appropriate and beneficial. "I actually thought I was helping myself," she says, "that going through every scenario, trying to figure out every possible outcome would help me manage my future. If I knew what to expect and how to respond, I would never be caught off guard or make a mistake." In fact, what had seemed like a productive use of her time was quite laborious and fruitless. Rather than helping, Liz's constant focus on her worries caused her to see possible danger and solitude lurking around every corner, which only strengthened her Uh Oh Center's alarm and fueled her fears further.

Once she saw that indulging the repetitive thoughts intensified her anxiety, Liz understood that worrying about her future was not helping her in the slightest. With time and the ability to Reframe these deceptive brain messages as *thinking errors* and the result of her bad brain wiring (not her!), Liz could understand *why* the thoughts, sensations, and urges were bothering her so much and began to *change* her relationship with these deceptive brain messages.

As she explains, with Step 2: Reframe, she finally could see that "the fiction in my brain was worse than whatever was actually going to happen. I was spinning my wheels and exhausting myself but I could not see it until I understood the errors my brain was making. Once I did, then I could stand up to the deceptive brain messages and say, 'No! The truth is that I will be able to take care of myself and that no matter what happens in my future, if I end up in a nursing home or not, alone or with lots of people around me, I can handle myself and find ways to make life meaningful.'"

What Liz so beautifully described is using Step 2 to learn how to see that the repetitive thought patterns were detrimental while simultaneously dispelling the notion that these thoughts must be true simply because they entered her consciousness. In other words, she began to embrace our adage *Don't believe everything you think!* In this chapter and the next, you will learn how to Reframe your experiences, just as Liz did, so that they no longer hold power over you or masquerade as the truth.

STEP 2: REFRAME

To change your perception of the importance of the deceptive brain messages, say why these thoughts, urges, and impulses keep bothering you: They are *false brain messages* (It's not ME, it's just my BRAIN!).

It Feels So Real, It Must Be a True Part of Me

Why did Liz have such trouble seeing that her deceptive brain messages and repetitive thinking were detrimental? Typically, this inability to identify the deceptive thoughts and repetitive thinking patterns as unhelpful or destructive occurs when they are tightly linked with your Self-Referencing Center. As you know, when the unhelpful aspects of the Self-Referencing Center are overactive, it inhibits or even blocks your ability to clearly see that the thoughts, desires, cravings, impulses, and urges are false and unhelpful. Instead, the deceptive brain messages seem like a part of you and absolutely true, especially when they appear to be linked to reasonable and presumably helpful actions, like repetitively "planning" (i.e., overanalyzing) your future. When you are in this mind-set, there appears to be no reason to change your behaviors or challenge the thoughts entering your head. As a result, you are stuck in the perpetual, highly deceptive belief that everything you think and feel is true. We refer to this scenario as the *"part of me" mode* because you are blinded from the truth with such brain-based falsehoods as "Why change a thing? Nothing is wrong and there are no problems here."

In psychological terms, this inability to see that the unhelpful brain messages are deceptive and incorrect—to be in the "part of me" mind-set—is referred to as "ego-syntonic." *Syntonic* comes from the Greek word *syntonos*, meaning attuned, and *ego* refers to the self. Therefore, when your sense of self is attuned with your thoughts, impulses, desires, cravings, and urges, you are operating in an ego-syntonic manner. When you are in this mode, you believe that the deceptive brain messages *are who you are and that they are correct or true.*

The opposite of this term, *ego-dystonic,* is derived from the Latin prefix *dys,* meaning "bad." In this case, *dystonic* implies being badly attuned, poorly aligned, or not consistent with your sense of self. When you operate in this mode, you have some sense that the deceptive brain messages are not a part of you, even though they feel so strong and true. You can more easily see the deceptive brain messages as *false foreign invaders.*

FALSE FOREIGN INVADERS OR AN
ACCURATE DEPICTION OF YOU?

"Part of me" mode (ego-syntonic)—These thoughts, impulses, cravings, desires, urges, and sensations are real and true! They are a part of me and I'm good with that. They reflect how I see myself and are acceptable to me. There's no reason to change what I am doing.

False foreign invader (ego-dystonic)—These thoughts, impulses, cravings, desires, urges, and sensations are uncomfortable and I do not like them. They are not part of me and they do not reflect how I see myself, but they *feel* real and true. I need to change something.

To get a sense of what it's like to *realize* you are dealing with false foreign invaders and begin to change your relationship to them, let's meet George, a forty-seven-year-old man with obsessive-compulsive traits who has recurring thoughts that if he does not check certain things at the right time, something bad will happen to someone he cares about. George's deceptive thoughts and impulses started in college and became so bad that he had to drop out of classes for a while. As he remembers, "I started getting these weird thoughts. I remember the first one: If I did not put something a certain way, someone in my family would die. It's a pretty traumatic thought. I had never had it before and I thought, 'Jeez, what's going on here?' This would continue and the sensations and anxiety would get pretty intense until I actually went ahead and moved the object the way [my brain was telling me] I was supposed to."

Even at that early stage, George had some sense that the deceptive

182 | You Are Not Your Brain

thoughts were false and inaccurate, but the sensations were so strong and overwhelming that he felt compelled to keep following the mandates of his deceptive brain messages. He knew there was no real correlation between his arranging objects or checking things repeatedly and his family's safety, but he found the only way to get rid of the horrible sensations was to check or reposition things. It affected many aspects of his life, as he recalls: "When I went out of my bathroom, I had to check a couple times—the light, the heater, the fan—to make sure they were all off. Same thing with starting the car in the morning—I always have to check the lights (are they off or on?), make sure the brake's off, just double-check on things like that because my brain kept telling me if I don't do this, something bad will happen to someone. My brother might die."

As George entered the workforce, the content of his thoughts changed slightly, but the sensations remained just as strong. He had a growing sense that the deceptive brain messages were false and that the feared outcomes wouldn't come true, but he couldn't resist the impulses to check or arrange until he learned how to Relabel those deceptive brain messages with the Four Steps and see them as *false foreign invaders*. Having this insight and knowledge made it easier for him to start putting a wedge between his deceptive brain messages and automatically engaging in the unhealthy habits of checking and rearranging.

Once George became adept at using the Four Steps, Relabeling became relatively straightforward because the bizarre thoughts and unbearably uncomfortable sensations did not feel like a part of him anymore. He could rapidly Relabel them as false messages and Reframe them as part of his maladaptive brain wiring, as he explains in this example:

> There's a drawer at work where I keep my pen. After I get the pen out and I shut the drawer, I have this recurring obsessive thought. It's that my brother is going to die. So when I would go to shut it, I would open and shut it again a couple times, if I am not catching myself. If I catch myself, then I Relabel it. I say to myself,

"That's an obsessive thought," and I Reframe it as a *biological problem,* a *chemical imbalance.* [It's not me, it's just my brain!] Once I do that, it's not easy, but I'm able to shut the drawer and Refocus by continuing with my work so I don't go back and keep opening and shutting the drawer.

Moving from "Part of Me" Mode Toward Awareness and Truth

Compare George's story to Sarah's experience of feeling like her thoughts and feelings were a true and accurate part of her. Whenever Sarah would become depressed, her deceiving brain would tell her she was not deserving of love or affection. As the negative thoughts took over, Sarah would try to Relabel her depressive thoughts and urges to physically isolate herself, but she had trouble seeing that the deceptive brain messages were not true. The thoughts and sensations were overwhelming and took hold in a most tenacious manner. Instead of being able to see that these emotional and physical sensations—including negative ideas and feelings, headaches, body pains, and malaise—were the direct result of deceptive brain messages, she viewed them as a true representation of who she was. In her head, the negative body sensations and thoughts went hand in hand with how she saw herself, which prevented her from seeing them as false. As she explains, "The deceptive brain messages truly felt like they were part of me and what I deserved to experience because I was such a loser. Why would I challenge something that was me and what I thought I deserved? When you really think you're worthless and that life is hopeless, you can't see any other options or perspectives. I thought this was how life is and would be."

For Sarah to start changing her perspective, she had to learn to recognize the signs of depression so that she could start seeing that those negative thoughts and sensations were part of a brain-based condition that was not representative of who she was. As she explains, "Once I learned what depression was, I could Relabel the tiredness, body aches, and negative thoughts *as depression* and not a part of me." Sarah would then Reframe her symptoms in a variety of ways: "I could say to myself, 'Okay, these feelings aren't really me, this is some kind of problem with serotonin or who knows what in my brain.' Or, I could say, 'Oh, okay, so that's why I'm feeling like I hate myself. That's what depression is. Well, that's what I'm feeling and you know what, that makes a lot of sense.'" Reframing her depression in these ways helped, she says, "because now at least I knew why I felt that way. Now I can see that it's just the depression, not me."

Similarly, when Steve could only see the people in his life as needy and alcohol as his friendly release, he was not able to Relabel those deceptive thoughts and uncomfortable sensations. As long as he continued to believe that drinking was an effective way to manage stress and that the people in his life were helpless, he would not be able to address his addiction to alcohol or his avoidance of his family members. "I spent a lot of time believing those deceptive messages," he says, "and it got me nowhere. I wasted time and missed out on all kinds of opportunities with my family. I wish I could have seen the negative thoughts sooner, but I am glad I can see them now."

How can you start making distinctions between helpful, productive thoughts and behaviors and deceptive or unhealthy ones? Just like George, Sarah, Steve, and Liz, you start by acknowledging that there is a part of you that knows, at some level, that the deceptive brain messages you experience are false. The problem right now is that the good and true part of you—the healthy part—is not that strong or well defined. Although it wants to help you, you continually crush it down by minimizing or neglecting the truth. Said another way, you ignore the faulty logic of your brain and take the deceptive brain messages as proof of who you are and what you deserve. You live your life distanced from the truth and are stuck responding in unhealthy and unhelpful ways.

To change your relationship to those deceptive brain messages, you need to use Step 2: Reframe to help you separate the deceptive thought patterns and habits from your healthy thoughts and behaviors—those based on your true self. As you are able to do this, you will see how false and erroneous those deceptive brain messages truly are.

In this chapter and the next, we will teach you three fundamental ways of Reframing your deceptive brain messages: (a) by attributing them to your bad brain wiring or biology with the phrase "It's not me, it's just my brain!" (b) by realizing "I'm feeling rejected—this is social pain," and (c) by recognizing the patterns of inaccurate thinking you engage in, known as thinking errors. These methods of Reframing will help you begin to view the deceptive brain messages as nothing more than faulty brain thinking or wiring. To begin, let's look at the science that explains *why* deceptive brain messages associated with social situations feel so strong and overpowering and how Reframing can help.

Social Bonds Matter: The Science of Social Pain

Why is it that you feel pain whenever your needs are being neglected, ignored, dismissed, devalued, minimized, overindulged, or hyperfocused on? Researchers at UCLA, led by Naomi Eisenberger, Ph.D., wanted answers to these kinds of questions, so they studied what happens in your brain when you are socially excluded. In one such experiment, they asked participants to play a virtual ball-tossing game with two other people while in a brain scanner. The participants were told that their goal was to keep passing the ball around to the other two players (who actually were computer simulations controlled by the researchers)—in essence, to adhere to basic social norms by politely sharing the ball with their counterparts. Unbeknownst to them, the goal of this experiment was to break that social contract and see what happened in the participants' brains. When the inevitable moment occurred and the two other "players" stopped throwing the ball to the person in the scanner, that person reported feeling excluded. In those moments, the person's Uh Oh Center started firing—thus indicating that social exclusion had "registered."

What is most interesting about these findings is that the part of the Uh Oh Center that started firing is the *same area* that is activated whenever the body experiences the distressing aspects of physical pain. This means that *the same part of the brain that processes the emotions related to physical pains also deals similarly with social pains*—and it explains *why* the uncomfortable sensations associated with deceptive brain messages feel so strong and true: The Uh Oh Center intensely fires in both situations. In a very real way, your body experiences the pain of social distress in the same way as the pain of physical distress because the same area in the brain generates the feelings and sensations.

When you think about it, these findings make perfect sense from an emotional attachment and bonding point of view. For us to survive and thrive in the world, we need more than physical security. We need the 5 A's (Attention, Acceptance, Affection, Appreciation, Allowing) to enable us to feel safe, secure, and confident. Without that sense of social safety and acceptance, we feel threatened and alone, and this causes the Uh Oh Center to fire. In this way, social connectedness is as important to humans as physical safety because *social pain and exclusion can be as dangerous as physical pain* (especially when we are children). This is why our brains perceive it in the exact same way and our bodies feel it so intensely.

Taking Things Personally

Another important finding from Eisenberger's work is that your level of distress and feelings of social pain are correlated with how strongly the Uh Oh Center is activated. For example, in a landmark study, Eisenberger's team asked participants to track their social distress and how disconnected from people they felt at the end of each day. After ten days, the participants played the same ball-tossing game and Eisenberger watched what happened. Interestingly, the more distress the person reported during his daily social interactions, the more the Uh Oh Center lit up in the brain scanner during the game.

Even more intriguing, people who reported that they had more feelings of social disconnection (e.g., those participants who strongly disagreed with statements like "Today I generally felt accepted by others") had more unhelpful Self-Referencing Center activity while in the scanner when being excluded in the ball-tossing game. This meant that when the unhelpful aspects of their Self-Referencing Center fired, it associated the mild social rejection as having something to do with themselves. If the unhealthy aspects of your Self-Referencing Center are activated in a similar way, taking social pains too personally, then you are much more likely to feel generally unaccepted by others.[1]

And if you repeatedly "buy into" the deceptive brain message and overanalyze what happened in that social situation or how you should respond in the future, your brain will *wire* the overanalyzing response into its routines. Because you sharply focus your attention in these ways, a vicious cycle forms, which will drive your future responses, decisions, choices, and actions. So, the more your Uh Oh Center fires and the more you use your Self-Referencing Center to process the information as being personally related to you, the more likely you are to overanalyze the situation and conclude that the interaction means something is wrong with you.

As a result, an unhelpful brain pattern sets in: The deceptive brain messages that cause you to take things too personally will lead you to overanalyze and make assumptions. This bad brain pattern can then drive you to repeatedly respond to social distress with the same unhealthy reaction, such as more overanalyzing, leading to avoiding social interactions and other problematic responses to social pain.

---

1. If the unhelpful aspects of the Self-Referencing Center lead you to take perceived social rejections personally, you will be much more likely to remember them as feelings of social disconnection (not being accepted by others) when asked hours later about how you felt during the day.

- Increased Uh Oh Center firing results in more *momentary distress* during social interactions.
- The distressing aspects of physical and social pain are processed by the Uh Oh Center.
- The stronger your Uh Oh Center fires, the more distressing emotional sensations you will feel.
- The unhealthy aspects of your Self-Referencing Center can cause you to take things personally and lead to more end-of-the-day feelings of disconnection or experiencing a lack of acceptance from other people.

Relabel and Reframe Calm the Uh Oh Center and Strengthen the Assessment Center

How can you calm down the Uh Oh Center in healthy ways after it's been agitated by social pain, sadness, anxiety, cravings, or other states? With the Four Steps! Eisenberger's findings, along with the work of her colleague Matthew Lieberman, provide compelling reasons for why you should use the Four Steps whenever you can. Relabeling, as Lieberman showed, enhances the calming activity of the Assessment Center, as well as the helpful aspects of the Self-Referencing Center, which calms the Uh Oh Center—resulting in healthy ways to manage your emotional sensations that do not involve devaluing or belittling yourself.

Suppressing Your Emotional Responses Negatively Impacts You and Those Around You

In addition to Eisenberger's and Lieberman's brain research, James Gross, Ph.D., of Stanford University has found that changing your relationship to your deceptive brain messages and experiences (as you do when you

Reframe) can have a beneficial impact on your body and blood pressure. In one of his experiments, he showed people a "disgusting arm amputation" and then instructed them to (a) *reappraise* the situation in a way that makes the images less upsetting, such as telling yourself you are just "watching a medical video," (b) just watch (with no instructions provided), or (c) hide their emotional reaction so that it does not show on their faces (i.e., *suppress* their emotional reactions). Interestingly, he found that *suppressing emotional reactions led to increased blood pressure*, likely by increasing the levels of stress hormones, whereas just watching and reappraising did not.

Gross followed this work with an experiment that demonstrated that *suppressing emotions resulted in decreased memory of information and events.* Participants were shown slides depicting injured men while they received verbal information about each man shown. When the participants were later given memory tests related to the stories of the men, the people who suppressed their emotions scored the lowest. Gross concluded from this experiment that suppressing your true responses is unhealthy because it causes the brain to dedicate significant resources to the act of suppressing, which results in less memory of events and impaired learning of new information.

As significant, Gross showed that suppressing or hiding your reactions can negatively affect those around you. In this study, he showed a movie to pairs of women and asked them to discuss their reactions with each other. One of the women in the pair was told to suppress, reappraise, or respond naturally, while the other woman was in the dark about these instructions. Interestingly, Gross found that *when the women suppressed their reactions, their counterparts experienced significant increases in blood pressure.* This did not happen when the women reappraised the videos or watched naturally.

Taken together, Gross's work demonstrates that *suppressing* emotional reactions leads to:

- Increasing your blood pressure (likely through stress hormones being activated)
- Decreasing your memory of events—thus impairing learning
- Increasing the blood pressure of those around you

From our perspective, the main point of Gross's work is that the more you try to suppress your reactions to deceptive brain messages (i.e., deny, neglect, or dismiss your true self), rather than accept that they are present and use the Four Steps to constructively deal with them, the more your blood pressure, stress levels, and uncomfortable sensations will rise and the worse you and those around you feel.

Reframing: A Way to Change Your Experience of Deceptive Brain Messages

Combined, the work of Eisenberger, Lieberman, and Gross demonstrates that the way to deal with deceptive brain messages, uncomfortable sensations, and maladaptive habits is to change your relationship to them *without trying to suppress your responses to the sensations, urges, impulses, cravings, or desires.* This is the goal of Step 2: Reframe—to use your knowledge that these are just deceptive brain messages, not a real part of you, to explain to yourself why they are bothering you so much. As you do this, you will be able to change your perception of the deceptive brain messages and uncomfortable sensations.

So, when you use Step 2 to Reframe your experiences in an accurate way, you begin to see how false the Uh Oh Center's alarm is. It's at that point that you begin seeing them as the false intruders they truly are. At that point, you will no longer feel compelled to act on the automatic unhealthy habits or responses. Instead, you will see what's really going on—that it's the *power you give* to these false messages and *how you associate* those thoughts with specific outcomes or meanings that's the problem.

As this happens, you change your relationship to the deceptive brain messages and uncomfortable sensations in a positive and beneficial way.

What's more, *Relabeling and Reframing can change the Self-Referencing Center from a nagging scold to an empowered enabler, helping to calm the Uh Oh Center.* Rather than causing you to take things too personally and feel a lack of acceptance, putting a true label on emotions and Reframing the situation help the Assessment Center enlist the healthy aspects of the Self-Referencing Center to calm down the Uh Oh Center's anxiety-provoking responses. Reframing also reminds you to invoke your Wise Advocate so that you can reevaluate the situation from a healthy, loving perspective.

Although Gross's work is intriguing and makes practical sense, there is one major difference between his version of reappraisal and Step 2: Reframe: Reappraisal includes anything you tell yourself to decrease your emotional and physical sensations—including creating a false reality to calm yourself down. Obviously, this is not something we want you to do, since we are trying to teach you how to align your actions with your true self and stay firmly rooted in the truth. Therefore, we want you to Reframe your experiences based on what's really happening *and let the sensations be there without acting on them.* You do not want to try to change the sensations or make them go away. Rather, your goal is to change your experience and perspective on the deceptive brain messages and uncomfortable sensations—to gain a better understanding of their cause and learn that through constructive and adaptive actions your reactions and responses can change in dependable and durable ways.

We know this is no easy task. As our patients have told us time and again, sitting with the uncomfortable sensations without attempting to act to directly relieve their distress by engaging in harmful behaviors can be extremely difficult and painful. To deal with the discomfort, they remind themselves of how detrimental it is, biologically, to give in to the sensations by acting in unhealthy ways. As John explains, "I would remind myself that the deceptive brain messages and sensations are part of the mechanics of my brain. I would look at it more mechanically and say, 'My brain is going through that but it won't be there forever. It's just a momentary, passing cloud.' By doing that, I'm looking toward the future, looking at those other times when these sensations will not be there, when it will not be the case that I will react in this way to whatever the false messages are telling me."

Similarly, Steve experienced the deceptive brain messages as causing "a sensation that feels very bad and you really want to get rid of it—that's why you do those [unhealthy actions] again and again. It's an unending cycle. So, the first thing would be to live with the uncertainty, the fear, and the pain that the deceptive brain messages and uncomfortable sensations leave you with." Rather than fighting them or denying their existence, Steve says, you need to "stay with the intense feelings until you are able to look at them more objectively, from another perspective—then the deceptive brain messages and sensations are less damaging or upsetting." The act of Relabeling and Reframing can actually make the deceptive brain messages less damaging by weakening the brain circuitry associated with those unhelpful thoughts, urges, impulses, and desires.

To help you understand that uncomfortable, upsetting sensations do pass on their own, try the following exercise.

EXERCISE: LEARNING THAT SENSATIONS WILL PASS

A major theme in classical mindfulness training is learning that physical and emotional sensations will pass on their own, even if you do nothing about them. For example, if you are sitting in meditation and notice an itch arise in your leg, you are taught to notice the itch, including how it feels and what it's like, but to not give it any special significance or try to change the sensation in any way—much like what we tell you to do with the uncomfortable physical and emotional sensations that arise because of deceptive brain messages.

If you think about it, intuitively, this principle makes sense. How many times have you noticed an itch or slight pain that seems to stop bothering you when you focus your attention elsewhere?

To make this point more clear, complete the following exercise: Think back on an event (or events) that occurred in the past few weeks that evoked a strong reaction in you at the time it occurred. As you look back at that event (or events) now, answer these questions:

- What happened?
- Why did you react the way you did? What upset you?
- Thinking about it now, does it still cause the same reaction in you? If so, why? If not, why not?
- When you think about the situation now, do you still have the same emotional and physical reactions you did at the time? Why or why not?

Completing this exercise should help you see that in many cases (though not all), your initial strong reaction is based on your brain's reaction to social pain and is not a result of some true problem or danger. The more you complete exercises like this, the more you will be able to see that in many cases, what seems like a big deal in the moment is not that important in the grand scheme of life—and that acting impulsively when the sensations arise tends to make things worse.

The goal, as you saw in our discussion of the biology of Relabeling and Reframing, is to change your relationship to the event so that you can see what happened with clear eyes and not believe the false alarm coming from your Uh Oh Center. The truth is, the less you personalize the incident, the more your perception of what transpired changes in a productive way. As this happens, you are less likely to become upset because you are not automatically equating the negative event with something *you did* or that you perceive is being *done to you*.

We'll talk about this more when we discuss thinking errors in the next chapter—the point for now is to see that your memory and perception of events change with time and that reacting impulsively or automatically in the moment likely is not the best strategy (unless you truly are in danger).

Option #1: Reframe the Biology— It's Not Me, It's Just My Brain

As we mentioned, you can Reframe in innumerable ways as long as you are seeing what's really happening and basing your actions on your true goals and values. One of the most effective ways to Reframe, especially at the beginning of your work with the Four Steps, is to focus on the biology— specifically the bad brain wiring that resulted from your repeatedly responding in the same way to the deceptive brain messages.

In the most simple of Reframes, our patients would simply say, "I'm having a bad brain day," "It's not me, it's *just* my brain," or "It's just *the* brain." The more they did this, the more they were able to *separate* their healthy, adaptive side from the deceptive brain messages and accept that while some days would be more difficult, they would not derail them or stop them from continuing on in a healthy direction. This ability is at the heart of a concept we mentioned in chapter 1, that biology (or your current brain wiring) is not destiny.

Whether you say it's *just your* brain or *the* brain makes little difference as long as you are clear that the initial thoughts, impulses, urges, and cravings are beyond your conscious control. When you are able to conceptualize the deceptive brain messages and sensations in this way—as coming from your brain, but not representative of you or who you are—you are able to change your behaviors without shaming yourself in the process. For example, just like you would never tell a person with Parkinson's disease to stop their tremor or to feel bad because they keep shaking, you should not berate yourself for having these deceptive thoughts and impulses. Similarly, you would never tell someone with cancer to "just get over it" or that they brought it on themselves.

This same logic and compassion holds true with anxiety, depression, addictions, and anything that evokes deceptive brain messages—you did not ask for them to be there. Rather, *the deceptive brain messages stem from biological problems that developed despite you, not because of you.* It's not your fault that they are present and bothering you, but fortunately, unlike many medical conditions, you can do something about your deceptive brain messages that results in permanent, positive changes in your brain.

How can you start Reframing biologically? Let's look at how some of our patients Reframed their deceptive brain messages as being part of their biology, not their true self. Abby says she often did so in this way: "I would say to myself, 'This certainly feels real, but no, this is just the brain's synapses firing.' Of course it feels true because my brain is sending those signals, but those signals are coming from something that is not really real. There's no need for those signals to be there [because there is no real danger]. But they are there, so I have to deal with them [by not taking them at face value or paying attention to them]. I realize that if I keep reacting to them [in unhealthy ways] the signals only get stronger and I cannot afford to do that."

Similarly, Steve, who often experienced physical cravings when he had the impulse to drink alcohol, says, "The trick is not to react to the deceptive brain messages because doing so is not going to stop the pain. Even though I feel physical pain and craving, I know it's coming from my brain and it does not have to be acted on. There is no injury and there is no real need to fulfill that craving, but yet the little nerves in my head are just going wild. So, I told myself, it's the brain that is making me crave alcohol right now."

Likewise, for those dealing with depression, you can Reframe the fatigue, low motivation, urge to isolate, and so on as being caused by the brain. For example, Sarah says, "When I have the de-energizing feelings, I Reframe them as symptoms of depression . . . it's a medical issue. It's not me. It's not that I'm lazy or weak, it's that I have certain chemical imbalances. I Reframe it for myself with Step 2 as something that has a bio-logical origin and a psychological origin, too. Either way, it's something the brain is doing that I do not have to listen to."

Similarly, when dealing with panic attacks, Sarah would Relabel those experiences as "anxiety," "panic," or "rapid heartbeat," and then Reframe the reason why she was distressed by saying to herself, "Hey, the brain is causing this anxiety that's making my heart beat faster and making my palms sweat . . . it's just a brain thing that causes the heart pounding and sweating—it's not me."

Option #2: Reframe the Social Pain—"I'm Feeling Rejected, This Is Social Pain"

As she became more adept at using Step 2, Sarah began to note all the times in her day when the uncomfortable sensations, emotional and phys-ical, were triggered by social pain and feelings of rejection. This helped her understand why she felt so nervous or even awkward in some social situ-ations and allowed her to see that she did not have to respond by over-analyzing.

With increasing insight, generated by repeatedly using the Four Steps in social situations, Sarah started employing a more advanced version of Reframing that allowed her to recognize that her true emotions and needs were being masked by overpowering emotional sensations coming from her experience of social pain generated by the brain. In these cases, Sarah would recognize the uncomfortable sensations she experienced in social situations as being related to *social pain.* With this knowledge, she could *reinterpret* her anxiety as a helpful *signal* that she was somehow ignoring, denying, or neglecting her true emotions and true self in those situations. In doing so, she would acknowledge that part of her reaction (and social pain) had roots in her childhood when her mother or brother evoked similar pains in her (related to her true emotions), while another part was coming from her brain and how it inaccurately interpreted the current social situation as dangerous. When she was able to do this, she could recognize that the anxiety she experienced was telling her two things: (a) she was dismissing or disavowing a true emotion or a part of her true self and (b) she was dealing with a deceptive brain message.

With this understanding, she would use the anxiety to help guide her—to allow a true emotion to surface or recognize that she was squelching one of her true wishes, values, or interests. What she did not do is personalize that pain too much, agree with any deceptive brain messages that accompanied it, or act in a destructive, unhealthy way because of it. Rather, she would acknowledge the discomfort and Reframe the anxiety as a healthy signal that she was about to ignore her true self yet again. When she Reframed in this way, she was able to see that her brain was simply responding to the social interactions in the same way it responded to physical pain—that's why the sensations felt so strong and intense. From this more balanced view, she could Refocus on a healthy activity and allow her true emotions to arise, knowing that the anxiety was a helpful signal encouraging her to pay attention and tend to her true self.

Option #3: Reframe Your Thinking Errors

A third and highly effective way Sarah dealt with her deceptive brain messages was to note the thinking errors that occurred throughout her day. By seeing when and how her brain inappropriately filtered information or applied meaning to situations that did not warrant such conclusions to be drawn, she was able to list yet another reason why the deceptive brain messages elicited such strong uncomfortable sensations. Given how important it is to recognize them, we'll take an in-depth look at those *thinking errors* in the next chapter.

For now, let's review what you have learned about Step 2: Reframe:

- Reframe answers the question: *Why* do these deceptive thoughts and uncomfortable sensations keep bothering me?

- When you cannot see that the thoughts, urges, sensations, impulses, or cravings are deceptive, you assume they are a part of you.
- Your goal is to change your perspective and start seeing those deceptive brain messages as false foreign invaders.
- Social pain is generated by the Uh Oh Center, as are the distressing aspects of physical pain.
- Taking things too personally is often a deceptive brain message coming from the unhealthy aspects of the Self-Referencing Center.
- Relabel and Reframe enhance the Assessment Center and calm the Uh Oh Center, thus helping you make healthier choices by seeing that the sensations are false.

CHAPTER 10

Reframing Your
Thinking Errors

In chapter 9, you learned to Reframe many of your deceptive brain messages as resulting from bad brain wiring by saying: (a) "This is *just* my brain" or (b) "I am experiencing *social pain*." By doing this, you were answering the question, "*Why* do these thoughts, impulses, desires, urges, and sensations bother me so much in a biological way?" While helpful in many situations, biology is not the only way you can Reframe your experiences. You can also use your Wise Advocate to help you see *how* your brain is *misinterpreting* and *misperceiving* information and making many thinking errors. This kind of Reframing is powerful because invoking your Wise Advocate helps you see how false and destructive those deceptive brain messages can be.

Commonly referred to as *thinking errors*,[1] these are ways your brain distorts information and causes you to see life through the lens of deceptive brain messages:

---

1. Other terms you may be familiar with for these same processes include *cognitive distortions, automatic thoughts,* or *negative thoughts.*

Ways your brain erroneously and inaccurately filters information or applies meaning to situations. When you engage in thinking errors, your brain distorts or misinterprets what's happening, causing you to make inappropriate and false conclusions about people, situations, and yourself.

Why are thinking errors important to catch? First and foremost, thinking errors are *actions*, not thoughts. In this way, they are habitual, *automatic ways* you respond once a deceptive brain message comes into your head. This means you can do something about them. Remember, the repetitive overthinking and overanalyzing occur *after* an initial deceptive brain message arises. So, even though overanalyzing and other forms of thinking errors *feel* natural and appropriate, they are quite detrimental habits and actions. The truth is, once the initial thought or impulse emerges, you actually do have control over whether you follow that first deceptive thought with endless loops of analysis fueled by thinking errors or whether you stop the progression of thoughts before they get out of hand.

The second reason thinking errors are important to identify is that your inaccurate beliefs about yourself are entwined with these negative thought processes. Remember, your Self-Referencing Center is active whenever you engage in thinking about yourself, which means the more you repetitively think about what you've done (or haven't done, but should have done) and the more you focus on the false aspects of your self, the more the unhealthy aspects of your Self-Referencing Center are negatively activated and the more distress you will feel (because of the extremely strong links to your Uh Oh Center). Rather than diminishing your distress, you perpetuate it further and, in the process, as Eisenberger found, you end up remembering the negative aspects of your experience. *These memories, caused by taking things too personally, lead you to propagate and maintain a negative concept of yourself and act in unhealthy ways*—thus taking you further away from your true self, goals, and values.

The good news is that once you are aware that you are engaging in these patterns of thinking, you can *choose to focus your attention* differently—not to indulge the thinking errors and their endless thought loops and instead Refocus your attention in healthy, constructive ways. That's why assertively Relabeling and Reframing your deceptive brain messages is so important—it is your gateway to awareness and making new choices.

Psychiatrist and author Dr. David D. Burns, who has studied desire and effort, categorized these thinking errors to make them easier to spot (and Reframe) in his bestselling book *Feeling Good*. To help you incorporate knowledge of thinking errors into the Four Steps, we recategorized Burns's initial ten thinking errors (i.e., cognitive distortions) into the six listed below and then added two of our own: faulty comparisons and false expectations.

Why? Three of his thinking error categories, *filtering, minimizing,* and *personalizing,* are universal processes related to all deceptive brain messages. Remember what we told you in chapter 6: Deceptive brain messages cause you to ignore, minimize, dismiss, neglect, or devalue yourself and your healthy needs (or the opposite, to overvalue and excessively focus on them). Whenever you listen and respond to a deceptive brain message, you are inherently *filtering* the information, *minimizing* your (or someone else's) contributions or worth, and *personalizing* the interaction in a way that makes you think something is wrong with you (or the other person). Therefore, we do not see these as separate thinking errors, but a by-product of living with deceptive brain messages and having an overactive Uh Oh Center and the unhelpful aspects of your Self-Referencing Center in charge. Let's look at each of the thinking errors in more detail.

ERROR #1: ALL-OR-NOTHING (BLACK-OR-WHITE) THINKING
When you engage in this thinking error, you evaluate information (including situations, people, and yourself) in extremes, such as perfect or ruined,

excellent or horrible, the best or the worst, and so on. In particular, this kind of thinking tends to go hand in hand with perfectionism, as Sarah knows all too well. She describes using all-or-nothing thinking to inappropriately guide many of her actions. For example, in the past if she couldn't do something perfectly, she probably wouldn't do it at all. As she explains, "I had days where I got absolutely nothing done or other days when I got everything done, but seldom were there happy mediums. That made it hard because there were days I needed to get specific projects done but I just felt like no matter what I did, it would be wrong, so I just didn't do it. This led to procrastination and a lot of stress around deadlines. So, whenever I noticed it, I Relabeled the procrastination as a habit I engaged in and then Reframed it as all-or-nothing thinking."

Thinking in all-or-nothing terms can also easily be turned on oneself. When that happens, people view themselves as either doing really well or horribly—again, there seems to be no in-between. In fact, what happens most often is that people repetitively devalue themselves, which results in their seeing themselves as "all bad" while simultaneously seeing others as "all good." When done repeatedly, this leads you to see any misstep or mistake as proof of your inadequacy and to set high, likely unachievable expectations of yourself.

Similarly, that all-or-nothing thinking often is applied to the people around you and opportunities in your life. For example, because of perfectionism you might miss out on a great romantic partner—someone who could be much more than "good enough" for you, who could connect with your true self, cherish you, and treat you well. Kara often experienced these kinds of deceptive thoughts and regrets the toll they took on her life. As she explains, "I spent a lot of time waiting around for the 'perfect' man to come along. This led me to think to myself, 'I can't date this guy because what if there's a more perfect person coming along?' It caused me to miss out on a lot of great people and waste a lot of time."

Perfectionism can also wreak havoc on your career, as it did to Liz. In terms of choosing jobs, all-or-nothing thinking can lead you to hold out for a mythical employment opportunity that never exists. For instance, Liz always wanted to work overseas as an executive director for a human rights foundation or watchdog group, but never found the "perfect" opportunity. She had received many offers, but the countries or the particulars of the job were not exactly what she hoped for. "I ended up passing on all these great options," she laments. "I wish I had just taken one of them for the experience, but no, my thinking was that it had to be the best or I was not going to do it at all. I wish I could have Relabeled those deceptive thought processes and Reframed them as black-and-white thinking, but I just didn't realize I was doing it at the time."

Another way all-or-nothing thinking can derail you is in terms of making decisions. Many of our patients have come to us saying that they became virtually paralyzed when they had to make even the smallest, seemingly inconsequential choice, like picking where to go to dinner. While they initially were very frustrated by this indecision, when they reflected back on their lives, they usually could remember being ridiculed for making the wrong decision or for having important people second-guess, or be disappointed in, their choices. As Ed remembers all too clearly, "My mom always gave me the message that no matter what I did, it wouldn't be right. Say, for example, I actually did make a choice, like where we were going for dinner. Once I made the choice, then she'd say, 'Well, we could have gone here.' Even after the dinner was over, she'd go on for hours saying, 'Well, you could have done this, too, you know. I mean, your choice is fine, but you should have also considered this.'" These interactions led Ed to view himself as a "second-class citizen" and perceive himself as "flawed." To deal with this kind of all-or-nothing thinking, Ed would say to himself, "You're doing it again. You're thinking in absolutes and are not taking in the truth—you are a good person and you are allowed to make choices that are best for you. Stop the all-or-nothing thinking, make a decision, and don't look back."

ERROR #2: CATASTROPHIZING (AKA FORTUNE-TELLING OR WORST-CASE-SCENARIO THINKING)

When you catastrophize, you *exaggerate or amplify* your current experiences or predict that *something bad has happened or is going to happen.* Often, this kind of thinking is referred to as *fortune-telling* or *worst-case-scenario thinking* because it causes you not to see other explanations, possibilities, or outcomes—just the ones suggested by your deceptive brain messages. For example, if you were giving a speech and slipped up on a word or two—despite the rest of the presentation going extremely well— you might assume that everyone noticed your mistakes and that when you were done your boss was going to call you over and fire you. Similarly, if you were studying for a big exam and told yourself that you had to get an A on this test or you weren't going to get accepted into grad school, you would be catastrophizing as well.

Obviously, people who overanalyze, overthink, and engage in lots of "what-if" thought processes rely heavily on catastrophizing, fortune-telling, and worst-case-scenario thinking. As Abby explained, "My brain would go to the worst-case scenario over and over." Whether it was worrying about the safety of her children or how to structure a deal at work, this repetitive thinking and analyzing was an unhealthy habit Abby engaged in to try to alleviate her anxiety. Unfortunately, it never worked out the way she hoped. Instead, she says, if she solved the problem or stopped worrying about one thing, "My brain would find another scenario to worry about. No matter how I tried to solve the problem, my brain would just find something else to worry about." And, regardless of what initial thought started the chain of overthinking and overanalyzing, the result was always the same: "I constantly worried that something bad was going to happen and that if I could only figure it out, I could somehow prevent it." But, the truth, Abby reminds herself, "is that in most cases, what I worry about doesn't come true or isn't as bad as I think. I worry myself sick for no reason at all. The more I Reframe those false thoughts as catastrophizing and overthinking, the less true those [repetitive thoughts] seem."

Like Abby and Liz, Sarah's brain would "mull things over" to the point that she would worry about even the most far-reaching scenarios. As she recalls, "If there was even a remote possibility it might happen, I would worry about it." With her boss, she was often worried that he would find some glaring flaw—something he had until now overlooked but soon would realize—and fire her, despite the fact that she had been working with him for five years and had received only glowing annual reviews and a promotion within the last year.

Similarly, John's catastrophic thinking and fortune-telling about Alicia and their relationship is what led him to compulsively check his e-mail and constantly worry that Alicia would figure out she was too good for him. To deal with this erroneous thinking, John Relabeled his urge to check e-mail as "reassurance" and Reframed the experience as "catastrophic thinking" or "fortune-telling." As he explained, "If I looked at the urges and negative thoughts objectively, I saw that I really have no evidence for the fortune-telling or catastrophic thinking. Therefore, I tell myself, 'Don't pay attention to it,' and a few moments later, all of a sudden, I have a different perspective on those urges, negative thoughts, and uncomfortable, anxious sensations."

ERROR #3: DISCOUNTING THE POSITIVE

In this thinking error, you take minimizing, ignoring, and devaluing to the extreme by severely downplaying your positive qualities, attributes, or contributions, or by failing to notice the positive reactions someone is having toward you. Going back to our presentation example, if someone says he likes the way you presented the information, but all you can think about are the two minor errors you made, you are discounting the positive information coming in. Somewhere in your brain, you assume that because you are thinking poorly of yourself for making those mistakes, the other person is doing the same and is "only being nice" by saying he liked the presentation. If you were able to see things from his perspective, you would realize that he really did enjoy the presentation and never even noticed the two minor mistakes you made—to him, it really was great, but you cannot take that information in and cannot believe it is true because your brain discounts the positive aspects of your experience before those positive aspects can ever reach your mind.

Ed knows all too well what happens when you discount the positive. Despite often receiving rave reviews for his performances and booking many jobs, he never thought he was good enough or that his performances actually were well received. As he recalls, "I would have these directors telling me, 'God, you're such a wonderful performer,' and in my head I was thinking, 'That was a horrible performance. What the hell is he talking about?' I realized that my brain was projecting my negative thoughts and assessments, which weren't true, onto these other people. What was happening was so weird because what people were telling me was not matching up with how I felt about my work or myself. My experiences were tainted by these deceptive brain messages and the horrible sensations, but I just couldn't see it until I started using the Four Steps and began separating *how my brain was making me feel,* which wasn't true, from the reality of the situation—that I had done a good job and that these reviews from others were accurate." Although Ed has largely conquered his stage fright and avoidance of auditions, whenever such negative thoughts come into his head, he Relabels them as "false thoughts and misleading sensations" and Reframes them as "being caused by my tendency to discount the positive."

Another dangerous area where discounting the positive emerges is when you make *faulty comparisons.* These comparisons can be with other people, as is often the case in the "grass is always greener" syndrome, or it can be with the life you imagined you would have. This is something Liz struggled with, despite living comfortably and being successful financially. As she explains, "The fact is I have an Ivy League degree, acted in leadership roles, live in a nice place, and have great friends—those are all things to celebrate. But I compare my life as it is with the dream life I had constructed as a kid. I compare my life as it is now to that life I imagined and that discrepancy really fuels the deceptive brain messages. Instead of being able to look at what I have and say, 'Isn't that great?' I focus on what I have not done, what I have not achieved, and what I do not have. It's a miserable way to live because no matter what I did, it was never enough." Now, if such thoughts arise in her head, Liz Relabels them as deceptive brain messages and Reframes them as "comparisons" or "dismissing the positive."

Obviously, discounting the positive can also be deceptively and inappropriately directed toward other people, such as when Steve cannot see the ways his family and coworkers are taking care of themselves and acting independently.

ERROR #4: EMOTIONAL REASONING

Many of the thinking errors our patients described result, in part, from emotional reasoning, just as Ed's discounting the positive came from his overwhelming negative feelings about his performances. Remember what we have been telling you—when dealing with deceptive brain messages, *don't believe everything you think or feel.* As you have seen time and again, the deceptive brain messages often are what's causing your Uh Oh Center's alarm to go off, not some real danger. This is the biggest problem with emotional reasoning—it causes you to buy into your Uh Oh Center's alarm and assume that what you feel is true and accurate. This causes you to believe that those uncomfortable sensations are signaling some kind of real danger or indicating that there *is* something wrong with you (or the people in your life). In these cases, your erroneous and false thought process would include some variation of the following: "If I feel like this, something *must* be wrong (with me or the world)." It is the role of your Wise Advocate to correct any distortions and thinking errors that are bubbling (and sometimes gushing!) up from the depths of your brain.[2]

---

2. Of course, your Uh Oh Center could be firing and generating anxiety because you are neglecting a true need or emotion. In that case, you need to acknowledge the true emotion (or need) and use your Wise Advocate to disarm any deceptive brain messages that accompany or fuel your unhealthy habit of ignoring, minimizing, or neglecting your true self.

Similarly, if you are not living up to excessive and unreasonable expectations of yourself, your Uh Oh Center likely will fire repeatedly and cause similar uncomfortable sensations that lead you to believe that something is wrong with you. Blindly listening to the Uh Oh Center in those situations takes you down a path that is unhealthy and leads to irrational or harmful behaviors that are not based on the truth of what is actually transpiring. The key is to *notice whenever you are about to do something based solely on how you feel, rather than what's in your best interest. If you find that you are dealing with a deceptive brain message and are about to act in an unhelpful way, immediately Relabel and Reframe those experiences and then Refocus on a healthy, constructive behavior.*

To Reframe such thinking errors, our patients often would simply say to themselves, like Liz, "If I am making a choice from the energy of the deceptive brain message, it's going to be an unhealthy choice. If instead I make it from an adult rational perspective, from the Wise Advocate, that would be a good, healthy choice."

ERROR #5: MIND READING

Mind reading overlaps with several of the other thinking errors, such as catastrophizing and discounting the positive, but it is given its own category because of how often people engage in this inaccurate thought process and how destructive it can be in relationships. Mind reading is defined as assuming you know what the other person is thinking, feeling, or believes based on either (a) your behavior (what you are saying or doing, how well you are communicating, your physical or emotional sensations, and so on) or (b) how you are interpreting the other person's gestures, language, tone, or behaviors. For example, when Ed went to auditions, he would watch the casting agents closely and often thought he knew what they were thinking. In one case, he saw an agent who had a puzzled look on his face, which prompted Ed to think to himself, "That guy in the middle can see that I'm sweating, that I'm scared. He knows I can't act and is going to tell the others to pass on me and choose someone else." Here, Ed jumped to conclusions and catastrophized while also believing he could read the agent's mind.

Similarly, if Alicia looked away while she and John were talking at dinner, he says, "I would get the sense that she didn't like what I said or that she was bored with me. I would become anxious and guess that she was thinking of ways of ending the dinner early or was daydreaming about being with someone else. Of course, this wasn't the case, but I made all these false assumptions just based on one look off to the side. It was agony when I did that. Now, I Relabel the anxiety I feel and then Reframe why it's bothering me as me 'jumping to conclusions' and 'mind reading.'"

ERROR #6: "SHOULD" STATEMENTS

Similar to mind reading, "should" statements are abundant and often accompany other thinking errors. The major problem with thinking in terms of "should," "ought to," or "must" is that they often are based on *false expectations* of how things should be, not what they actually are. For example, if you believe there are only certain ways to act, and you are not able to live up to those standards all the time, you are bound to feel demoralized and guilty because you are not acting according to your inordinately high standards. While it may be true that it would be good for you to behave in a different way, shaming yourself into action helps no one and actually has the opposite effect—it ignites negative emotional and physical sensations (most notably depression, anxiety, or anger) that can paralyze you.

Sarah often reminds herself, "What I need to do is stop rehashing the past. What's happened has happened and I cannot change it. And overanalyzing it isn't going to change the way I feel right now. I need to be moving toward positive things in life, not focusing on all these false expectations and 'shoulds.' All it does is make me feel worse." And it causes Sarah to discount all the positive things she is doing in life, the good choices she's making, and the healthy ways she acts that are in accordance with her true self.

When they are inappropriately applied (i.e., meant to shame you, not spur you to act in accordance with your true goals and values), "should" statements and false expectations directed toward yourself tend to cause feelings of guilt, remorse, regret, sadness, or anger *toward you*. When repetitively applied, this kind of "should" thinking often causes you to feel hopeless or helpless, resulting in depression, anxiety, addictions, or other maladaptive sensations and behaviors, just as Sarah's perfectionism led to periods of depression and anxiety.

Similarly, when the "should" statements and false expectations are incorrectly directed outward (e.g., you hold inappropriate expectations of other people or society to fulfill needs that you can provide yourself), you experience anger, resentment, or frustration *toward others*. This can occur in benign situations, such as when someone is driving too slowly in front of you in the fast lane, or it can be more serious, such as what often happened to Steve when he dealt with his coworkers or his family. As mentioned previously, Steve often became frustrated by his inaccurate perception that everyone was incapable of taking care of themselves, which led him to adopt the stance that the people in his life *should* be able to handle more on their own. "If only they were more capable," Steve thought, "then I would not be this stressed out all the time. I am so annoyed by all of them!" His response to these "should" thinking errors (which we know were not based in the truth, since his coworkers and family did many things independently and effectively) was to become angry and drink often. In this way, his "should" statements and false expectations were controlling his life and his perceptions.

The way many of our patients Reframed these kinds of thinking errors was to call this process "the Should Monster" or use some similar name. By doing this, they took the sting out of the emotional sensations and separated what was truly happening from what their brains were trying to tell them to do. After they Relabeled their thoughts and sensations, they would Reframe the *why* of the deceptive brain messages to thinking in terms of *false expectations*, *"should" statements*, and not seeing the truth.

False Expectations and Faulty Comparisons

Clearly, false expectations and faulty comparisons can profoundly affect your life, especially if you are not aware of their presence. One particular place where these deceptive brain messages and thinking errors can wreak havoc is in relationships.

For example, what would happen if you inappropriately try to get other people to fulfill the 5 A's (Attention, Acceptance, Affection, Appreciation, and Allowing) for you more than 25 percent of the time? Most likely those well-intentioned people will be unable to meet your expectations, and you will quickly become disappointed and likely quite frustrated. Why will you not get what you want? When you expect and desire too much from other people, you are placing an unreasonable and *false expectation* on the other person to take care of you or put you first, rather than appropriately caring for yourself and prioritizing your needs in a healthy and constructive way. Granted, there *are* times when you will need someone to care for you— that's not what we're talking about. Nor are we talking about genuine love and affection that is freely shared. Rather, we are referring to things you *can* do for yourself, but choose not to for some reason. Usually, this kind of behavior stems from childhood and is an unconscious attempt to obtain the 5 A's we did not receive as children. Although it's understandable why you might do this (just remember how important emotional attachment and social bonds are for all of us), it's not a healthy way to seek out affection or attention from others. The way to constructively deal with these desires is to call them what they are, such as "I'm trying to get someone else to take care of me" or "false expectation," and remind yourself that you can and must learn how to meet your own needs on most occasions.

If you don't believe that expectations can have such strong effects, consider the research analyzed by James Gross, Ph.D., and Kevin Ochsner, Ph.D. (of Columbia University). In their review of scientific studies dealing with emotional regulation, they found that *anticipating* (expecting) something negative, like pain, heat, or an injection, can provoke that same part of the Uh Oh Center that processes social and physical pain to fire and actually makes you feel pain when no painful stimulus is applied. In essence, *if you anticipate or expect that a specific outcome will occur, your brain prepares for and can actually cause those sensations (physical and emotional) to arise in your body.* This likely explains why just thinking about a loved one makes you feel warm and comforted and why conjuring up a scary image causes you to experience fear.

When viewed in this way, false expectations and faulty comparisons are also thinking errors. When you anticipate or expect a certain result, all you can see and look for is that result (or evidence that it's not going to happen). Similarly, when you inappropriately compare yourself to others, all you can see is what the other person has or what you do not have. This causes your brain to filter the incoming information, just like with the other thinking errors, which clouds your ability to see the truth and results in harmful sensations or actions. In short, false expectations and faulty comparisons bias you and your brain from seeing the truth. The way to deal with such problems is to Reframe them as "expectations," "desires," or "comparisons," or note the specific thinking error associated with the inaccurate expectation.

To see how prevalent expectations are and how they unconsciously guide your behaviors, complete the exercise below. This will help you start noticing your expectations, which will allow you to begin making new choices based on the truth, not the "fiction of my brain," as Liz likes to think of it.

WHAT ARE YOUR EXPECTATIONS?

In this exercise, we want you to start becoming aware of your expectations to try to "get" things "from" other people or achieve a specific result on your agenda. Find someone who is willing to set aside time to practice talking with and listening to you. To start, have your partner talk—uninterrupted—for two minutes about anything he or she wants. During this time, you cannot speak. Instead, listen closely to what the person is saying and notice any reactions you are having. Specifically, notice if you have the impulse to jump in and say something, if you have the thought to correct the other person, if you are empathizing with the person, or if you are disagreeing with what the other person said. Then, switch roles and you talk for two minutes without interruption. As you talk, notice what emotional or bodily sensations arise—do you feel comfortable, scared, anxious, sad, upset, irritated, or something else?

Throughout the exercise, as you notice any reactions you are having, allow the associated sensations to be there while you remain focused on the person, how he or she is communicating and what is being said. When you are done, ask yourself these questions:

- How did I want the other person to react? What did I want the person to say?
- What was I trying to achieve (e.g., connection, understanding, empathy, transfer of information, receive the 5 A's)?
- What did I want the person to understand or take from what I said?
- What did I want the person to do with that information?

Becoming aware of what happens when you communicate with others will help you see what situations (e.g., unfulfilled expectations, specific interactions, or specific content) trigger your emotional sensations, physical sensations, deceptive brain messages, and habitual responses.

With time, you can increase the time spent talking and listening, such as one person talking for five minutes at a time or increasing the number of times you switch between talker and listener. As with all mindfulness exercises, the more you practice this in your everyday interactions, the more you will become aware of what triggers your uncomfortable sensations and how ⌐ your expectations and desires affect you and your actions.

Now that you have experienced learning how to examine your expectations, let's review all of the thinking errors that can negatively cloud your perception and lead to deceptive brain messages.

THINKING ERRORS—SEEING LIFE THROUGH THE LENS OF DECEPTIVE BRAIN MESSAGES

In every case of a thinking error, the brain is *filtering* out information that could be helpful to you (because the maladaptive aspect of the Self-Referencing Center is in charge) and making you look solely through the lens of deceptive brain messages. In these cases, you *minimize* the positive attributes or contributions of yourself or others and *personalize* events or interactions to somehow make them your fault or see them as *occurring* to you (as if you are a victim or helpless, when in fact you are not). In a word, at these times, your false self (i.e., deceptive brain messages) is in control of your thinking.

All-or-Nothing Thinking: Evaluating situations, events, people, or yourself in the extremes of perfect or horrible. Also called black-and-white or polarized thinking. Example: "If I do not do this perfectly, I have failed."

Catastrophizing: Blowing events out of proportion (exaggerating what happened) or taking it as proof that something bad is going to happen. Also called fortune-telling or worst-case-scenario thinking. Includes "what-if" thinking. Example: "What if Keith realizes I made a mistake yesterday on the project and he fires me"—even though Keith thinks highly of you.

Discounting the Positive: Devaluing your (or others') positive qualities, attributes, or contributions, or failing to notice the positive reactions someone is having toward you. Example: "Even though I helped Keith move today and he was appreciative, I am still a loser because I forgot to bring the packing tape."

Emotional Reasoning: Believing something is wrong with you or with your life because you are experiencing uncomfortable emotional or physical sensations generated by your Uh Oh Center. Example: "If I feel like this, something *must* be wrong (with me/the world)."

Mind Reading: Assuming you know what the other person is thinking, feeling, or believes based on your behavior (what you are saying, doing, how well you are communicating, your sensations, and so on) or how you are interpreting his gestures, language, tone, or behaviors. Example: "He looked away when I said I was happy to see him. He must be mad at me."

"Should" Statements: Believing that there are only certain ways to act, behave, or interact with others. Also includes "must" or "ought to" statements that reflect and generate false expectations. When "should" statements are directed toward you, you experience guilt, remorse, regret, or anger toward yourself. When "should" statements are directed outward (e.g., other people, society), you experience anger, resentment, or frustration toward them. Example: "I should help Keith with his move today or I am not a good friend."

The above thinking errors are adapted from David D. Burns, *Feeling Good* (New York: Harper, 1999).

Faulty Comparisons: Believing that your current situation is somehow worse than someone else's or how you imagined it would be. When you compare,

e positive and rely heavily on "should" statements (among

rrors).

ons: Allowing your anticipation of a specific result to nega-

r brain and body. Often occurs with "should" statements,

ith any of the thinking errors and can equally apply to you,

to the people in your life.

our Thinking Errors?

f interacting with the casting agent who he thought did

lear that more than one thinking error can occur at the

t example, Ed was simultaneously using emotional rea-

soning, mind reading, and fortune-telling/catastrophizing. How do thinking errors affect you? Use the exercise on pages 218 to 219 to identify all
the thinking errors you use on a regular basis. If it is helpful to you, copy
this form and fill it out at the end of your day or when you've just experienced an upsurge in uncomfortable emotional or physical sensations.
The goal of this exercise is to help you become familiar with and rapidly
spot when your brain is making a thinking error.

IDENTIFYING YOUR THINKING ERRORS

Describe the situation/event: _____

_____

_____

_____

_____

Describe the emotional and physical sensations: _____

_____

_____

_____

_____

Describe the thoughts: _____

_____

_____

_____

_____

Check off all of the thinking errors involved:

☐ Catastrophizing, Fortune-Telling, Worst-Case Scenario

☐ All-or-Nothing

☐ Discounting the Positive

☐ Emotional Reasoning

☐ Mind Reading

☐ "Should" Statements

☐ Faulty Comparisons

☐ False Expectations

How would the situation be different if you removed those thinking errors and viewed the situation from the perspective of your Wise Advocate?

_____

_____

_____

_____

_____

To consolidate your knowledge of thinking errors and how they affect you, review the following table of Sarah's thinking errors and then complete the blank table on your own. Note: As we discussed above, you may not use all of these thinking errors, but try to come up with at least one example for each category (if needed, use the same one for overlapping thought processes, such as having a specific false expectation that includes a "should" statement). Remember, the goal is to help you see that these thinking errors occur frequently and that more than one can be in play at the same time.

TAKING STOCK OF WHERE THINKING ERRORS
OCCUR IN MY LIFE: EXAMPLE FROM SARAH

Thinking Error	Example(s) and Where They Occur (or with Whom)	Result
All-or-nothing	I must be perfect at all times with everyone in my life, especially my boss.	I place high standards on myself and am never satisfied.
Catastrophizing	If I make a mistake, my boss will fire me.	I worry constantly that something bad will happen, which is exhausting.
Discounting the positive	I made a mistake on the presentation and it sucked, which means I suck.	Depression, frustration—I'm never good enough.
Emotional reasoning	I am anxious and feel horrible, so something must be wrong.	Hopelessness and helplessness, despair—will I ever feel differently?
Mind reading	My friend tensed up when I said I missed seeing her, so she must be mad at me or not want to hang out with me anymore.	I will do whatever I can to fix the situation, or maybe I will avoid her so that I don't have to feel this bad again.
"Should" statements	I should be able to do all this work and help my friend tonight.	I push myself too hard and disappoint myself and my friend when I can't come through.
Faulty comparisons	Everyone else at work seems to be doing fine. What's wrong with me?	I feel inadequate and push myself harder, rather than see that everyone is struggling a little but doing just fine—including me!
False expectations	If my mom really loves me, she'll call this weekend—and I really want her to call because I am feeling low and sad right now.	She doesn't call and I conclude that she does not care about me as much as I want her to and that I really am all alone. I get upset and angry at her, but later find out she was waiting for me to call her.

TAKING STOCK OF WHERE THINKING
ERRORS OCCUR IN YOUR LIFE

Thinking Error	Example(s) and Where They Occur (or with Whom)	Result
All-or-nothing		
Catastrophizing		
Discounting the positive		
Emotional reasoning		
Mind reading		
"Should" statements		
Faulty comparisons		
False expectations		

The Wise Advocate

Now that you are well versed in thinking errors, you are ready to learn more about the Wise Advocate and how to take full advantage of it whenever a deceptive brain message strikes.

What is the Wise Advocate? As we mentioned previously, it is an ally that can help you see the truth even when you strongly doubt that the deceptive brain messages, uncomfortable sensations, or habitual responses are false and harmful to you. It does this by giving you the ability to step outside what your deceptive brain messages are telling you and examine them from a rational, calm perspective—like a seasoned judge deciding a case. And, as we mentioned in chapter 6, its goal is to advocate for you to ensure that your true needs are met and true emotions are expressed in a loving, healthy way.

WISE ADVOCATE

The aspect of your attentive mind that knows what you are thinking, can see the deceptive brain messages for what they are and where they came from, understands how you feel (physically, emotionally), and is aware of how destructive and unhealthy your patterned, automatic responses have been for you.

The Wise Advocate wants the best for you (such as you receiving and giving the 5 A's), so it encourages you to value your true self and make decisions in a rational way based on what is in your overall best interest in the long term.

The best way to think of the Wise Advocate, Liz says, "is to imagine a loving figure, someone who cares about you and wants the best for you. This person is only going to make decisions that are in your best interest and will see the falseness of the deceptive brain messages. There's no way a loving figure like that would let you believe those negative things your brain is telling you—no way." For example, Liz thinks about her grandmother, whereas Ed wonders how his best friend would respond. Similarly, many of our religious patients have found that using God or Jesus as the Wise Advocate can be beneficial and comforting. We've even seen young children effectively imagine their pet dog as the Wise Advocate. The key is that the *Wise Advocate is a being whom you genuinely believe loves and cares for you.*

The main point to keep in mind is that regardless of the person being imagined, the Wise Advocate chosen must be a moral agent who is acting in your best interest based on your genuine desire to achieve specific goals and embody certain values. As we often say, *the Wise Advocate does not sympathize with bad behavior*, such as lying, stealing, cheating, or harming another person. More significant, even if the Wise Advocate can sympathize with the motives or desires for wanting to engage in a bad behavior, he or she will never condone the *actual doing* of the behavior. In this way, the Wise Advocate can be thought of as a helper that encourages rational, wholesome, and adaptive behaviors—in a phrase, it is the good friend within.

That said, we recognize that there are times when doing something to help yourself conflicts with what another person wants or needs. Often, people will expect unreasonable things from us that we cannot accommodate. These are the instances where the Wise Advocate is crucial because this is when your deceptive brain messages will creep in and tell you that to be "a good person" you must sacrifice your needs for someone else (unless, of course, you have signed on to put another person's needs before your own, such as being a parent, mentor/teacher, judge, or other role where this kind of self-sacrifice while performing your duties is the norm). Barring those exceptions, do not make the mistake of thinking you have to act in others' best interests before your own. Rather, use the Wise Advocate in these moments to figure out whether your intended action is aligned with your true self or whether you are basing your choices on desire, impulse, craving, anxiety, a sense you "should" do something, or another uncomfortable sensation or thought. Remember: The Wise Advocate wants you to act in a constructive, balanced way, which requires that you don't act like a victim, but rather in a manner that is consistent with your true goals and values. Even more to the point, the Wise Advocate never wants you to be either manipulated or a manipulator.

In John's case, he often put other people first and wanted to make sure they were satisfied before he was, which is why he had been living such a limited life. Rather than saying he wanted to play basketball with his friends when Alicia would ask if he wanted to go to dinner, he would cancel his plans. As he admits, "I just couldn't disappoint her, ever." When John started using his Wise Advocate, "everything changed," he says. "I used the image of my grandpa—he was a very active guy who loved his family, but who also had his own interests. When I started looking at it from his perspective, I could see that doing things that I enjoyed wasn't hurting Alicia. My grandma never got upset that he spent time with me or other people and they had a good relationship. Looking at my actions from the perspective of the Wise Advocate made me realize I could have my own interests and still have Alicia in my life. That it was just the deceptive brain message telling me that I couldn't or that I would hurt her immensely if I did something for myself."

Similarly, Sarah sees the Wise Advocate as a counselor and friend. As she explains, "There's this calming quality inside me telling me to be patient and reminding me that there's this great picture that I am missing because I am focusing on the problems. I have great attributes and there's so much more to me." She uses this force to remind herself that "I have no choice about the urge to talk to people perfectly or get that right feeling of 'I got it,' but I do have a choice of attitude, of how I view my interactions with people. This helps me Relabel my anxious sensations as they come up and Reframe the entire thing as 'perfectionism' or a problem in the brain. Then, I can Refocus on something important to me."

For Ed, the Wise Advocate reminds him "that one mistake doesn't invalidate an entire project and that this uncomfortable sensation I have when I am auditioning is something that will pass. It's not true, there is no danger, but my brain is making me think there is." So, rather than stewing in his thinking errors, Ed uses the Wise Advocate to tell himself, "I know that this is one of those deceptive-brain-message feelings and it will go away within an hour or one day, but definitely, it will go away. Don't act on it. Refocus on learning your lines or connecting with the people in front of you."

Abby, who worries about doing the "right" thing, realized with the help of the Wise Advocate, "I didn't need to figure it all out—I didn't need to own or take responsibility for everything. All I can do is tell people what I think and how I feel about them and then let them make their own decisions. I can't protect my kids from every possible harm. And, if I did, they would never learn anything on their own. It's actually best for me to give them my advice and perspective, but then to let go and let them decide what's best for them on their own. Then, I need to do the same for myself! That's what the Wise Advocate has taught me."

Encouragingly, the more you use the Wise Advocate, the stronger it becomes. Even more heartening, regularly using your Wise Advocate literally rewires your brain to become your ally. As Steve explains, "Rather than figuring it all out on my own, I turn to the people in my life whom I love and trust and I really listen to them now, to what they say and to their opinions about things. I take what they say and then look at myself so that I can honestly evaluate things in myself accurately, impartially. I take all that data and use it to strengthen my own Wise Advocate. It strengthens my ability to have rational faith when I am trying to be impartial with myself, these deceptive thoughts and urges, to respond in habitual ways."

With these stories in mind, use the following exercise to determine how your Wise Advocate would respond to your deceptive brain messages, uncomfortable sensations, and habitual, unhealthy behaviors.

EXERCISE: In the table below, write down some of your deceptive brain messages and what they tell you to do. Then, write down how the Wise Advocate would view the situation instead. If it is difficult for you to objectively respond, think about what a loving, caring figure would say if you honestly told him what you thought, how you reacted to the deceptive brain messages, how strongly you believed in the uncomfortable sensations, and so on. We have provided you with some examples to help you get started.

Deceptive Brain Message and Intended Action	Wise Advocate Response (e.g., Loving Figure)
I feel like crap. I had a horrible day, I am so stressed out. I need a drink.	You are trying to escape the pain. The drink is a temporary distraction, nothing more. Don't drink—go do something healthy instead.
Playing blackjack feels so good! The rush is amazing. So what that I am down $400—I'll make it up on the next few hands.	You are actually $10,000 in debt from playing this game. It is masking your sadness and grief. Walk away from the table and spend time with your family.
Jane is mad at me. I could see it in her body language. I'm so anxious now. I need to fix this somehow. I just need to figure it out, what happened. What if I . . .	You are anxious for no reason. You do not know she is upset with you and are engaging in "what-ifs." Stop the thinking errors and ask her directly if she's upset with you.
Joe was so rude and after everything I've done for him! I should receive better treatment than this. I'm never helping him out again.	Your anger is clouding your ability to hear what he said. He was in a rush because his friend was just in an accident and he did thank you. You're filtering his words through your expectations and not seeing the truth. Take all the information in before you make a decision to ostracize him.

I am so exhausted and drained. I just don't think I can go to the party tonight. Plus, I won't know anyone and likely won't have any fun. I'll just stay home.	You have been isolating yourself for weeks and are depressed. Your brain is telling you that you are tired and can't do things. And, you're fortune-telling and using emotional reasoning. Go to the party with an open mind—you may meet some really nice people and your depression probably will improve a little.

Our patients have used the Wise Advocate to think about a situation in one of the following ways:

- I look at how someone else deals with the same issue in a healthy way and try to emulate what they do. I ask myself, how would somebody else react to this?
- I ask myself how people who really love me would think about the situation and what they would advise me to do.
- I ask myself: Why am I about to go do this? Is it because I am listening to a deceptive brain message or because I am following my true self?
- If the situation is going on right now and other people are involved, I look at them, at how they actually are reacting. Most often, the other people are not reacting as strongly as I am and I bet they are not having the same uncomfortable sensations I am. This "reality check" helps me Relabel and Reframe the situation.
- Sometimes, I do not really know what's happening or why I am reacting the way I am, but I know that it's out of proportion to the event. In those cases, I use the Wise Advocate and Reframe it as a "restless, irritable feeling" and just try to move on.

Repeatedly using the Four Steps and incorporating the Wise Advocate into your decisions (especially in how you focus your attention), you will more strongly believe that you are worthy of the 5 A's (Attention, Acceptance, Affection, Appreciation, Allowing) and living a life that reflects your true self. In fact, the more you strengthen your Wise Advocate, the more you will be able to instantaneously see deceptive brain messages for what they really are and truly understand that the uncomfortable sensations are nothing more than the *feeling of a deceptive brain message*—and certainly not something that must be acted upon. This ability to see the deceptive brain messages as they truly are, without any misconception or misperception, is the ultimate goal of the Four Steps and is the essence of Step 4: Revalue and progressive mindfulness. To get there, you need to learn ways to strengthen the Wise Advocate so that you can effectively put a wedge between the deceptive brain messages and your true self. One such technique is Recognize, Dismiss, and Accept.

Strengthening Your Wise Advocate: Recognize, Dismiss, and Accept

In our previous work, we taught people to anticipate and accept that the deceptive brain messages would arise and cause uncomfortable sensations. Unfortunately, many people misunderstood what we meant by *anticipate*, which led them to engage in habitual patterns of scanning their environments and overthinking. Rather than understanding that *anticipate* meant "to recognize" (via Relabel and increasing levels of mindfulness) when deceptive brain messages or uncomfortable sensations have surfaced, they thought it meant to mentally prepare for the onslaught of negative sensations and deceptive thoughts they knew inevitably would come. When used in this way, "anticipating" quickly becomes a form of overthinking or overanalyzing and results in worsening, not helping, the maladaptive brain circuits and habits.

Therefore, instead of passively anticipating, we want you to learn how to actively use Recognize, Dismiss, and Accept as an assertive, intensive way of applying and synergizing the first two steps:

RECOGNIZE, DISMISS, AND ACCEPT

- Recognize the deceptive brain message or uncomfortable sensation (Relabel).
- Dismiss the faulty logic or strong pull to act on the sensations (Reframe).
- Accept that deceptive thoughts, urges, impulses, and sensations will arise, but that you do not have to act on them.

A wonderful example of Recognize, Dismiss, and Accept comes from Liz and her worries about her future. She described having considerable anxiety whenever she would wonder if she will end up, as she fears, "alone in a nursing home with no one to take care of me." Whenever Liz would engage in this fortune-telling and catastrophic thinking, she says, "I constantly had this thing in my head. It would pounce on me like a tiger and I would get so anxious." When the sensations became strong, Liz recalls, "I would worry that the feelings would never go away and that there was no way out." She would become desperate and feel helpless. "I couldn't concentrate and my work and relationships suffered. My only escape was to shop because for a while it would lift away all the pain I was feeling."

When we taught Liz how to Recognize, Dismiss, and Accept, she exclaimed, "Oh, so what you're saying is that I need to *recognize* the deceptive brain messages, *dismiss* the faulty logic/realize the thoughts are not true and have no meaning with the Wise Advocate as my guide, and then *accept* that the feeling will be there [and though it does not readily go away, it doesn't have to control how I think and act]. My goal isn't to get rid of the feeling, but to work around it and continue on with my life. By doing this, my brain will change and the sensations won't be as strong in the future!"

We agreed with Liz's assessment and summarized how to use the Four Steps for her in this way:

The deceptive thought sucks you in. What you need to do at that point is use Step 1 and *Relabel* the thought as a deceptive brain message and the anxiety as fear that you will be alone. You then allow the thought to be there and do not try to alter it in any way. The reason you allow the thought to be there is that it is just coming from your brain and is a false message. You use Step 2: Reframe to say, "This thought—this is just the brain sending false messages. It's not me, it's just the brain." You also Reframe the thinking error as fortune-telling and catastrophic thinking. You then Refocus (Step 3) on a health activity. Finally, you use Step 4: Revalue to see that this is all a thinking error with no validity. In other words, you listen to your Wise Advocate when it tells you this is a false interpretation of the sensations and thoughts you are having. You have been interpreting the sensations as having a meaning that you are going to end up alone, that somehow this thought is a fact and will come true. This is false and can be categorized as a negative prediction (e.g., fortune-telling) or catastrophic thinking. The feeling does not mean you will be alone, and if you listen to your Wise Advocate, you know it will tell you the same thing. You are a good person and have many loving family members and friends. You are never really alone and must not indulge the deceptive, harmful brain messages trying to tell you otherwise. You will get better by accepting that the feeling will be there but that it is a false message with no real meaning.

From Liz's example, it's clear that Recognize, Dismiss, and Accept is essentially a summary of the first two steps in an alternate form. Recognize is most analogous to Relabel, while Dismiss is much like Reframing.[3] In this way, you can think of Recognize, Dismiss, and Accept as a shortcut

---

3. Note: Do not dismiss your true emotions and needs, only the faulty logic of the deceptive brain messages.

when dealing with your deceptive brain messages, uncomfortable sensations, and unhealthy habits. Additionally, using Recognize, Dismiss, and Accept as outlined above *is an intensive exercise for building up and empowering the Wise Advocate* because it helps you quickly assess the deceptive brain messages and engage the perspective of the Wise Advocate to counter them in a healthy, loving way.

Acceptance

As you can probably see by now, acceptance is one of the most important aspects of the Four Steps. Although it is definitely difficult to accept that the deceptive brain messages, uncomfortable sensations, and gnawing urges to engage in unhealthy habits are unavoidably present, it is critical that you do so. These feelings certainly are bothersome and even painful. However, accepting them for what they really are (bad brain messages!) and *not* engaging in futile efforts to make them go away (i.e., unhealthy habits and actions) is vital to overcoming them. The key point is this: Accept that these bothersome feelings are *not* who you truly are. They are deceptive brain messages, nothing more or less, and you can think of them as occurring as part of a "bad brain day."

Without this kind of acceptance, you will be stuck in a futile and endless loop, trying to make the deceptive brain messages, sensations, and habits go away, rather than charting a new course for yourself based on your true goals and values.

True acceptance means letting go of the false expectation that you can somehow make these deceptive thoughts, impulses, urges, desires, and sensations disappear and just go away. It also means letting go of expectations related to yourself and other people that are not aligned with your true self. Rather than clinging to and desiring specific outcomes, accept that things may not work out the way you want right now and keep moving forward toward your goals and values.

As Sarah explains, "Acceptance is huge and it's about accepting all the deceptive brain messages as a whole. You need to accept that you have them. You're not trying to be in denial or fight them anymore. Rather than focusing on the problems, I have to accept that I am doing the best I can today. I'm going to take myself, along with this brain problem, and I am going to go to my job, the gym, et cetera. Wherever I am going, it's going to be there, but I'm not going to stop living my life. And, when I am having a hard time accepting the way things are, then I have to accept that, too. I'm doing the best I can."

Steve reminds himself that he cannot control everything. He uses the deeply insightful analogy of trying to stop the ocean waves to bring into perspective that acceptance is, as he says, "all I've got." As he explains, "I tell myself, 'These thoughts and sensations, I have no control over them. *They are not me and I have no more control over these deceptive brain messages and sensations than I have over being able to stop those waves in the ocean.*'" Interestingly, one well-known psychologist speaks of "surfing the urge" (i.e., not responding to the urges) as a way of managing the terribly uncomfortable feelings of deceptive brain messages. When seen from this perspective, Steve's insightful image really makes the relevance of that phrase come to life.

Like Steve, Abby often reminds herself that she can't control what others do, especially when dealing with her kids. As she explains, "What I need to accept is that there are things in life I cannot control. I cannot control that people will die or make bad choices. I can't control the fact that these things will happen someday. I can't change the rules and I can't control other people at all, but I have to let them try to take care of themselves. When they need me, they will come to me. I remind myself that I am trying to control the uncontrollable, which is impossible. So accept that I can't control these things, but that I can give people my input and hope they make decisions that are beneficial to them."

Accepting can also mean grieving the time you lost following your deceptive brain messages and vowing to make changes as you go forward. As Liz explains, "I need to get to an acceptance that I will not get the last thirty-five years back. I won't, but it doesn't mean I have to keep listening to the negative messages and lose more years of my life." Similarly, John tries to turn the seriousness of his deceptive brain messages into a positive in this way: "For someone who had these deceptive brain messages, as serious a case as I had, the fact that I achieved so much is incredible. I have come so far and am grateful that I was able to start seeing and dealing with these false messages. I am getting my life back!"

Finally, as Ed knows, acceptance means asking for help and acknowledging that the brain is sometimes working against your true goals and values. As he describes, "I try to just accept it and acknowledge that I needed help . . . this is in my brain, I don't know why it is in my brain, but I just need to accept it. I try to take the Zen approach and just let the deceptive brain messages and sensations go by." We sometimes call this "working around" the deceptive brain messages because you are not trying to change them, but allow them to be present while you continue on with your day.

TRUE ACCEPTANCE VERSUS FALSE ACCEPTANCE

TRUE ACCEPTANCE INCLUDES

- Accepting that the deceptive brain messages and uncomfortable sensations will come, but that you do not have to act on them and you should not engage in futile efforts to try to make them go away.
- Knowing that the deceptive brain messages are not representative of you or your true self—they are false, foreign invaders.
- Acknowledging and grieving the time you lost while following the deceptive brain messages' commands, all the while remembering that things can change going forward.
- Listening to your Wise Advocate.

- Giving up by knowingly letting the deceptive brain messages take over and saying, "This is just how it is." This kind of false acceptance usually happens when you are feeling demoralized or exhausted.
- Believing that you are to blame or at fault for having these deceptive brain messages.

Reframing Your Deceptive Brain Messages

Throughout this chapter and the previous one, we have provided you with many ways to answer the question: *Why do these thoughts, impulses, desires, urges, and sensations bother me so much?* As you know, you can Reframe these experiences as being a part of your bad brain wiring or you can attribute them to thinking errors. Regardless of how you Reframe, your goal is to use the Wise Advocate to help you see the false nature of your deceptive brain messages and uncomfortable sensations so that you can make new choices based on your true goals and values. And, to strengthen your Wise Advocate, you can use the shorthand approach of Recognize, Dismiss, and Accept, as many of our patients successfully have.

We'll leave this chapter with this summary quote from Sarah, who describes how she uses the Four Steps at work.

> I know when I am upset or anxious, so now I say to myself, "These are unpleasant feelings I am getting" and I Relabel them that way. I'm aware of the unpleasant feelings and that they are being caused by what is going on right now. Once I Relabel, I ask myself, "So, why am I getting these unpleasant feelings? Well, because I want to be perceived as doing a good job, but, hey, I probably AM doing a good job. I'm just getting this feeling nevertheless." I Reframe it to a concern that I have that isn't valid and I try to reorient myself

by asking, "If this happened to another person, how would I be evaluating this?" That's where the Wise Advocate comes in and helps me separate the malfunction in my thinking from the reality of whatever I am doing. A lot of times I will be hypercritical of myself or be anxious about little things with my job. Or things will be said constructively and I may be concerned and take it more critically than was intended. So I can Reframe those things to thinking errors and my desire to do a good job. With the Wise Advocate's help, I then can Refocus on my work, knowing that the sensations and thoughts are false, and use rational faith to believe I am a good person who really is performing well.

Summary

- You can Reframe in many ways, including:
  - It's not me, it's *just* my brain.
  - I'm feeling rejected—this is social pain.
  - These are thinking errors.
  - Seeking the 5 A's from another, rather than providing it to yourself.
- Thinking errors result from deceptive brain messages. In addition to causing you to ignore, deny, and neglect your true emotions, they can result in the following unhelpful and inaccurate thought processes:
  - All-or-nothing/black-or-white thinking
  - Catastrophizing/fortune-telling
  - Discounting the positive
  - Emotional reasoning
  - Mind reading
  - "Should" statements
  - Faulty comparisons
  - False expectations

- The Wise Advocate is your ally and can be anyone or anything that helps you recruit your healthy side to act in your genuine best interest.
- Recognize, Dismiss, and Accept is another way you can quickly assess your deceptive brain messages so that you can Refocus on a healthy activity. It also strengthens your Wise Advocate.
- Acceptance includes acknowledging that the deceptive brain messages and sensations will arise, but that you do not have to act on them. Rather, you can let them be present while continuing on with your day.
- Listen to your Wise Advocate.

CHAPTER 11

The Power Is in the Focus

Step 3: Refocus

After Abby had been using the Four Steps for about a month, she realized that something was off. Perplexed, she came to us and said, "No matter what I do, I keep getting caught up in these upsetting thoughts: Will my husband's high cholesterol, increased stress, and lack of exercise give him a heart attack? Will my son get injured playing football and never make it to college? Will my career be in jeopardy because of the bad economy? It's just so frustrating because I know there's nothing I can do about these 'what-ifs,' that there are no definitive answers, yet no matter how I Refocus, I can't get them out of my head!" When we asked her to elaborate, she described how she was using the Four Steps with her most recent difficulty related to her daughter.

"It all started a few weeks back," Abby told us, when she learned that a former babysitter, Stacy, had been placed on probation by her college for marijuana possession. "The minute I found out," Abby remembers, "I immediately started worrying." What was the problem? Abby's fifteen-year-old daughter, Katie, had idolized Stacy and always thought highly of her, adopting Stacy's mannerisms, dress, and even some of her activities. Abby's brain took these two pieces of information and merged them together. That's when Abby's thoughts began to spin out of control: Does Katie now want to smoke pot as well? Would she think it's "cool" because Stacy did it? Does Katie understand the dangers of marijuana and how it can damage her brain? What if Katie did try it and she got arrested? Her life could be ruined! Then what would happen? Would she never get a college degree? Abby's brain was unrelenting and seesawed from those worries about what might happen to what Abby could to do prevent such feared consequences. The ensuing anxiety was unbearable and the "what-ifs" ran the gamut: What if I searched her room every day? Read her diary? Made her take drug tests? Took her out of all her extracurricular activities and only allowed supervised visits to the movies or the mall? And so on.

Although Abby could Relabel her anxiety and distress and accurately Reframe her deceptive thoughts as the thinking errors "catastrophizing" and "what-ifs," she did not completely understand what the Refocus step was trying to achieve. Throughout this chapter, we will teach you the basics of Step 3: Refocus and demonstrate how to use the various forms of Refocusing through some of our patients' stories. For example, we will explore how Refocus can help with:

- Steve's urges to drink
- Ed's avoidance of auditions
- Abby's overthinking
- Sarah's panic attacks and depression

With this background, you will be able to figure out what the best ways are for you to Refocus whenever your deceptive brain messages strike.

Direct your *attention* toward an activity or mental process that is productive—even while the false and deceptive urges, thoughts, impulses, and sensations are still present and bothering you.

What Is the Purpose of Step 3: Refocus? How Does It Help?

As Abby's story demonstrates, your attention can easily be grabbed by all kinds of unhealthy thoughts, impulses, desires, urges, and sensations that cause you to become stuck in repetitive cycles of overthinking, overchecking, drinking excessively, overeating, or other unhealthy behaviors. Step 3 is meant to be the antidote for such destructive uses of your attention and is designed to help you rewire your brain in ways that decrease the power and influence of the maladaptive brain circuits while strengthening healthy, adaptive ones associated with wholesome, constructive behaviors.

The premise behind Step 3 is that you can change how your brain is wired based on the collective forces you learned in chapter 3: Hebb's law ("neurons that fire together wire together"), neuroplasticity (brain functions and circuits can change), and the quantum Zeno effect (*attention* stabilizes brain circuits so they can fire together and wire together). More than anything, Refocus gives you the confidence—through experience—to see that you *can* continue on with your day despite whatever deceptive thoughts, impulses, desires, urges, and sensations you experience. As important, it teaches you that you do have choices, no matter how you are feeling, and that you can act in ways that positively impact your life.

Even more significant, Refocus strengthens your Wise Advocate so that you feel empowered to make healthy choices on your own behalf. Refocusing is the most powerful way to change your brain, and the act of Refocusing with the Wise Advocate in mind strengthens your belief in your true self (i.e., that you have the right to follow the path of your true emotions, interests, and needs in a balanced, healthy way).

As John explains, Refocusing helped him considerably with his repetitive concerns that Alicia might be upset with or possibly leave him. The deceptive brain messages "were so intense," John says, "but my Wise Advocate was growing stronger, telling me that everything in my relationship was fine and that I needed to learn how to focus more energy on myself. What I eventually realized is that when you have a deceptive brain message, there's this energy and you have to do something with it. Whether it's anxiety, a thinking error, whatever, doesn't matter. No matter what, that energy is there. So, you can channel it in productive or unhealthy ways—it's ultimately up to you. What you learn with the Four Steps is that when you Refocus [rather than give in to the deceptive brain message], you process that energy in a healthier way. It's the same energy, but now you are doing something different with it that empowers you and makes the deceptive brain message less overwhelming or strong."

Ed agrees with how Refocusing has helped him continue on with his day despite uncomfortable sensations and strong desires to avoid certain situations. For instance, whenever he wanted to go to an audition or ask a woman out, he would become flooded with deceptive thoughts that he was not good enough and needed to avoid the situation. Refocusing helped Ed realize the following: "If I were to avoid going to an audition, that would be running away and letting the deceptive brain messages win. Instead, I need to keep going because there are certain things that I need to get done and I'm not going to get booked for a job by staying in my house. I can't stay in bed or stay still. I need to keep on moving and do some activity. Even if I can't go to an audition right then, I could still call up my agent, look for upcoming auditions, or something else because I have to go on. I can't stay stuck and in avoidance."

Refocusing: The Basics

How do you Refocus? After you Relabel your deceptive brain messages with mental notes and Reframe them, you need to *actively place your attention* on something of your choosing that is healthy, constructive, and beneficial for you—even while (and *despite* the fact that) the deceptive thoughts, impulses, urges, sensations, and cravings are present and screaming for you to act on their maladaptive behalf. Although this sounds obvious and easy to do, as Liz knows, it's anything but that: "It seems so simple, and in some ways it is, but in others it really isn't. It's not about putting your body somewhere else [though no doubt that sometimes helps!], it's about working to make sure that your *mind* and *attention* are focused on something good for you."

What does Liz mean? You've actually experienced it yourself when you completed the breathing and thought awareness exercises in chapter 8. Every time you made a mental note of when your attention wandered and then brought your focus back to your breath, you were Refocusing. That's why we emphasized these exercises and recommended that you practice them every day—doing so is the ultimate training ground for Refocusing and learning how to clearly see that your deceptive brain messages and uncomfortable sensations are *false* and do not need to be followed.

To help you hone your Refocusing skills, here are a few of the tips and recommendations that will help you on your way.

NOTICE WHERE YOUR ATTENTION IS FOCUSED

In chapter 8, we spent considerable time teaching you about mindfulness, being lost in thought, and how to train your mind to Refocus your attention on your breath whenever your thoughts begin to wander. Aside from assisting you in Relabeling and Reframing, being able to notice when your attention is drifting away and proactively doing something to bring your attention back to the object you have chosen is vital for Step 3. This act of Refocusing on healthy, adaptive activities is what changes your brain in positive ways. As we mentioned in Part One, the Habit Center is easily "trained" by your repetitive actions and does not know healthy from unhealthy—it simply responds to how you behave and where you focus your attention—and adapts accordingly. Therefore, *how you act and what you focus on shapes your brain in powerful ways.*

For example, consistently depriving the brain of an unhealthy substance or action that "feels good" results in weakening those brain circuits and eventually extinguishing those cravings (as long as you continue to abstain or, in the case of food, only consume the item once in a while). If you've ever consistently overindulged in ice cream, but then stopped eating it for a while, you know what we are talking about. The less ice cream you eat, the less you crave it. Eventually, if enough time passes, your craving for ice cream becomes sporadic and no longer holds the power over you it once did. But, if you resume eating ice cream on a semi-regular basis, your brain will start strongly craving it again. The key for such cravings, when possible, is not to indulge them or to have the item only when you're not actually craving whatever it is (so that the unhelpful association among craving, getting the item, and feeling better is not revived).[1]

This means that being aware of when your brain is trying to take you down an automatic and well-worn path, like eating ice cream without your full awareness, is so important. The same holds true for any repetitive behavior you engage in, from checking to overanalyzing to drinking alcohol. Relabeling, Reframing, and Refocusing once is not enough and letting your body "go through the motions" without being mindful and aware of what you are doing takes you down a familiar yet dangerous and unhealthy path. The answer to dealing with the insidious way your brain works is to continue to Relabel and Reframe whenever those thoughts, urges, desires, cravings, and impulses strike—even if you are in the middle of Refocusing—and to choose Refocus activities that capture your atten-

---

1. With highly addictive and potentially dangerous substances like drugs and alcohol, you want to abstain, rather than use in moderation. Twelve-Step programs can really help in these situations.

tion in healthy, beneficial ways. Therefore, notice where your attention is focused as much as possible and especially when you are Refocusing.

REFOCUS ACTIVITIES—MAKE A LIST

One of the most helpful things you can do when you begin Refocusing is to make a list of potential Refocus activities you could use *before* a deceptive brain message actually surfaces. The unfortunate reality is that once the deceptive thoughts, desires, impulses, and sensations emerge, it's difficult to start thinking up ways to Refocus your attention in that moment. Therefore, we strongly suggest you make a list of different ways you can constructively Refocus your attention when you are not in the midst of dealing with a deceptive brain message.

Our patients' activities spanned from going for a walk to tossing cards into a hat to exercising to spending time with friends to working. You can literally choose any constructive, helpful behavior that engages your mind and holds your attention. Here are some ideas to help you get started:

- Go for a walk—focus on your feet striking the ground (e.g., mindful walking).
- Go for a walk—notice the scenery and environment (e.g., feel the wind on your skin; notice the color of the trees, the grass, the birds).
- Exercise alone or with others (something with strategy is better).
  - Lift weights.
  - Go for a run, swim, hike, bike.
  - Play basketball, tennis, soccer, etc.
  - Stretch.
  - Class: yoga, spinning, Pilates, etc.
- Play a game like Sudoku, solitaire, a crossword puzzle, etc.
- Read.
- If you are at work, Refocus on what you need to accomplish that day.

- Watch a wholesome or educational TV show or movie.
- Spend time with someone (friend, coworker, family member).
- Spend time with your pet.
- Write/blog.
- Call someone.
- Cook a healthy meal.
- Pursue a hobby you enjoy (knitting, train models, etc.).
- Learn a new skill, sport, or game.

One of the key points is that choosing an activity that requires strategy or interests you tends to be the most engaging and helpful, especially when you are just starting out with the Refocus step. Involving strategy in your Refocus is particularly beneficial because it causes the Habit Center to work constructively to wire the new routines you are learning into the brain, which deprives the maladaptive circuits of the attention they need to stay strong.

As Steve recommends, "The best Refocus is something that is enjoyable. For example, I might go out and play soccer with my son, maybe watch a TV show that I like, listen to some music, something that's fun." The same advice holds true for depression, as Sarah found out. "The only Refocusing that was helping me was exercising," she recalls. "This is what depressed people are supposed to do, they're supposed to go out and do pleasurable things when they are feeling low," so exercise or spending time with people, she says, is usually best.

Therefore, whenever possible, choose a Refocus activity that is enjoyable or involves strategy. That said, if you are already at work or working, you need to learn how to *Refocus on your work* like John did. As he explains, "Until I really understood Refocus, I thought that I had to go do something different—go to another place and get away. I couldn't do that when I was supposed to be at work, so I felt stuck." When we told John that Refocusing on your work is an excellent activity because it is constructive and usually can engage your attention effectively, he tried it out and found that he was more productive. Of course, any aspect of your work that you can do at the moment is helpful—it doesn't have to be something difficult when you are already stressed—anything constructive is good.

Remember, the goal is to choose an activity that will capture your attention in a positive, healthy way—so make sure you have a mental list on hand for whenever deceptive brain messages arise. We included the exercise below to help you do so.

EXERCISE: In the space below, write down various Refocus activities you can use when deceptive brain messages surface. We have provided some categories for you, but come up with anything that *will capture your attention and interest in a healthy, constructive way*. No matter what you choose, be specific about what you will do. Don't say simply "Read" but specify what you would read, such as "CNN website headlines" or "the new Dan Brown novel." Whenever possible, include strategy or learning something new (but not too complex or difficult) while Refocusing—this makes your Habit Center kick into overdrive to incorporate the new skill into your brain's repertoire, thus depriving the maladaptive brain circuits of their essential fuel—your attention!

- Individual or group exercise (gym, swimming, basketball, soccer, walking)
- Play a game (Sudoku, crosswords)
- Read (book, newspaper, website)
- Work (specific project)
- Spend time on your hobby (knitting, model building)
- Watch something (TV, movie, birds, sunset)
- Write (journal, blog, novel)

- Spend time with or call a friend
- Other (e.g., cook a healthy meal)

IT'S *NOT* ABOUT BEING DISTRACTED

When many people learn that Refocus means to deliberately place your attention somewhere, they mistakenly conclude that Refocus means to distract yourself or somehow avoid situations that cause you anxiety. When properly understood, Refocusing is *not* a form of simply distracting yourself. We are not telling you to run away from your deceptive thoughts or sensations and we do not, under any circumstances, want you to try to "just" get rid of or diminish the deceptive brain messages or sensations in the short term. Rather, we specifically tell you to *let the sensations, thoughts, impulses, desires, urges, and cravings be present while you engage in another activity that is healthy and good for you.* What we are trying to teach you is how to constructively *manage your responses* to the bothersome thoughts, sensations, impulses, desires, and so on. In fact, we developed an intensification of Step 3 called *Refocus with Progressive Mindfulness* to specifically address this misunderstanding and ensure that you know how to confront and deal with situations you typically would avoid.

FIFTEEN-MINUTE RULE

Try to wait at least fifteen minutes (or as long as possible) between when a deceptive brain message or uncomfortable sensation strikes and when you act. If possible, do not act on the thoughts or impulses at all and instead choose to engage in a healthy behavior. When the fifteen minutes is up, try another fifteen minutes.

FIFTEEN-MINUTE RULE AND MINDFUL CHECKING

Another helpful guideline is the fifteen-minute rule, which probably is similar to how your parents dealt with you as a child when you announced you wanted a snack immediately after dinner. In essence, the rule simply asks you to wait fifteen minutes between the time you experience a deceptive thought, impulse, urge, desire, or sensation and when you act. The idea is to put as much time as possible between your deceptive brain message and the automatic habit to immediately respond in an unhealthy way. Obviously, if you can resist the urge entirely, all the better. However, if you find that you cannot withstand the strong sensations, your second-best response is to wait as long as possible and then *mindfully* engage in whatever activity your deceptive brain message is demanding of you. For example, if John could not hold out for fifteen minutes to resist the urge to check if Alicia e-mailed him, he would check while saying to himself mindfully, "I am checking. I am afraid she is going to leave me and I am looking for reassurance. Even though I gave in this time, that's okay. I just need to be aware of what I'm doing and try not to give in next time." The key here is to be honest with yourself—if it is checking, Relabel it as checking, and resolve to try to wait longer the next time. That said, it is important to have compassion for yourself and patience—to call things what they truly are and be honest with yourself while actively accepting that you are doing the best you can and encouraging yourself to wait longer the next time.

Dealing with Repetitive Thoughts When You Refocus

When Abby began learning how to Refocus, she chose spending time with friends as one of her Refocus activities. Unfortunately, because she did not fully understand how to Refocus, she did not realize that excessively talking about what was distressing her, like Katie's potential use of marijuana, was the wrong approach. Rather than helping her brain focus on something constructive (like discussing the latest movie she saw, good places to go to dinner, or what to do this weekend), Abby was fueling the deceptive brain messages further whenever she excessively focused on their content. Much of the hard work she had put into Steps 1 and 2 was being washed away, brain-wise, when she let the deceptive brain messages take over her attention so quickly and run the show. Additionally, she admitted, she was unwittingly hoping that Refocusing would help her feel better, calmer. Unfortunately, all this unrealistic expectation did was frustrate her more and make her feel like the Four Steps weren't working.

As we explained to Abby, the way to deal with the *inaccurate expectation* that she *should* feel better (two thinking errors) was to endeavor to *never try to make the uncomfortable sensations or feelings go away*. Remember, we told her: *When dealing with deceptive brain messages, it's not what you think or how you feel that matters, it's what you do that counts!* You are not trying to make the feelings go away—ever—and your goal in Refocusing is to *direct your attention* toward a healthy, wholesome activity *while* the thoughts, impulses, urges, and sensations are present. The goal is not to try to distract yourself, but to engage your attention in a constructive activity so that your brain rewires in a healthy, adaptive way via the quantum Zeno effect. This is the only true and reliable way to really change the uncomfortable sensations and feelings, but it takes time. The key point to remember is that trying to make the feelings go away in the short term (or strongly overidentifying with them) only makes things worse in the long term because *focusing your attention on the uncomfortable feelings and sensations further entrenches the unhealthy responses and more strongly wires them into your brain.*

We summarized for Abby that her difficulties in Refocusing were rooted in three missteps: (a) she was still repetitively thinking about things, such as Katie's future, when she talked with friends, went for a walk, or Refocused on another activity; (b) she was trying to make her feelings go away; and (c) she was not continuing to Refocus *her attention* every time the deceptive brain messages or pull to overanalyze struck. To fix the problem, Abby needed to do these three things instead:

1. Choose a Refocus activity that would strongly engage her attention and did not involve talking or thinking about Katie (or discussing other deceptive brain messages).
2. Continue Relabeling and Reframing her deceptive brain messages whenever they came up.
3. Never attempt to make the uncomfortable sensations go away.

Ways to Refocus

When you begin working with the Four Steps, Refocusing in one of the ways we described above (what we call regular Refocus) likely will be the best. That said, we have learned from countless hours of working with patients that a one-size-fits-all approach does not work for everyone, especially if you are avoiding specific situations, people, or events. That's why we developed variations on Step 3 that are designed to assist with problems such as being repetitively lost in thought or avoiding situations. Regardless of which form of Refocus you choose, the same rules apply— your goal is to sharply focus your attention on healthy, constructive activities while the deceptive thoughts, urges, impulses, desires, and cravings are present. Here are three versions of Refocus you can try, depending on what you are dealing with:

1. Refocus: Engage in a different activity without distracting yourself from the sensations, thoughts, urges, impulses, or desires (what you learned above).
2. Regulate & Refocus: Focus on your breathing or another activity that, as a side effect, decreases your physical or emotional sensations (i.e., do not engage in the activity with the sole purpose or intent of calming yourself down—it's about Refocusing, not just calming).
3. Refocus with Progressive Mindfulness: Continue in an activity that triggered your deceptive brain messages and uncomfortable sensations, or face a situation that you normally would avoid and that is beneficial for you.

In general, it's much easier to start with regular Refocus or Regulate & Refocus because when Refocus with Progressive Mindfulness is done properly, it tends to significantly intensify deceptive brain messages and uncomfortable sensations at first. For this reason, we consider it an advanced practice. You've already learned about regular Refocus, so now let's look at how Regulate & Refocus can help with anxiety, uncomfortable physical sensations, and overthinking.

Regulate & Refocus—Especially Helpful with Anxiety and Overthinking

What is Regulate? It's a form of Refocusing that emphasizes ways to calm down your body's intense physiological reactions to stress or upsetting situations. Specifically, it encourages self-care and learning how to Refocus your attention when no other constructive activity is available. In reality,

Regulate activities are no different from other forms of Refocusing—they all are attempting to get you to sharply focus your attention in ways that are beneficial to you. The reason we specifically point them out is that they have been scientifically shown or demonstrated clinically to calm your nervous system and decrease the uncomfortable sensations that often accompany deceptive brain messages. *This happens, though, as a side effect or by-product of focusing your attention properly—feeling better or calmer from Refocusing, as Abby learned, should never be your goal.* Rather, your purpose in Refocusing is to retrain your attention in constructive ways that rewire your brain. The end result of following the Four Steps is improved mental health, but this result should not become an intense *desire* as you use the Four Steps. As we've mentioned previously, intense desires for immediate (short-term) results definitely tend to get in the way of sustained, long-term progress.

Two great Regulate activities you already know are focusing on your breathing and meditating. They are particularly powerful Regulate activities because they capture your attention in a very specific way that helps if you tend to overanalyze, overthink, and get lost in thought. From her experiences of going down the "what-if" path ad nauseam, Abby knows that Regulate is a powerful and valuable way to Refocus. As she explains, "I'm really kind of a novice, but I have seen that meditation is a very effective way of strengthening my Wise Advocate. I find the more I do it, just like the more I apply the Four Steps, the better I get at it and the more awareness I get. It does help me a lot, meditation—I feel calm, more insightful. I'm able to Relabel faster and Reframe my thinking errors; I can see them so much clearer now. Meditation definitely is a useful tool and maybe is one of the most useful tools there is for strengthening your Wise Advocate—for example, when these thoughts would start coming in, I had a sense that they were garbage and could Refocus on something that was good for me."

In addition to helping you see more clearly, Regulating your breathing can also help you center yourself when you experience acute anxiety, such as a panic attack, or other intense physical sensations. The most effective way to Regulate if you are hyperventilating is to use a variation of the breathing exercise we taught you in chapter 8, where you breathe in on a 4 count and out on an 8 count *through your nose*. Why? Breathing in for 4 and out for 8 elongates and smooths normal breathing patterns, and naturally calms in a way that other kinds of activities cannot. Just as significant, breathing through your nose ensures that you will not over-breathe or hyperventilate (thus setting off more uncomfortable sensations, such as shortness of breath, that you may incorrectly associate with another anxiety attack). In short, breathing in for 4 and out for 8 is a simple, reliable way to replicate and achieve the calming effects of traditional forms of breathing meditation when you are hyperventilating. When you are not having trouble with your breathing patterns, it is best either to note your breath or to use a 4-IN, 4-OUT breathing cycle.

Sarah agrees that Regulate & Refocus is beneficial, especially for anxiety attacks. At the beginning of her work with the Four Steps, she found that focusing on her breathing helped immeasurably when the uncomfortable physical and emotional sensations emerged. As she explains, "I shifted my attention to my breathing and tried to take slow, deep breaths through my nose. The [4-IN, 8-OUT] thing helped a lot. As I Refocused in this way, I also reminded myself [via the Wise Advocate] that everything was going to be okay. I shifted my attention to reassuring thoughts like 'It's fine, you've been through this before, you don't have to worry about this.' I reassured myself [without intensely desiring for the uncomfortable feelings and sensations to go away] with the knowledge that it's going to be okay. This is going to pass, just like the other [anxiety attacks] did."

While you should not cling to a desire to be calmed or comforted by any Regulate or Refocus activity, you likely will find that focusing on your breath does indeed calm down your nervous system and body, something Dr. Herbert Benson of the Benson-Henry Institute for Mind Body Medicine at Massachusetts General Hospital has convincingly shown in his studies of the Relaxation Response.

Relaxation Response is a term Dr. Benson coined that refers to any method or technique that results in decreased blood pressure, heart rate, or breathing rate—activities that are associated with a state of physiological rest, as opposed to the amped-up responses seen in the fight-or-flight response. Scores of techniques that have been used for millennia can elicit a Relaxation Response, including many forms of yoga, meditation, repetitive prayer, breathing exercises, progressive muscle relaxation, guided imagery, and Qigong.

What's most significant about the Relaxation Response is that it has been shown through many studies to have powerful effects on stress-related disorders and to decrease the number of stress-related genes that are activated and used. *This means that if you incorporate a Relaxation Response technique into the Four Steps, you may actually change the way your body and brain react to stress in positive and beneficial ways.*

THE RELAXATION RESPONSE: WAYS TO REGULATE & REFOCUS

- Any method or technique that results in decreased heart rate, blood pressure, and breathing rate or in more relaxed muscles (i.e., less muscle tension)
- Methods can include (but are not limited to):
  - Yoga, Qigong
  - Meditation
  - Repetitive prayers or mantras
  - Breathing techniques
  - Muscle relaxation
  - Guided imagery
- Relaxation Response is composed of two parts:
  - Repeating a calming word, sound, phrase/prayer, or muscular

activity for ten to twenty minutes in a manner linked to awareness of in-and-out breathing

- Passively disregarding everyday thoughts that come into your
head and trying to focus on repeating the calming action during that time period

- The Relaxation Response can influence how much certain genes associated with stress are expressed. In particular, when people practiced the Relaxation Response for eight weeks, their bodies decreased
the number of stress-related proteins and chemical messengers that
were made—meaning that the Relaxation Response may actually reverse some of the negative effects of stress.

In other words, you might be able to reverse some of the negative effects
of stress in your daily life by consistently practicing the Four Steps with
meditation or another form of Relaxation Response as your Refocus activity.

MENTAL NOTES CAN HELP YOU REGULATE

As we mentioned in chapter 8, mental notes are a powerful way of accurately, effectively, and efficiently Relabeling your deceptive brain messages.
An important effect of Relabeling, much like what Lieberman found in his
experiment, is that using a word to label an emotion can calm your Uh Oh
Center's alarm. Granted, you should never make a mental note with the
exclusive goal of just trying to make yourself feel better, but if you practice
this skill regularly, you will find that it does indeed result in beneficial changes.

To see what we mean, let's look at the following example: Say you are
driving down the freeway and someone cuts you off. If you are like many
people, you might become angry, even enraged, over this event. If you did
become angry, typically you would then get lost in a series of thoughts

about the driver, how rude he was, that he had no right, and so on, rather than simply noting what is happening inside you. As you go down this negative-thought cascade, you fuel the deceptive brain messages further and personalize the interaction in a way that is detrimental to you.

Instead, if you made the mental note "anger" when this happened, you would have described your immediate reaction without getting too involved in any thought process about it. If you then kept mindfully repeating the word you chose, you would find that your bodily sensations and experience of the event change to something that is more neutral. This happens because you decrease the overthinking associated with the angry deceptive brain messages and instead view them from the perspective of the Wise Advocate. For example, the Wise Advocate may look at the situation and say, "Yes, you were angered because you were scared. You thought you might be injured by the reckless maneuver he made, but stewing about it doesn't help you at all. It just makes you angrier and more upset. Instead, focus on your driving and keeping yourself safe—don't waste your energy on that guy. Don't allow him to make his problem your problem."

Try it. The next time you are angry, simply make the mental note "anger . . . anger . . . anger" slowly and watch what happens inside your body. Usually within five to thirty seconds, your physical sensations change and you no longer feel the sensations of anger (again, as long as you are *not* just trying to make the sensations go away, but literally are focusing your attention on making the mental notes of your experience).

Why does this happen? When you are no longer caught up in the thoughts, you've taken the fuel away from the proverbial fire. By focusing on the process, rather than allowing your thoughts to run wild, you are starving the brain of the one thing it needs to keep those uncomfortable sensations and deceptive thoughts flowing: your attention!

The trick with mental notes—and it is an important one—is that *you cannot focus on wanting or intensely desiring a specific outcome or result.* You must simply note what is happening and see how your experience changes.

Refocus with Progressive Mindfulness

As we mentioned earlier, Refocus with Progressive Mindfulness is a more advanced form of Refocusing because it asks you to deliberately confront or deal with something that causes deceptive brain messages or uncomfortable sensations to arise—which often intensifies them at first. Therefore, we recommend that you start with regular Refocusing or Regulating & Refocusing before you attempt Refocus with Progressive Mindfulness. Once you have a good sense of how to use regular Refocus and Regulate & Refocus, you can begin using Refocus with Progressive Mindfulness to enter into situations that cause you distress and evoke deceptive brain messages.

What is Refocus with Progressive Mindfulness? It is a technique that asks you to enter into or remain in a situation that activates your deceptive brain messages and uncomfortable sensations so that you learn how to work around the distress you experience. By doing so, you learn how to remain in that situation (and with those sensations) longer and strengthen your Wise Advocate. For example, if you experience a rapid heartbeat and shortness of breath whenever you enter an elevator, Refocus with Progressive Mindfulness would suggest that you gradually face your fear of elevators. This could mean first walking near elevators, then walking on and off an elevator, then taking the elevator one floor, then several floors, and so on *while allowing the sensations to be present* and using Regulate (e.g., if hyperventilating, breathe in for 4, out for 8; if not, use the 4-IN, 4-OUT pattern) as your object of Refocus. (Note: Regulate is often used in these instances because inside an elevator there are very few constructive, healthy objects for your attention and we do not want you to focus on the elevator itself or your distress.)

If you are familiar with a specific cognitive-behavioral therapy technique known as exposure and response prevention, Refocus with Progressive Mindfulness may seem similar. In some of the mechanics, it is—you are entering situations that distress you. However, the important distinction lies in what you do once you are in that distressing situation. The major difference between the two approaches is that exposure and response prevention asks you to enter a situation and then sit with—but do nothing about—your uncomfortable sensations. You do not focus your attention on a healthy behavior or attempt to regulate your sensations in any way. The presumption of exposure and response prevention is that your brain is no different from an animal's and that to change your behavior, all you need to do is experience incredibly intense spikes in your anxiety or distress level and then allow them to come down on their own—thus "teaching" your body and brain to no longer associate that specific situation with a threat or danger. When exposure and response prevention is done in that way, all your brain learns to do is calm down your Uh Oh Center and not associate *that* upsetting situation with danger, but it does not strengthen your Wise Advocate.

In contrast, Refocus with Progressive Mindfulness encourages you to first face situations you currently are avoiding or to continue in an activity that causes you distress and *then focus your attention on constructive, healthy activities while you are in that situation.* This process results in your brain rewiring itself in ways that are beneficial to you and that adaptively retrain your Habit Center to work toward your true goals and values. Most important, it strengthens your Wise Advocate so you can apply what you learned about the falseness of your deceptive brain messages in this situation to other places in life where deceptive brain messages arise.

REFOCUS WITH PROGRESSIVE MINDFULNESS

1. Place yourself in a situation that causes your deceptive brain messages and uncomfortable sensations to emerge, or remain in a situation that has already evoked your deceptive brain messages.
2. Allow the deceptive sensations, thoughts, urges, impulses, desires, and cravings to be present but do not act on them.

3. Instead, Refocus on another healthy, constructive behavior while you remain in the distressing or upsetting (but nondangerous or nonthreatening) situation.

4. If you cannot find a constructive object or activity for your attention, use Regulate & Refocus to turn your awareness to your breathing (e.g., by using the 4-IN, 8-OUT method for short periods of hyperventilation and the 4-IN, 4-OUT method for all other situations).

5. Continue with your life and daily activities without avoiding (as much as possible).

Kara describes Refocus with Progressive Mindfulness in this way: "The purpose of Refocus with Progressive Mindfulness is to really go through an event and live with the anxiety—getting into that dark area and getting to know it a little more, sort of like living with it and stretching your ability to be in that space for a little longer each time." She says that Refocus with Progressive Mindfulness is "really helpful because you basically are exposing yourself to the very thing you are anxious about or that is triggering your obsession or your craving and sitting with that, the discomfort, and watching it pass. With the Wise Advocate, you are watching the transient nature of it and that it's not really you. If you sit and observe it and don't buy into it and are mindful, you see how it detaches after a while. You can see it for what it is and it's not really you." As this process continues, your Wise Advocate strengthens and you start making healthier choices in many aspects of your life—not just the one situation you currently are encountering. In this way, Kara says, Refocus with Progressive Mindfulness is useful because it helps you get "to the point where whatever you are avoiding becomes more of a common thing, less scary or upsetting, which makes it easier to encounter and do. In reality, I think it can be applied to many things in life."

WHAT CAN REFOCUS WITH PROGRESSIVE MINDFULNESS HELP WITH?

- Anything you avoid
- Anything you want to be doing, but are not
- Anything you are afraid to do, but know would be good for you
- Learning how to deal with uncomfortable physical sensations
- Ensuring that you do not miss out on parts of your life because of the deceptive brain messages or uncomfortable sensations
- Learning how to take care of yourself in relationships by managing and regulating feelings of rejection or social pain
- Dealing with perfectionism by deliberately making small mistakes

NEVER USE REFOCUS WITH PROGRESSIVE MINDFULNESS FOR HIGHLY ADDICTIVE AND DANGEROUS BEHAVIORS SUCH AS DRINKING ALCOHOL, TAKING DRUGS, OR GAMBLING.

Although Refocus with Progressive Mindfulness is highly effective, one point that we must make absolutely clear is that you should *never use Refocus with Progressive Mindfulness for highly addictive and dangerous activities*, including those related to alcohol, drugs, sex, or gambling addictions. Instead, use regular Refocus or Regulate & Refocus. Why? The biological forces are just too strong and overpowering and the stakes are too high in such situations. That's why the conventional wisdom of Alcoholics Anonymous and related traditions has always been to never take a drink or go into a situation that will make you crave alcohol (which is why Steve only used regular Refocus and Regulate & Refocus, but never Refocus with Progressive Mindfulness to deal with his cravings for alcohol).

With that important caveat, let's see how Ed used Refocus with Progressive Mindfulness with his performance anxiety and avoidance of auditions.

Refocus with Progressive Mindfulness and Avoidance

Avoidance is one of the most destructive behaviors you can engage in because of how much it limits your life and how easily you can rationalize away your lack of action with myriad thinking errors. For instance, you can readily tell yourself, "Oh, I don't really need to do X," or "I can do it another time." The problem with this approach, of course, is that your choices are being made on the basis of your deceptive brain messages rather than your Wise Advocate and true self. When that happens, it is difficult to observe and be mindful of what is occurring and you become stuck. That's what happened to Ed, who stopped going to auditions. As he let his deceptive brain messages take hold and dictate his life, he developed an almost immobilizing fear of and anxiety related to performing. Sadly, because he did not challenge or notice his deceptive brain messages for some time, his anxiety generalized to the point that he could no longer even go to an acting class or call his agent.

When he began telling us about his difficulties, we suggested that Refocus with Progressive Mindfulness would be helpful to him because it would teach his brain that the negative thoughts, fears, and social pain related to auditioning were false and that he could succeed on the stage. This would happen, we told him, as his Wise Advocate grew stronger and he had more experiences of confronting the deceptive brain messages with the Four Steps and seeing how inaccurate they were.

To start the process, Ed inventoried his deceptive brain messages and identified his true goals (using the tables provided in the previous chapters). We then asked him to write down the situations that triggered his fear and distressed him the most. While he was doing this, we encouraged him to specifically think of any performance-related activity, event, person, or place he avoided or that he encountered reluctantly because of his significant distress. Here is an example of his initial list:

ED'S INITIAL LIST OF SITUATIONS HE AVOIDS OR THAT DISTRESS HIM

Calling my agent
Going to an acting class
Going to an audition
Telling someone their performance was not that great
Reading a review of my work
Talking to a casting agent
Asking for feedback on my performance

After Ed compiled the list above, we asked him to rate his fear and distress of those situations on a scale of 0 to 100, using figure 11.1 as a guideline:

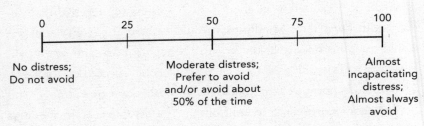

Figure 11.1. Distress and Avoidance Scale

As Ed assigned distress and avoidance ratings to each of the events or actions on his list, we instructed him to be specific about what aspects of each situation distressed him and to separate out the different components of an activity so that he could see how *what he did/the role he served* in an activity affected how distressed he might become. For example, if he was anxious being in an acting class, was it the actual performance that was distressing? Watching others? Critiquing others? Receiving critiques? Similarly, for other activities, what were the most distressing aspects for him? The actual performance? Being evaluated? Concern that he would not be accepted? Fear of making mistakes and being ostracized? And so on.

Here's an example of how Ed rated his distress with those parameters in mind:

ED'S LEVEL OF DISTRESS RELATED TO AUDITIONING AND PERFORMING

Activity	Distress and Avoidance Level
Reading a review of his performance while the musical is still running	100
Performing in the musical	90
Auditioning for a musical	85
Calling a casting agent	70
Calling his agent	60
Reading a script for a musical he may audition for	50
Participating in a singing or acting class	50 (watching) 60 (critiquing others) 70 (performing) 85–100 (receiving critique about his performance)
Reading other people's reviews in the same performance/musical	30
Talking to a friend about a recent performance	30
Looking at the *Playbill* of a performance he is in	15

As you can see from the chart above, Ed rated the following items below 50: reading others' reviews, talking to friends, or looking at the *Playbill*. These low ratings meant that they likely were not things he often avoids. He could engage in those activities at least 50 percent of the time and they were not limiting his life, so Refocus with Progressive Mindfulness was not needed in these cases. In contrast, the items he rated at 50 and above *were* the activities he had been avoiding and these were the ones we wanted him to target with Refocus with Progressive Mindfulness.

We helped Ed develop a list of situations that he could deliberately encounter with the express purpose of increasing his distress and evoking deceptive brain messages. He made a list of the activities associated with distress ratings from 50 to 100 (in order from least distressing to most distressing)—this became his Refocus with Progressive Mindfulness plan. Weekly, he attempted to enter into a new situation on the list (starting at the top of his list and working down) and remain in the situation long enough for his distress level to spike to its maximum and then slowly decrease over time. When his level of distress was less than 50 percent of its maximum for that situation on that day, Ed could then leave the situation or remain in it if he was enjoying it or found the activity interesting. The ultimate goal of this and other Refocus with Progressive Mindfulness exercises was to have Ed use the Four Steps with his Wise Advocate as his guide, which helped him see how useless and inaccurate his deceptive brain messages were.

On page 265 is an example of a list similar to the one he followed at approximately one-week intervals (i.e., one list item per week, starting at the top and ending at the bottom).

ED'S REFOCUS WITH PROGRESSIVE MINDFULNESS LIST

Original Distress Level	Refocus with Progressive Mindfulness Plan
50	Go to an acting class and watch (do not perform or critique)
60	Call my agent and just talk (no agenda)
60	Go to an acting class and provide my opinions/critiques
65	Call my agent and deliberately make a mistake (e.g., mispronounce someone's name)
70	Participate/perform during the acting class as an extra or supporting player (not the main character)
75	Call a casting agent and ask for basic information
80	Read an old review from two years ago
85	Call a casting agent and express interest in an upcoming audition
90	Audition for a musical
100	Perform in a leading role in acting class and receive critiques— allow the Wise Advocate to take in all the positive as well as constructive comments made.
100	Read the reviews of my performance the next morning while using the Wise Advocate to remind me of how well I performed

As Ed entered each of these situations, he would use his Wise Advocate to notice and Relabel his anxiety and the negative, deceptive thoughts. He would then Reframe them as "false brain messages," "social pain," "inaccurate fear of failure and discounting the positive," and so on. He would then Refocus on the activity at hand, such as watching others perform, and try to remain focused on and interested in that activity. If his thoughts started to wander or if he became caught up in his sensations, he would remind himself to Refocus on the actors who were performing or to focus on his breathing for a minute and then return to watching the actors. If the deceptive brain messages and sensations became intense and overpowering again (as they often do when you use Refocus with Progressive Mindfulness), he would again Relabel and Reframe, then Refocus on the actors or his breathing. What he would not do is leave the situation when his distress levels were high (50 or higher). Instead, he would repeat the cycle of Relabel-Reframe-Refocus until his distress level decreased by at least 50 percent from its maximal point.

After approximately twelve weeks of using Refocus with Progressive Mindfulness, Ed was able to go to auditions and has since been booking jobs with regularity. As he explains, "Refocus with Progressive Mindfulness helped me because I was avoiding situations that had to do with people . . . I couldn't get away from people or their potential judgments. So, Refocus with Progressive Mindfulness meant to me that I had to be in the situation and keep going and be mindful. I had to accept these feelings as nothing more than deceptive brain messages—not the truth—and continue on. For me, this changed the meaning of the brain messages to something I could handle. Learning how to use the Wise Advocate to help me out, and see how wrong those negative messages about me were, was an incredible asset. Although it's not fun to put yourself into those distressing situations, it's a whole lot better than being stuck in your life and not achieving anything."

We hope this example of Refocus with Progressive Mindfulness is helpful to you and increases your understanding of how you can use Refocus with Progressive Mindfulness throughout your day. In the next section, we will provide you with the necessary tools to help you evaluate your levels of distress related to things you avoid. However, as we recommended, *it is best for you to learn how to effectively use regular Refocus and Regulate & Refocus FIRST*. Once you have become proficient in those options, then you can begin using Refocus with Progressive Mindfulness to your advantage.

Developing Your Refocus with Progressive Mindfulness Plan

Refocus with Progressive Mindfulness can be used effectively in a wide variety of situations where your current behavior (or lack of action) is harming or inhibiting you. This includes panic, anxiety, avoidance, and relationship problems. Given that there are many ways to use Refocus with Progressive Mindfulness, we have provided you with some helpful general guidelines. In Part Three, we will provide you with examples of other ways you can apply Refocus with Progressive Mindfulness so that you can creatively use Refocus with Progressive Mindfulness whenever you need it.

For the purposes of this exercise and these tables, we will use the term *avoidance* to mean anything you are averse to doing out of fear or distress (but would like to engage in) or anything you would like to be doing but are not (e.g., changing your eating patterns or changing how you act in relationships).

To begin developing your plan, think of situations that you avoid and write them down in the table below. When possible, specify what makes the situation easier or harder to deal with and examine your role or expected contribution to see if that affects your distress level. Add those qualifiers to your list to make it more complete.

THINGS THAT I AVOID OR CAUSE ME DISTRESS (INCLUDE SPECIFIERS)

1.	
2.	
3.	
4.	
5.	
6.	
7.	
8.	
9.	
10.	

Now, rate each activity (with qualifiers) according to how much distress engaging in the activity would cause (using the scale of 0 to 100).

LEVEL OF DISTRESS RELATED TO _____

Activity	Distress and Avoidance Level

Order the activities above based on their distress or avoidance level. Start with items at or near 50. Then, in ascending order, list all of the other activities up to 100. This ranked list, from least distressing at the top of the list to most distressing at the bottom (to be done last), is your Refocus with Progressive Mindfulness plan.

MY REFOCUS WITH PROGRESSIVE MINDFULNESS PLAN—A RANK-ORDERED LIST, FROM LEAST DISTRESSING TO MOST DISTRESSING ACTIVITY

Original Distress Level	Refocus with Progressive Mindfulness Plan
	1.
	2.
	3.
	4.
	5.
	6.
	7.
	8.
	9.
	10.

Complete one list item per week (if possible, but allow yourself more time if needed). Once you start the exercise (i.e., enter the distressing situation), you will notice that your distress level will increase, usually substantially (e.g., from 50 to 80 or 90), and then decrease over time and likely end lower than when you started. Remain in the situation until your distress level has decreased by at least 50 percent from its maximal level (e.g., distress level of 80 becomes 40, 90 becomes 45). Continue to Relabel, Reframe, and Refocus while you remain in the situation/complete the exercise. Repeat the exercise throughout the week until entering the situation no longer bothers you (i.e., your maximal distress level is less than 50) and you can use the Wise Advocate to see that this situation is not threatening or something to be avoided because the deceptive brain messages and uncomfortable sensations are false.

Gratitude Lists—Refocusing with the 5 A's in Mind

To end this chapter, we want to introduce you to one other way you can Refocus that increases your ability to see the positive achievements and qualities you possess: gratitude lists.

These are short lists you complete every night (or during a Refocus) that emphasize the positive aspects of your life—what you did well (though not perfectly) today, what you accomplished, what you are grateful for, what you appreciate, and so on. As Sarah describes, "Gratitude lists are about acknowledging what is right about me and getting away from the 'I am a sick person' dialogue. The gratitude helps me focus on who I really am and what I have in my life that is healthy and is good. Everybody has something like that. We all have gifts that we can look at."

And looking at what we do right is something we often neglect, as John so eloquently pointed out when he asked us this question: "Why can't I obsess on my assets like the way I obsess on my liabilities?" Seeing what you have accomplished helps you counter deceptive brain messages and dismiss unhelpful, damaging thoughts as nothing more than false chatter. In this way gratitude lists are a wonderful tool to help you activate the more constructive parts of your mind, provide yourself with the 5 A's (Attention, Acceptance, Affection, Appreciation, Allowing), and rewire your brain in positive ways—to see that you are a good person striving to achieve laudable goals.

GRATITUDE LISTS

Each night (or whenever you are Refocusing and cannot find another object for your focus and attention), write down:

- Ten things you are grateful for (e.g., the sun is shining; I Refocused twice today; I have wonderful friends)
- Five things you accomplished today (e.g., I was able to work all day despite the deceptive brain messages bothering me; I called my sister; I made a healthy dinner)
- Any positive changes you've noticed in your response to your deceptive brain messages (e.g., I did not avoid the market today, and went inside and bought one item)

Summary

In the next chapter, we will bring the Four Steps together by teaching you about Step 4: Revalue. Until then, review and remember these key facts about Step 3: Refocus:

- You already learned how to Refocus when you completed the breathing and thought awareness exercises in chapter 8.
- Refocus is designed to teach you how to place your attention and

focus on a healthy, constructive activity while the deceptive brain messages and sensations are present.

- There are many ways to Refocus including:
  - Regular Refocus
  - Regulate & Refocus
  - Refocus with Progressive Mindfulness
  - Gratitude lists
- Never use Refocus with Progressive Mindfulness for highly addictive and dangerous activities, like alcohol, drugs, sex addictions, or gambling addictions.
- You should start with regular Refocus or Regulate & Refocus at first, since Refocus with Progressive Mindfulness very likely will make your deceptive sensations, impulses, cravings, desires, and urges more intense at first.

CHAPTER 12

Progressive Mindfulness
and Step 4: Revalue

Before Sarah started using the Four Steps, her world was dominated by deceptive brain messages, thinking errors, anxiety, depression, panic, and unhealthy habits like overthinking and repeatedly checking to see if she made mistakes or upset someone. Perfectionism, shame, and guilt ruled her life and dictated her actions. She was miserable and exhausted, but she knew no other way of living. That is, until she started using the Four Steps and learned how to Revalue her experiences. As Sarah began to challenge the faulty logic of her thinking errors, disarm the hysteria coming from her Uh Oh Center, and refuse to comply with the Habit Center's automatic responses, she began to see just how limited and restricted her life had been when she viewed herself and made choices from the perspective of her deceptive brain messages.

She remembers the day when she finally realized that she truly did have *the power to choose.* Her options, she realized, were to listen to her healthy, loving side or the harsh and deceptive brain messages. Since she now could believe her Wise Advocate's assertion that there was nothing wrong with her, she knew that what she needed to do was change how she *viewed* what was happening inside her brain and body. That change in perspective was critical, she says, and only happened the more she used the Four Steps and Revalued her deceptive brain messages.

As she explains, "I tended to see the smaller picture [propagated by deceptive brain messages], like I made a mistake or didn't do something right, rather than see [from the perspective of the Wise Advocate] that I am trying to do the right things in life." When she remained bogged down by the negative and distracting false details, she allowed the deceptive brain messages to "prevent me from believing in my true self, in who I really am." However, when she stepped back and looked from the perspective of her Wise Advocate, she realized, "I'm already there. I am fine and a good person just as I am."

The key, Sarah recognized, was choosing to see life from the perspective of her loving and compassionate Wise Advocate. With this ability, her healthy side could shine through and help her see the larger picture—that she was worthy of leading a fulfilling and meaningful life and believing in herself. As important, when she stepped back from those distracting and unhelpful negative thoughts and allowed her loving, healthy side to recognize her positive attributes and accomplishments, her view of herself and life shifted in a fundamental way. No longer beholden to her thinking errors or self-doubt, she was liberated. "What I had to do, which is hard—the feelings will try to trick you—is not change anything about me, but change my *attitude, my belief about myself.*"

This idea of shifting your perspective with the Wise Advocate is what the Four Steps and especially Step 4: Revalue are all about. In essence, Revaluing encourages you to recruit and nourish your healthy, loving side on a consistent basis so that you can instantly see and dismiss the logic of the deceptive brain messages and make positive, constructive choices that emanate from your empowered, compassionate Wise Advocate. As Sarah explains, when she got to this point, she was able to say to herself, "I am fine with who I am. It's coming to terms with who I am and that I'm already okay because I am a moral person. It doesn't matter in the long run what my deceptive brain messages are or what thoughts and feelings they cause. My true self is who I am—I am a good person."

STEP 4: REVALUE

Clearly see the thoughts, urges, and impulses for what they are—simply sensations caused by deceptive brain messages that are not true and have little to no value (they are something to dismiss, not focus on).

When things happen in life, as Sarah now knows, you can respond in many ways that may be beneficial or harmful, but you essentially only have two ways of looking at a situation: from the broad view of your healthy, loving side or from the narrow and negative perspective of your deceptive brain messages. Ultimately, the *choice* of how to view events is up to you—and it really is a choice!

That's why learning to Revalue is so important—it is the final and ultimate step in your journey to clearly see what is happening in each moment of your life. When you take even the weakest, seemingly tamest deceptive brain messages seriously and address them directly, you not only have the opportunity to Revalue them from the perspective of your Wise Advocate, but also to literally change the way your brain works. By building your capacity to resist the habit of taking things too personally, buying into thinking errors, or automatically responding to deceptive brain messages in an unhealthy manner, you become more adept at taking away their power while simultaneously increasing your level of mindful awareness and ingraining positive automatic responses into your brain. It's no easy task, as Sarah knows, but the more you practice using the Four

Steps and allow the healthy side to break through your deceptive thoughts, urges, impulses, desires, and cravings, the easier it becomes.

Gaining Perspective Through Progressive Mindfulness

To develop that grander perspective of the Wise Advocate, however, requires that you realize and accept that you have been living life from a narrow point of view—that of the deceptive brain messages—and that seeing life in this way leads you to discount much of what you have achieved, not recognize how far you've come, not appreciate how monumental it is that you are seeking help and making positive changes in your life. Once you accept that this is what you have been doing, you can make a genuine commitment to change how you view the world and your experiences. When that happens, you are actively Revaluing in ways that are wholesome and beneficial to you.

The key to active Revaluing is learning how to operate from the perspective of your Wise Advocate on a consistent basis so that those positive patterns of thinking and behaving become ingrained in your brain. Remember, the brain cannot differentiate healthy from unhealthy behaviors on its own—it simply responds to the environment and where you actively focus your attention. This means that when you use the Four Steps and your Wise Advocate you are making your brain work to your advantage by teaching the Habit Center to choose new responses that are aligned with your true self.

As this happens, you will be able to *instantly* identify and dismiss deceptive brain messages while simultaneously *knowing* that the uncomfortable sensations are false and that Refocusing your attention on a healthy, constructive activity is your best option. This is the definition of *progressive mindfulness* and what we hope you achieve the more you use the Four Steps.

Using your Wise Advocate to gain deeper levels of mindful awareness (through experience) so that you can clearly see the bothersome feelings, urges, fears, worries, cravings, negative ideas, and thinking errors as nothing more than deceptive brain messages.

Progressive mindfulness is important because it is the crux of the Four Steps. In this way, it's a rather advanced application of the Wise Advocate, which is why we waited until Step 4 to introduce it to you. When you are using progressive mindfulness and actively Revaluing, you approach your experiences and feelings as *a direct object of observation.* As you do this, you firmly and assertively label and strive to *directly experience* the sensations as *nothing but* deceptive brain messages.

Now, we know this concept is hard to grasp at first—after all, Step 4 is experiential, just like Step 1: Relabel, which makes it difficult to describe or understand exactly how this process unfolds. That said, the best way to think of Revaluing and progressive mindfulness is that it is an *experience, feeling,* or *knowledge* that allows you to see what is transpiring in this very moment as it is happening without distracting concepts or deceptive brain messages getting in the way.

In short, learning to Revalue is much like learning how to notice when you are lost in thought—they are both forms of mindfulness. The biggest difference, and it's a huge one, is that Revaluing is designed to help you gain deeper levels of awareness and understanding with more experience (i.e., progressive mindfulness). As such, Revaluing and progressive mindfulness are *the* aim of the Four Steps and your ultimate achievement.

That's why after you make significant progress Relabeling and Reframing, your goal shifts from repeatedly and methodically going through each of the first three steps (e.g., Step 1, then Step 2, then Step 3) to emphasizing Step 4: Revalue. As you enter into the active Revalue stage, you want to move *beyond* a mere cognitive understanding of your deceptive brain messages and instead get to the point of *directly experiencing* the bothersome sensations as *nothing but* a deceptive brain message. When you are able to do this, you no longer will need to go through Steps 1 and 2; rather, you will directly feel the deceptive brain message as nothing more than a deceptive brain message and immediately Refocus your attention in a healthy way.

Although this seems complicated and confusing, remember that Revaluing is something that gets stronger and deeper with increasing amounts of time, insight, and practice. In fact, even a few seconds of truly Revaluing is a big achievement at first. And, with continued work and perseverance, Revaluing will happen more often and become easier. In the end, this becomes the most powerful step of all because it liberates you from the mandates of your deceptive brain messages and empowers you to face your fears assertively, courageously, and with confidence.

As with other forms of mindful awareness, until you actually experience it yourself—that deep knowing and progressive mindfulness that come with practicing the Four Steps—you will not fully understand what we mean. And it's okay that you don't, for the goal is not to know everything at once, but to slowly expand your knowledge and skills through experience and time.

Liz acknowledges that the process of achieving deeper levels of mindfulness through experience (i.e., progressive mindfulness) is difficult, but absolutely worth it. As she explains, "The more you use the Four Steps, the more it strengthens the Wise Advocate and the more mindful you become." The process, she says, happens something like this: "The deceptive brain message comes along and you *know that feeling.* You *automatically can identify* it as a deceptive brain message right away. Over time, you *know it and feel it as a deceptive brain message.*" At the same time, she says, you dismiss the logic and importance of the deceptive brain message and "try not to get so put out by it, to not get so stressed about it" because you know it's a false message that you do not need to follow or believe in.

Similarly, Abby remembers Step 4 being a challenge at first but says that it gets easier with time. As she explains, when she first started the Four Steps, she would recite the definition of Step 4: Revalue to herself, but did not truly understand what it meant. "At first," she says, "I was just kind of saying [the Revalue definition] to myself, but as you progress in mindfulness and keep on going with the Four Steps, you can actually see what that means. You can feel it as just being a deceptive brain message and then you're Revaluing because you're saying, 'Don't take it at face value.' Definitely Revalue was hard to grasp at first, but that's not something to get discouraged about," she says. "I think if you concentrate on doing the first three [steps] and especially the Refocus, then the Revalue will kind of come on its own."

With time, John says, Revaluing actually provides you with "a new way of looking at things" and the confidence to know that the uncomfortable sensations and deceptive thoughts will pass. As he explains, "You get to a point where you *know* it's a passing feeling. Although everything may look dark at that point, if you have the depth [and ability] to realize that it's just a passing feeling, you can go on because [these thoughts and sensations aren't] going to stay forever. You can focus on longer-term events or goals that you know are coming. [In this way, Revalue] kind of builds a bridge toward those better times outside of that emotional cloud. You can look forward and say, 'This is not always going to be the case—I am moving forward.' So that alleviates the pain of that emotional sensation at that time and gets you going in a positive direction."

Ed agrees and adds: "The whole process is a matter of getting your foot in the door between you and the deceptive brain message. Getting more and more time to look around within it, to not be defined by it any longer. But mostly [Revaluing helps you] start reacting differently to things, thinking differently about things, and having a different way of looking at something. Gradually over time, through using the Four Steps and through using mindful meditation, a person can really become the master, not over what emotions or thoughts come up, but be the master over evaluation of anything that comes into your head or into your body."

What Abby, Sarah, Ed, and John are describing is that *shift* that takes place somewhere along the line when you consistently use the Four Steps and actively Revalue your experiences. It's a shift that fundamentally alters how you approach what happens in your life and what you do with the information you receive. Instead of taking things personally and being overrun by your Uh Oh Center and the unhelpful parts of the Self-Referencing Center, your Assessment Center takes charge and assists your Wise Advocate in seeing life's events—and your self-worth—from a rational, healthy, loving perspective.

Learning to Take Care of Yourself

Along with developing deeper levels of mindfulness, another important goal of the Four Steps is to teach you how to care for yourself—to appropriately make your needs and goals a priority, without harming others, and to learn how to provide yourself with the 5 A's. This is so you make decisions from a secure, loving place, not from unwarranted fear, anger, sadness, or other deceptive emotional sensations. The key is to figure out when you are experiencing true emotions and when you are being ruled by unhelpful and inaccurate emotional sensations generated by deceptive brain messages.

TRUE EMOTIONS VERSUS EMOTIONAL SENSATIONS

True emotions—reactions or feelings that anyone would have in the situation. The Wise Advocate would tell you they are true and worthy of your attention—and that you need to *constructively* deal with those emotions in some way.

Emotional sensations—result from deceptive brain messages and almost always arise from a thinking error or negative messages you learned in life and especially in childhood. They are not based in reality and are not representative of who you are. The Wise Advocate would look at these emotional sensations and tell you they are not true and that you should not focus any attention or spend any time on them.

We know that this distinction between emotions and emotional sensations probably is one of the hardest to make, because for years you likely have been equating these erroneous emotional sensations—powered by thinking errors—with true feelings and emotions. What do we mean? When your deceptive side is in charge, it mimics what you learned as a child and causes you to ignore, minimize, and dismiss your true emotions and to replace them with the unhealthy emotional sensations you have been experiencing, such as anxiety, depression, and cravings. In doing so, *your deceptive brain messages dictate that you only take notice of and pay attention to your emotional sensations and not your true emotions.*

Even more damaging, if you did experience and display a true emotion in childhood, such as anger or sadness, your brain likely was programmed, like Sarah's, to automatically respond with a deceptive brain message telling you that somehow you were to blame or at fault—thus activating strong (and inappropriate) sensations of guilt and shame. Similarly, if you were overly coddled or smothered, your natural reaction to this excessive and overbearing attention on you likely would have been anger and a desire to be left alone, as in Steve's case. In response to those true emotions, your deceptive brain messages would have swiftly responded by telling you that you were ungrateful or otherwise acting inappropriately—thus triggering guilt and shame as well.

In short, these kinds of upbringings and environments would have taught you that emotional sensations were "safe," whereas true emotions were "dangerous" because they threatened your caregivers in some way. Coming from this perspective as a child, it would then be very difficult as an adult to tell what was a true emotion or an emotional sensation. This is precisely why using the Wise Advocate to help you discern the difference is so critical as you start to deal with your deceptive brain messages.

For example, whenever John was concerned that Alicia might be leaving him, he was flooded with anxiety, fear, and distress. Clearly, John *felt* a lot when the deceptive thoughts arose, but they were not true emotions. Rather, they were emotional sensations related to, and based on, his repeated experiences of social pain and rejection that emanated from his childhood marching orders that to be loved and accepted, he needed to put others first at all costs. If he did not do this, he learned as a child, he would lose the important people in his life (like Coach) and be abandoned. Because of these experiences, John's brain concluded that putting people first was his "job" and that if he did not accomplish this goal, he should feel guilty and ashamed. Sadly, this meant that John either spent his time anxious and preoccupied with others or guilty and ashamed for not fulfilling inappropriate and unreasonable expectations.

What John was not consciously feeling, but was present underneath the surface, were anger and outrage over having to fulfill this one-sided contract, and sadness over never feeling like he could simply do what he wanted and still be loved. Those were his true emotions, but he dismissed, minimized, and ignored them at the behest of his deceptive brain messages. In this way, even though John *felt* something, they were emotional sensations (anxiety and distress) based on false messages and thinking errors, not his true emotions (anger and sadness).

The key to figuring out whether your experience is the result of a deceptive brain message or a true emotion is to use your Wise Advocate (or a friend or counselor if you are just starting out). The question to ask yourself is *whether a reasonable person would respond in a similar way to how you actually responded.* Would the other person get anxious, feel like he had done something wrong, or experience guilt and shame for having not lived up to some exalted expectation? Or would he respond with anger or sadness?

If we applied this question to John, we would conclude that another person likely would look at John's behavior and say that there's no reason for John to feel guilty or ashamed. He'd done way more than he should have and, in fact, most people would feel angry if they had to constantly take care of others at their own expense. When seen from this impartial perspective, John would then be able to conclude that (a) the anxiety, guilt, and shame are the result of deceptive brain messages that do not need to be acted on and (b) unlike what his deceptive brain messages told him, he does not need to suppress or disavow his true emotions, such as anger or sadness, but can feel and deal with them in a constructive, healthy way.

Similarly, when Kara began using the Four Steps, she often was confused as to whether something she experienced was a deceptive brain message or a true emotion. "I had spent years believing that anxiety, depression, fear—all of these things—were real emotions. I never saw them as the result of thinking errors or deceptive brain messages. They were all I knew and I thought they were true." What was actually happening was that Kara was suppressing her true emotions—her anger and grief—over what had happened in her life and replaced them with more "socially acceptable" emotional sensations, such as anxiety, fear, panic, and depression. Just like John, Kara was subtly taught that any expression of her true emotions, such as anger, disappointment, or sadness, were not going to be tolerated under any circumstances and were punishable with loss of love, acceptance, or affection.

For example, if as a child Kara expressed anger over her mother not fulfilling a promise, her mom would emotionally withdraw and not speak to Kara for a day or longer. This left Kara feeling alone, sad, and scared. In her child brain, she equated her mom's emotional withdrawal with abandonment and serious risk of potential harm or death. Given the dire situation Kara faced emotionally and the considerable social pain she felt in those moments, she very quickly learned that to keep her mom around and caring for her in even minimal ways meant suppressing her true emotions and covering them up with anxiety and fear instead. This inability to feel her true feelings and to instead ignore, minimize, and neglect them certainly ensured that she stayed away from feeling the emotions she actually felt as a child—anger, resentment, sadness—and kept her locked in the same harmful patterns and unhelpful emotional sensations.

To counteract that negative childhood programming, Kara had to start seeing her anxiety as an emotional sensation and a *signal* that a true emotion was lingering under the surface—an emotion that up to that point in her life was punishable by abandonment and loss. For example, when her mother announced that she would be giving Kara's sister $50,000 to help her and her husband purchase a new home, Kara became anxious and depressed. Rather than feeling her outrage at the inequality (her mother had not helped her when she bought her first house), Kara retreated into her well-defined and highly deceptive responses of anxiety and depression— the "acceptable" emotional sensations that would not have provoked her mother's withdrawal response. Because of her overwhelming anxiety, Kara started to stress-eat and was flooded with questions of self-doubt: What's wrong with me? Why doesn't Mom love me as much as my sister? Why doesn't she treat me the same way? What did I do? And so on.

When we pointed out to her that the stress-eating and beating up on herself were preprogrammed responses from her childhood that were designed to keep her from actually being angry with her mom, Kara was astonished. With this insight, she was able to tell us that whenever she did experience any anger toward her mother, "I would immediately feel guilty and ashamed." And therein lies your dilemma, we said: Remain anxious and depressed (one set of emotional sensations) or allow some anger to emerge and then feel inappropriately guilty and ashamed (another set of emotional sensations). Not surprisingly, this is almost identical to John's experience and, like John, Kara was vacillating between two sets of deceptive emotional sensations and was never truly feeling her emotions. When we pointed out her quandary—to be anxious or to be angry followed by inappropriate guilt—she saw the problem and asked how she could change the way she responded to such situations.

The first and most important step, we told her, was to use her Wise Advocate to look at the situation from another person's perspective and to Revalue the situation from that point of view. The goal, we said, was to help her see that the deceptive brain messages were condemning her for trying to feel her true emotions and dictating that she continue to experience uncomfortable emotional sensations instead.

The best and most effective way to do this, we told her, was to *think about how she would react if the same event happened to someone else she really cared about*—not her. What would she feel about that person's situation and why? If that person told her that she felt exactly the way she did right now, what would she say to her? Would she tell her she should feel guilt, shame, or anxiety, or would she tell her she had a right to experience her anger and let it flow through her body without acting in damaging ways? Would she encourage her to discover her true emotions or to continue allowing the emotional sensations to take hold and obscure her ability to make rational decisions that are in her best interest? The point of this thought exercise, we told Kara, was to use her Wise Advocate to see *why* she might have learned to react this way as a child so that she could use that information to allow her actual emotions to come through and help guide her choices based on her true goals and values.

Steve also found that this approach of understanding where the deceptive brain messages originated (i.e., by figuring out what happened to him as a child whenever he tried to express his true emotions) was helpful in dealing with *his excessive and inappropriate* anger (emotional sensations) toward his coworkers and family. In his case, despite growing up in privilege and being indulged in every material way possible, Steve's parents were not affectionate with him and never asked him how he felt. If Steve mentioned that he was upset or sad, his father responded to his comments by telling him to quit being a "sissy" and to "toughen up." Adding insult to injury, his parents doted over his little sister and legitimized her needs. These experiences caused Steve to resent his sister's expression of feelings, desires, or interests and left him feeling alone, depressed, and sad, especially since the only way he could get his parents' attention was by being angry or acting out in an inappropriate way (e.g., drinking, using drugs, staying out all night).

A consequence of his parents not listening to him and prioritizing his sister's needs was that Steve received the message that his true emotions (such as sadness and a longing to connect emotionally) were unimportant. As a result, he learned to either withdraw from people or become angry whenever he perceived that their needs would trump his (as his sister's did when they were growing up). Unfortunately, these patterns of responding with excessive anger in a desperate attempt to get attention (and his needs met) would continue into adulthood and cause him to feel alone, isolated, or disconnected until he was able to allow his true emotions of sadness and longings to connect to come through.

Now, if he realizes he is becoming excessively angry, Steve asks himself *how another person would react to the situation he was in.* For example, would that person become *this* angry? How would he view what is happening? Would the situation be so bad that it would drive him to drink alcohol and emotionally withdraw from the people around him? Or would he see that he was overreacting to the situation because of thinking errors and childhood programming and choose to Refocus on a healthy, constructive behavior instead?

We will continue to discuss how to differentiate true emotions from emotional sensations in the next chapter, as this distinction is probably one of the most difficult, yet critical, to make. The key, no matter the situation, is Revaluing, using your Wise Advocate, and truly believing in yourself.

One point that must be made is that stress—in any form—can make your deceptive brain messages worse. Why mention this now? As you use the Four Steps and begin to notice more deceptive brain messages, you may feel like you are actually getting worse. This is not the case, as Abby mentioned in chapter 7, but it often concerns many people. Similarly, when you are stressed, your deceptive brain messages can try to take over and make you feel like "nothing is working." The truth is that almost all medical and psychological symptoms get worse when someone is more stressed. For example, you might find that when you're stressed your chronic pain gets worse, your stomach is more upset, your heartburn occurs more often, the number of deceptive thoughts per day increases, or your uncomfortable sensations intensify.

What you need to remember is that the culprit of your increased sensations likely is stress and not an indication that you are relapsing.

Although no one knows for sure why overloading the brain with stress causes increased physical and emotional sensations, clinical experience proves that it does happen—likely because stress causes your brain to recruit its old, hardwired routines to go into overdrive. That's why you experience more intense or frequent sensations or experience deceptive thoughts and urges you haven't experienced for a while. The old brain pathways somehow are gearing up and taking over (this is especially true when you are just starting to use the Four Steps and those pathways have not been replaced with healthier brain wiring yet).

What you need to remember is that the whole point of the Four Steps is to wire new, healthy routines into your repertoire and into your brain—including the physical memory and habitual response *to use the Four Steps* whenever deceptive brain messages arise. This means that when you are stressed, you want to be even more diligent about using the Four Steps so that your brain learns to recruit these healthy pathways *under stress* in the future.

A key to achieving this increased awareness is to remind yourself that (a) you can Reframe your experiences as being caused by stress and (b) the increased sensations are not an indication that you are relapsing. Therefore, when you are stressed, Reframe your increased negative thoughts, urges, impulses, desires, and cravings as being caused by how your brain is responding to the stress. It's the faulty, overloaded brain wiring that's the problem—not you—and just because you experience increased deceptive brain messages does not mean that everything you learned is lost or that you will never improve. Rather, *you are continuing to move forward and are making progress every time you use the Four Steps.*

So, when you are stressed, Reframe your increased and intensified deceptive thoughts as the result of your brain going into a maladaptive overdrive and Refocus on a healthy, constructive activity.

Summary Tables

Now that you understand the Four Steps and how to apply them to your deceptive brain messages, you can use the following tables whenever a deceptive brain message surfaces. In fact, we would recommend that you make copies of these tables and use them throughout your week to help you identify and deal with your deceptive brain messages, uncomfortable sensations, and habitual responses.

The first table is designed to help you identify what happens to you when deceptive brain messages strike. We ask you to describe the situation/trigger, how distressed you were, what emotional and physical sensations you experienced, what your automatic thoughts (i.e., deceptive brain messages) and unhealthy responses were, and how the Wise Advocate would have approached the situation. In the second table, we ask you to think about how you could Relabel, Reframe, Refocus, and Revalue the situation. We hope these tables will be helpful to you as you work with the Four Steps.

SUMMARY TABLE #1: IDENTIFYING YOUR DECEPTIVE BRAIN MESSAGES AND DEFINING THE WISE ADVOCATE'S RESPONSE

Item	Your Responses
Circumstance/trigger (i.e., location, environment, people)	
Distress, anxiety, or avoidance level	Circle one: 1 2 3 4 5 6 7 8 9 10 Not intense ————————→ Very intense
What are the emotional sensations?	
What do I think or feel like I need to do? (i.e., what is the deceptive brain message saying to me or telling me to do?)	
Wise Advocate: What would a caring, loving person, whom you trust and knows everything about this situation, say?	
What did I do?	
What would my Wise Advocate say to me and suggest I do?	

SUMMARY TABLE #2: APPLYING THE FOUR STEPS

Step 1: Relabel	
What are the deceptive thoughts?	
What are the urges, desires, cravings, impulses?	
What are the sensations (i.e., how do your body and brain want you to act or respond right now)?	

Step 2: Reframe	
Why does this keep bothering me?	
Is this a false message?	
Am I using any thinking errors?	
Is there social pain involved?	

Step 3: Refocus	
What activity can I do right now to turn my attention toward something that is healthy, constructive, or beneficial?	
Would Regulate & Refocus be the best?	
Should I use Refocus with Progressive Mindfulness? Am I avoiding something I want to do?	

Step 4: Revalue	
Using the Wise Advocate, sum up what is really happening.	
Is this thought, urge, impulse, craving, or desire true or is this the feeling of a deceptive brain message only and not something that must be followed blindly?	
In other words, is this a true emotion that reflects my true self or is it a false emotional sensation?	

The Horizon

To end our discussion of Step 4, let's review this wonderful summary provided by Bhante Gunaratana that describes the goals of mindful awareness and choosing actions that are based on your true self, not the deceptive brain messages:

[The deceptive brain messages] are just perceptual mental habits. You learn to respond this way as a child by copying the perceptual habits of those around you. These perceptual responses are not inherent in the structure of the nervous system. The circuits are there, but this is not the only way that our mental machinery can be used. That which has been learned can be unlearned. The first step is to realize what you are doing as you are doing it, to stand back and quietly watch. [That is the goal, to be able to] learn to watch the arising of thought and perception with a feeling of serene detachment. We learn to view our own reactions to stimuli with calmness and clarity. We begin to see ourselves reacting without getting caught up in the reactions themselves.[1] [This is progressive mindfulness!]

As we have emphasized throughout this book, becoming aware of your deceptive brain messages is no easy task. In addition to consistently noticing what is happening in your brain and how you are reacting, you have to figure out how to deal with all the negative aspects of your experience you are now observing with your increased levels of mindful awareness. As our patients have told you time and again, you need to be tolerant and gentle with yourself—using the Four Steps can be a humbling and challenging undertaking, but the results are immensely positive and beneficial to your life.

We can tell you from experience that people do improve the more they use the Four Steps. We have had the privilege of witnessing this transition happen time and again. It is remarkable to see the progress people make when they directly confront their deceptive brain messages with the Four Steps. To watch their struggles and see them succeed based on their consistent efforts and dedication to themselves is extraordinary and heartwarming, especially considering where many of them started. It is staggering to think that some of these people were nearly devastated by their deceptive brain messages when we met them, their lives virtually in shambles, and that after making a commitment to themselves and steadily applying the Four Steps, many of them now are leading full, productive lives with families, jobs, graduate degrees, commitments, and myriad outside interests. Seeing them finally liberated from the oppressive commands of their deceptive brain messages and making unrestrained choices—ones that are in their best interest and based on their true goals and values—is the most meaningful result we could wish for them to achieve.

---

1. Bhante Henepola Gunaratana, *Mindfulness in Plain English* (Boston: Wisdom Publications, 1992), p. 36.

We hope that through these chapters you, too, have learned how to develop a strong, healthy Wise Advocate who can travel with you, like a good friend, teacher, or counselor, and help you consistently make decisions that are in your best interest and based on your true self. To send you off to the best start possible, we have dedicated the final section of the book, Part Three, to applying the Four Steps to a variety of deceptive brain messages or situations you may encounter.

This choice in structuring Part Three around deceptive brain messages—as opposed to standard "symptoms" or "diagnoses"—was deliberate because we wanted the book and your learning of the method to mirror the real world, not a textbook. One thing we have realized from our clinical experiences is that deceptive brain messages can manifest in any number of ways depending on the individual, which means they do not fit neatly into predefined categories. For example, a deceptive brain message can cause one person to become anxious and have panic attacks whereas another person may become depressed or start drinking alcohol. Therefore, we chose to focus on what drives the behaviors and how they play out in the real world, rather than organizing the chapters around specific psychiatric diagnoses, such as depression or panic disorder.

Most important, in Part Three we will walk you through how to choose which problems to address first, when Refocus with Progressive Mindfulness might be helpful, and how to chart your own self-guided Four Step program.

PART THREE

Applying the Four Steps to Your Life

We are what we repeatedly do.
Excellence, then, is not an act, but a habit.

—ARISTOTLE

CHAPTER 13

What Is Going On Here?

Is This a True Emotion or an Emotional Sensation?

W e have often heard people say that one of the most difficult things for them to determine is whether they are dealing with a true emotion or an emotional sensation. Being able to differentiate true emotions from unhelpful and often destructive emotional sensations is critical in helping you clearly see what is happening so that you can appropriately and constructively respond to any situation that arises in a way that is consistent with who you are and how you want to be in the world (i.e., your true self). To that end, we discussed the role your upbringing and childhood interactions may have played to help you see that your brain likely has been *ignoring, minimizing, dismissing, neglecting, or devaluing your true needs and emotions* and causing you to employ many thinking errors to your detriment. These thinking errors, when not properly Relabeled and Reframed, often cloud your perspective and cause you to conflate difficult or upsetting experiences from your past with the current people in your life.

Since our goal is to increase your insight and ability to spot deceptive brain messages on your own (i.e., without a therapist in many cases), let's take one more in-depth look at three of the most common and confusing emotional experiences to differentiate when you begin working with the Four Steps: anger, sadness, and anxiety. We'll also take a closer look at "should" statements.

Anger: Healthy or Unhealthy?

Anger can be a friend or foe depending on the situation and the intensity. When it is all-consuming and used destructively, anger can wreak havoc on your life, ruin relationships, and cause you to act in unhealthy ways. It may lead you to yell at people for no good reason, numb yourself with drugs or alcohol, push people away, act impulsively, and so on. However, when it is used constructively, anger is a mobilizing force that advocates for you to care for yourself and ensure that you are not being taken advantage of.

Steve, the fifty-five-year-old executive, is an example of excessive and inappropriate anger leading to harmful actions, such as drinking alcohol to relax and escape. When Steve was beholden to a series of deceptive brain messages that led him to believe that everyone around him was needy and inept, he was unable to see those people and events as they truly were. In those instances, Steve was clouded by all-or-nothing thinking, discounting the positive, and "should" statements, which left him feeling frustrated, stressed, used, and disappointed. In his brain, it was as if no one actually *saw* Steve and who he was, which led to intense and inappropriate anger that built up throughout Steve's day until he made it home to the bottle and the inevitable, but harmful, release that ensued.

In short, Steve's inability to identify his deceptive brain messages, Revalue his experiences, and see life from the perspective of the Wise Advocate caused him to act in detrimental ways that ultimately hurt him (and the people around him, given his level of emotional withdrawal). Had he been able to realize that his brain was operating under false assumptions and was clouded by thinking errors, he could have seen that the people in his life were trying to provide him with the 5 A's[1] (rather than trying to get something from him) and that his anger was inappropriate and excessive because it was *not leading to any productive changes in his life*. It was not empowering him to take care of himself, but was causing him to neglect his needs and emotions further.

If instead Steve had realized that some of his misdirected anger was the result of his ever-increasing loneliness and longing to connect with the important people in his life, the true emotions underlying his anger might have emerged. In that case, he might have constructively dealt with those true emotions by allowing himself to really feel the grief associated with isolating himself, no matter how painful, and to sit with those emotions—without overidentifying with them or acting in unhealthy ways. Similarly, had he recognized and constructively dealt with his sadness instead of ignoring, minimizing, and neglecting his own needs, he likely would have been motivated to proactively change his life in positive ways, such as telling people what he wanted and needed, spending more time with his family, ensuring he had more time off from work, and so on.

How anger affects you—what it causes you to do—is the hallmark of whether it is healthy or unhealthy. When anger encourages you to work harder on your own behalf and in accordance with your true self, it is healthy and helpful. For example, when Connie used her frustration and anger to motivate her to redouble her efforts and try a specific physical therapy exercise again, it was advantageous. Conversely, when she would become angry with herself at her lack of progress in physical therapy, her anger was unhealthy. In those cases, she was operating from the perspective of deceptive brain messages (i.e., "should" statements and false expectations), rather than seeing the truth of how far she'd come with her Wise Advocate. These thinking errors caused her to minimize her progress and become inappropriately angry, thus keeping her farther from her true goals.

---

1. Attention, Acceptance, Affection, Appreciation, Allowing. See pages 122–23.

No less damaging, but harder to initially spot, was how John dealt with his true emotions. In his case, not feeling anger was as bad as feeling it excessively. By not allowing himself to feel anger or denying that it was there, John locked himself into a series of deceptive thoughts and harmful behaviors that resulted in his putting others first and living a subservient life. He was stuck and nothing would change until he could see his deceptive brain messages for what they were. Like Connie, once John was able to uncover his anger and use it to spur him into wholesome action on his behalf (e.g., spending time with people other than Alicia; doing things for himself; expressing his interests, likes, and dislikes), his anger became healthy and productive.

As you can see from these examples, anger is not all-good or all-bad and it does not fit neatly into one category. It is an emotion when it acknowledges some true harm that came to you and spurs you into action to care for yourself and it is an emotional sensation when it is based on deceptive brain messages that cause you to act in unhealthy ways.

HEALTHY ANGER VERSUS UNHEALTHY ANGER

Healthy anger—recognizes that you are being taken advantage of (or were hurt) in some way and encourages you to take care of yourself in a respectful, compassionate manner. It is a mobilizing force that helps you notice that you are not following the path of your true self for some reason and that you need to make a healthy change.

Unhealthy anger—is clouded by deceptive brain messages, especially thinking errors involving false expectations and "should" statements. It causes you to see people or events from a skewed perspective and then to act in a destructive way that hurts you (and potentially others) and takes you farther away from your true goals and values.

Sadness: Grief Versus Depression and Self-Hatred

Sadness, too, can be a helpful and cathartic true emotion or a damaging emotional sensation. The difference lies in whether you are truly experiencing some form of loss (i.e., grief) or whether you are beating up on yourself for who you are, what you have not accomplished, or what you believe about yourself because of deceptive brain messages (i.e., depression or self-hatred). For instance, Sarah's negative beliefs about herself and the recurring thought that she was a "loser" were emotional sensations that kept her away from seeing her true self and locked into a "depressive dialogue" that fueled self-hatred and physical inactivity (e.g., lying in bed, not going to the gym). These kinds of emotional sensations were persistent (i.e., they could last for weeks or months at a time and never be completely resolved) and focused on the negative aspects of herself.

Compare this scenario with Liz's true grief over the time she lost when she was under the spell of her deceptive brain messages or the sadness she felt when a good friend or relative died. In Liz's case, her sadness and grief came in waves and decreased over time. Equally important, these true emotions were based on specific losses that honored Liz's true self—the part of her that connects with people on a deep emotional level and that strives to give and receive Attention, Acceptance, Affection, Appreciation, and Allowing (the 5 A's). When she constructively dealt with her sadness, she was acknowledging how important the loss was and was living in accordance with her true goals and values.

In both of their cases, Sarah and Liz felt sad. The major difference is that Liz was *honoring a true loss and a true part of herself* whereas Sarah was beating up on herself because of deceptive brain messages. The distinction in their sadness, and in yours, lies in whether you are seeing and honoring reality as it truly is, from the perspective of the Wise Advocate, or whether you are seeing life through the lens of deceptive brain messages and acting in unhealthy ways.

GRIEF AND SADNESS VERSUS DEPRESSION AND SELF-HATRED

Grief and sadness—healthy, true emotions that allow you to experience and process loss and pain. The grief may be the loss of someone close to you or a change in your roles in life. Similarly, the sadness can be related to not having your true needs and emotions tended to as a child or acknowledging the time or opportunities you lost over the years when you were subservient to your deceptive brain messages. In all respects, grief and sadness are a normal part of our experience and are the result of honoring our true self— the part of us that wants to connect with people on a deep emotional level, give and receive the 5 A's, and live in accordance with our true goals and values. These emotions do not ridicule or judge you, but acknowledge the human condition and your incredible ability to connect and love. Processing these emotions in a healthy, respectful way—feeling the pain, but continuing to move forward—allows you to heal and grow stronger. These kinds of true emotions tend to come in waves, are time-limited, and are related to specific situations or losses.

Depression and self-hatred—result from deceptive brain messages and thinking errors that berate, belittle, disparage, or otherwise demean who you are, what you care about, or what you are trying to achieve. These negative thoughts are the direct opposite of how your Wise Advocate and anyone who loves you actually sees you. They damage you by keeping you from advocating for yourself or engaging in actions that are beneficial and healthy for you. These types of emotional sensations tend to be persistent and incorporate a negative view of you.

Anxiety: Productive or Destructive?

Another vital emotional experience to distinguish is anxiety, because it can be helpful in some cases. We know that many people think of anxiety as always being a destructive force, but this is a limited way of looking at anxiety. The truth is that anxiety can be a very important warning sign or motivator in many instances. Whether anxiety is helpful or harmful depends on the context and reason for its emergence. When anxiety and worry lead to no productive or helpful outcome, such as when Abby would worry excessively about her family members or Sarah would replay conversations and her actions over in her brain, it was destructive and needed to be dealt with via the Four Steps.

Conversely, when anxiety serves as a *signal* that alerts you of potential danger, it should be heeded and evaluated with the Wise Advocate. For example, if you are feeling anxious or stressed because someone asked you to do something that is not in accordance with your true self or that puts you in an awkward situation, such as turning a blind eye to inappropriate behavior or compromising your principles and values to help someone out, you need to take that anxiety seriously because it is telling you that you are about to act in a way that is not consistent with who you are or how you want to be in the world.

Similarly, when anxiety alerts you to the fact that you are ignoring, minimizing, or dismissing another important, true emotion, such as appropriate anger, sadness, or grief, you should view the anxiety as a guide and helper. In this case, it is informing you that a vital true emotion is lurking under the surface that needs to be constructively dealt with by allowing the true emotion to arise and sitting with the pain that accompanies it—without overidentifying with it or acting in a destructive way.

Finally, stress can also be your friend when you need short-term motivation to achieve a specific result or outcome. For instance, if you are working on an important deadline and are feeling anxious about getting the project done on time, the stress in that situation is healthy. The short burst of chemicals that course through your body in response to the stress heighten your thought processes and make you more alert—thus helping you complete the project on time. In this way, discrete periods of stress, what some authors call "optimal stress," can make you better able to do your job when time is of the essence.

The key is to determine whether the anxiety or stress is going to lead you to act in a constructive, positive way or if it is simply derailing you. When it is arising to warn you, motivate you, or make you aware of other important true emotions, it is healthy and must be paid attention to. Conversely, if it is going to lead nowhere and waste your time, use the Four Steps to effectively deal with it and move forward.

PRODUCTIVE ANXIETY VERSUS DESTRUCTIVE ANXIETY

Productive anxiety—a signal that something *is* wrong or possibly dangerous or threatening. It could be that you are close to missing an important deadline, you are truly about to make a mistake, or you are acting in a way (or submitting to treatment) that is not healthy or good for you. This kind of anxiety or stress is limited and spurs you into action by encouraging you to align your actions with your true self.

Destructive anxiety—leads to no positive or healthy outcomes. It is repetitive, relentless, and nonsensical when viewed by the Wise Advocate. This kind of anxiety and stress does not encourage you to take proactive healthy actions, but instead causes you to waste time, act in unhealthy ways, and miss out on positive, constructive activities and events. For instance, it can make you constantly worry about things over which you have no control, engage in repetitive behaviors (including alcohol and other addictions), avoid people/places/events, and so on.

Balance Is the Key

As the examples above demonstrate, emotional experiences are not cut-and-dried, and a one-size-fits-all approach to emotions does not work. This is precisely why the Wise Advocate is such a powerful ally. By using its perspective (or that of close, emotionally well-balanced, loving, and rational people in your life), you can quickly determine whether the emotional experience you are having is a true emotion that should be tended to and constructively dealt with or whether it is a damaging emotional sensation that should not be fueled further, but rather dealt with via the Four Steps. In all cases, healthy emotions spur you into appropriate, wholesome actions (including honoring loss through grieving and pain through sadness) that are aligned with your true self, whereas emotional sensations cause you to dwell in unhelpful states that result in unhealthy behaviors.

"Should" Statements—When Are They Useful?

Should. It's a word we use all day long, yet we probably do not think about how influential or upsetting it can be. In some instances, *should* inspires us and launches us into positive action, potentially reaching heights we never thought were possible, such as Connie going further in her physical therapy than anyone believed she could. In other cases, *should* shames us, makes us beat up on ourselves, incites anger, evokes strong emotional sensations, and causes us to become stuck, such as when Connie became angry if she could not achieve a physical therapy task and momentarily gave up. One little word with so much potential power.

Similar to emotional experiences, *should* is helpful when it spurs you to proactively take care of yourself and it is harmful when it slows you down, berates you, causes you to inappropriately judge others, or makes you question who you are or what you have accomplished. As you've seen in the cases of Abby, Ed, Sarah, and Steve, indiscriminately believing in *should* can lead to destructive thinking errors, clouded perceptions, unhelpful emotional sensations, and unhealthy responses. For Abby, inappropriate "should" statements resulted in chronic worry, while for Sarah it meant constantly questioning her actions and worth. Ed's belief that he should be able to perform perfectly kept him out of auditions and Steve's "should" statements caused him to get angry at coworkers and his family for no good reason.

As is the case with our patients, you need to learn how to use *should* to your advantage because when it's applied in a healthy, productive way, *should* can be a wonderful ally. The key is to refuse to wholeheartedly believe the "should" statement as it is without digging a little deeper. Rather, look at the *intention* behind the "should" statement and evaluate whether the implied assertions are true or helpful before acting. For example, if someone says to himself, "I should lose ten pounds," the statement in and of itself is neutral and likely is simply a statement of fact. However, if you examine the intention behind that "should" statement, one of two possibilities tends to emerge. He will either follow the "should" statement about losing weight with the negative thought "because I am a loser like this" or "because no one likes me as I am," or with a self-affirming belief, such as "because I will feel better" or "because I will lower my cholesterol or blood sugar." In the first instance, the intention behind the "should" statement is to shame him into submission (which won't help at all and may in fact make things worse) and is based on deceptive brain messages, whereas the meaning of the "should" statement in the second case is to help him achieve a positive result—something that he wants and that is in accordance with his true self.

Helpful "should" statements—inspire and motivate you to act on your behalf in positive, constructive, and beneficial ways. When appropriately applied, "should" statements encourage you without shaming or berating you because the intention is true and pure. In those cases, the "should" statement acknowledges what you need to do and what is in your best interest. For example, positive "should" statements can prompt you to use the Four Steps, begin an exercise program, change your diet, stop drinking alcohol as a stress reliever, and so on.

Unhealthy "should" statements—shame, cripple, derail, or otherwise demoralize you (when directed toward you) or incite anger (when applied toward others) that leads to no productive outcomes. These statements are contaminated by impure intentions not related to your true self—such as getting you to do something for someone else or getting someone to do something for you. "Should" statements directed toward you make you feel bad about who you are or what you have accomplished (or not) and can readily lead to depression, anxiety, or other uncomfortable emotional sensations, whereas "should" statements directed toward others cause you to become irritable, angry, frustrated, dismissive, or intolerant of others. In all of those cases, your reaction is fueled by deceptive brain messages and thinking errors, not true intentions to help yourself or others.

Although "should" statements are analogous in many ways to how to approach true emotions and emotional sensations, there is one big distinction between them: You have far more control over when you use or invoke a "should" statement. Unlike emotional experiences that arise whenever certain situations or events transpire, you can proactively use "should" statements to spur you into positive action. In this way, you can turn a potentially paralyzing, damaging "should" statement into a helping, supportive coach, with the Wise Advocate, such as when Ed started using Refocus with Progressive Mindfulness to confront his fear of performing. When Ed encouraged himself to follow his Refocus with Progressive Mindfulness plan and reminded himself that he *should* do it because it would help him, he was using healthy "should" statements.

How can you use *should* to your benefit? By making sure you *only* use "should" statements to inspire and motivate yourself, not berate, belittle, or shame yourself or guilt someone else into doing something for you.

In the next chapter, we will review ways to continue moving forward with the Four Steps. In particular, we will show you some ways to adapt Refocus with Progressive Mindfulness and learn how to use the Four Steps in a variety of situations.

CHAPTER 14

Using the Four Steps to Help You Move Forward in Your Life

Now that you can reliably identify your deceptive brain messages and uncomfortable sensations with Step 1: Relabel, can change your perception of their importance and accuracy with Step 2: Reframe, can sharply focus your attention while the uncomfortable sensations are present with Step 3: Refocus, and are beginning to change your perspective with Step 4: Revalue, you are ready to use the more advanced Four Steps techniques. As we mentioned in chapter 11, we did not want to teach you too many advanced methods for dealing with deceptive brain messages until you had practiced with regular Refocus and Regulate & Refocus for a while. Our primary goal in delaying this information is that we wanted you to *experience firsthand* what it is like to deal with these bothersome, upsetting physical and emotional sensations in a new way—by becoming comfortable with allowing the sensations to be present while directing your attention elsewhere (i.e., Step 3: Refocus). The second reason for waiting until now is that you needed to have a solid understanding of true emotions versus emotional sensations so that you could design appropriate

Refocus with Progressive Mindfulness activities that will help move your life forward in positive ways.

What follows is a description of several creative ways you can use Refocus with Progressive Mindfulness and the Four Steps to your advantage. We have divided them according to general deceptive brain messages or themes, including:

- Standing Up for Your True Self in Relationships—Saying What You Really Think and Feel and Acting in Accordance with Your True Interests
- Resisting Momentary Rewards—Withstanding Cravings and Desires
- Perfectionism and the Fear of Rejection—Learning How to Make Small Mistakes
- Dealing with Apathy, Depression, Boredom, and Fatigue
- Achieving Optimal Performance
- Changing Unhealthy Habits

Standing Up for Your True Self—Saying What You Really Think and Feel and Acting in Accordance with Your True Interests

As you have seen, when your brain *ignores*, *minimizes*, or *dismisses* your true self, you end up neglecting your needs, goals, and values. In some cases, you may not even notice what is happening, but the cumulative effect of living your life this way can be substantial. When it becomes more of a repetitive approach toward yourself, you end up putting others first at your expense, just like John used to do. In his case, his repetitive fear that Alicia would leave him resulted in his not caring for himself well and putting virtually all of his attention on Alicia and her well-being. Although it's understandable why he had these fears and insecurities (e.g., his interactions with Coach), John's near-constant focus on Alicia clearly was not healthy for him and was not a balanced way to go through life. As he was able to bear witness to his own destructive behaviors and brain messages, he realized that he needed to make changes in his life, but he was not sure how to do it. The answer was to use Refocus with Progressive Mindfulness. Here's an example of how Refocus with Progressive Mindfulness could have helped him.

To begin the process, John needed to develop a Refocus with Progressive Mindfulness plan similar to Ed's in chapter 11. His first goal was to think about what self-care situations would distress him or keep him from doing things that were beneficial to him. After he completed such a list, he rated the situations based on how much it would upset him to engage in those activities. Here's an example:

JOHN'S LEVEL OF DISTRESS RELATED TO ATTENDING TO HIS NEEDS AND INTERESTS

Activity	Distress Level
Doing something Alicia likely will disapprove of or not like	100
Doing something for myself when Alicia says she wants to spend time with me or needs me	100
Checking e-mail/text every hour instead of every five minutes	95
Saying what I need	85
Checking e-mail/text every thirty minutes instead of every five minutes	80
Saying what I want to do	75
Waiting fifteen minutes to respond to Alicia when she calls/e-mails/texts	70

Activity	Distress Level
Making a decision	50 (inconsequential/no impact on Alicia) 75 (somewhat important/might impact Alicia) 90 (very important/very likely to impact Alicia)
Checking e-mail/text every ten minutes instead of every five minutes	55
Doing something for myself when Alicia is free but has other things to do	50
Doing something for myself when Alicia is busy	30

Once John completed the table above, he needed to think of enjoyable things he would like to do whenever the urge to care for Alicia or neglect himself might strike. Some of the things on his list included playing basketball with his friends, going to the gym more often, reading a book, watching "guy stuff Alicia doesn't like" (such as action movies and sports) on TV, and so on. With this in mind, he then could make a list of activities that he could use as Refocus with Progressive Mindfulness exercises. Here's what his list could have looked like:

JOHN'S REFOCUS WITH PROGRESSIVE MINDFULNESS LIST

1. At least once a week, do something for myself (e.g., exercise, meet up with friends) when Alicia is free but has other things she could be doing. With time, increase the length of time I spend in activities for myself or the frequency (up to something reasonable for both of us).

2. Check e-mail every ten minutes, then increase to fifteen minutes, thirty minutes, and so on until I am only checking personal e-mail twice a day. Let people know that if they have an urgent issue, they should call me. Put my cell in the "phone only" mode so that I do not hear when texts come in.

3. Unless it's an emergency, do not immediately respond to any texts or e-mails I receive. Rather, wait at least fifteen minutes and slowly increase the delay in response time for personal contacts during my workday. On the weekends, only respond a couple of times a day unless it's important or urgent. (Note: As you check personal e-mail less often, this will become less of an issue because the Habit Center's drive to immediately respond will not be as pressing.)

4. Make inconsequential decisions at least once a day. With time, increase the number of decisions and importance of those decisions. When I make decisions about where to go, what to eat, which movie to see, base them on *my* interests, not on trying to please someone else or guess what they want to do. Work toward making bigger decisions or stating my opinions over time.

5. Whenever possible, make plans with others based on what is convenient and works well for my schedule. Do not check in with Alicia about every little plan—she will tell me when important things need to be marked on my calendar. Do not wait to see what she's doing first—just make plans and live your life.

Since John's biggest problem was rarely putting himself first, his priority needed to be on pushing himself out of his comfort zone with Refocus with Progressive Mindfulness and doing things that would seem more self-directed than he was used to. Unsurprisingly, his deceptive brain messages tried to resist this plan at first, asserting that taking care of himself was "selfish." When we asked him to invoke his Wise Advocate with such thoughts, he reminded himself that his grandfather had outside interests and was well adjusted and balanced because of it. His grandfather never ignored his wife and he coordinated plans with her, but he did not live his life *solely for her benefit* the way John was doing with Alicia. John's problem was not being thoughtless toward others, it was being that way toward himself. Therefore, Refocus with Progressive Mindfulness in his case meant letting go of the strong pull and desire to care for Alicia at his expense. Of course, if his problem were the opposite—that he did not spend enough time with Alicia or did not attend to any of her needs—his Refocus with Progressive Mindfulness plan would look very different from this and involve his spending more time with her, not less. However, since this was not the case for John, his goal was to learn how to be more independent in making decisions and living his life while still being connected to Alicia.

Resisting Momentary Rewards— Withstanding Cravings and Desires

One of the most difficult patterns of behavior to change are those actions that involve the Reward Center, such as eating excessively or unhealthily, drinking too much alcohol, engaging in risky or dangerous sex, gambling, gaming, smoking, over-shopping, or other momentarily pleasurable activities that end up harming you in the long term. How can you learn to decrease the cravings over time and how do you deal with the strong impulses associated with the behavior, especially when you are feeling stressed out, uncomfortable, or upset?

The answer, in most cases, is to use Refocus with Progressive Mindfulness to learn how to withstand the cravings—to see them for what they are—and to not act on the impulses whenever they arise. By using Relabel and Reframe, you can more easily identify the cravings for what they are—a desire to feel better right now. Then you can begin to see that strong impulses coming from your brain do not have to be acted upon. That's when you can make a free choice regarding what you actually want to do (rather than mindlessly following the impulse).

How does Refocus with Progressive Mindfulness fit into this? Refocus with Progressive Mindfulness, when applied to cravings, helps you safely evoke the emotional sensations (e.g., cravings, desires, impulses) while simultaneously encouraging you to not act in ways that will harm you in the long run. Refocus with Progressive Mindfulness also does something else: It acknowledges the strong biological forces involved in generating cravings and helps you teach your body and brain to work for you, rather than against you. It does this by helping you to decrease your unhealthy or unhelpful behavior *slowly* over time, rather than all at once (i.e., "cold turkey"), so that the brain pathways associated with those cravings and actions wither. It's the exact same process we've talked about before with Hebb's law, Quantum Zeno Effect, and Self-Directed Neuroplasticity: The less attention you pay to something (either with your thoughts or through your actions), the weaker the brain circuits associated with that sensation or action become.

Consider the case of Nicole, a mid-thirties woman who smoked tobacco daily and responded to stress by overeating. She had tried to change both of these behaviors many times throughout her life, but always to no avail. Why wasn't she having success? In the past, whenever January 1 would roll around, she would resolve to quit her unhealthy habits all at once. On the same predetermined day, she would stop smoking and go on a diet. At first, this approach seemed to work. She would go many days without overeating and would not smoke. Unfortunately, these positive results never lasted. After about a week or two, her cravings would ramp up to the point that they were no longer tolerable, and Nicole would give in because of how overwhelmed and pained she felt. This left her feeling defeated and sure that no program or approach would ever work in the long run—at least not for her.

What else could Nicole have done? She could have started by tackling *one* of her behaviors, rather than both of them at the same time, and she could have decreased her intake slowly, rather than cutting herself off all at once. By doing this, her cravings would decrease slowly as she paid less attention to those impulses and desires—and, in the process, her brain chemistry and the pathways supporting those cravings would decrease as well.

What was Nicole's first step? She looked at her current behaviors and decided which one was more important to change first. In her case, smoking was having more of a negative impact on her life and was the higher priority. To quit smoking in a way that would ensure her cravings would not skyrocket out of control, Nicole needed to slowly decrease the number of cigarettes she smoked each day. When she started out, she was smoking about a pack a day (twenty cigarettes). Although her impulse was to just quit, without a taper plan, Nicole agreed to try to cut down by five cigarettes per week. She could do this in a number of ways, but realized that Thursday and Fridays tend to be her most stressful days. Given that she knew her cravings increase dramatically when she's stressed, she chose to cut out one cigarette a day Saturday through Wednesday, and then remain at the same number of cigarettes on Thursday and Friday. She did this for the first three weeks, and then more slowly decreased the remaining cigarettes in the last two weeks. Her taper plan looked something like this:

Week 1	Week 2	Week 3	Week 4	Week 5
Saturday: 19	Saturday: 14	Saturday: 9	Saturday: 4	Saturday: 1
Sunday: 18	Sunday: 13	Sunday: 8	Sunday: 4	Sunday: 1
Monday: 17	Monday: 12	Monday: 7	Monday: 3	Monday: 1
Tuesday: 16	Tuesday: 11	Tuesday: 6	Tuesday: 3	Tuesday: 0
Wednesday: 15	Wednesday: 10	Wednesday: 5	Wednesday: 2	
Thursday: 15	Thursday: 10	Thursday: 5	Thursday: 2	
Friday: 15	Friday: 10	Friday: 5	Friday: 2	

Regardless of how she chose to slowly taper off of cigarettes, we told her, *she needed to stick with her plan until she achieved her goal—that, in essence, was the Refocus with Progressive Mindfulness: to continue on with her planned changes no matter how strong the cravings became and to Refocus her attention whenever the impulses or urges to smoke struck.* (Or, if she did give in, analogous to the fifteen-minute rule, try to only smoke part of a cigarette, not the whole thing.) If she continued to do this, she would see noticeable changes in her cravings over time.

The key to staying on course with these kinds of changes is to chart (and celebrate) your successes and to notice that the cravings *do* decrease with time when they are resisted and not focused on.

Note: This approach works well for almost all behaviors, except for highly dangerous activities. As we've told you before, you should never use Refocus with Progressive Mindfulness to put yourself into a situation that will evoke strong urges to do something highly destructive, such as going to a bar when you are an alcoholic or attending a party where others are using drugs. Clearly abstinence, going to Twelve-Step meetings, and using regular Refocus or Regulate & Refocus in most of those situations is the best course of action.

Spurred by her successes with quitting smoking, Nicole then decided to move on to her eating habits, especially her tendency to overeat when she was stressed. To change how she ate in general, and especially in response to stress, she needed to engage in a process very similar to that used by Ed or John, with one twist. Rather than looking at how much she avoided a situation and how much distress it caused her, Nicole needed to assess how intensely she craved certain foods (especially when she was stressed) and how much they satisfied her. Figure 14.1 shows what the scale in the case of cravings and desire looks like:

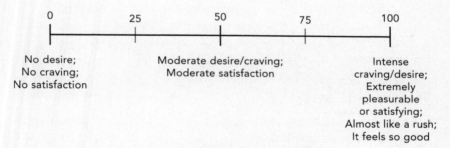

Figure 14.1. Craving and Desire Scale

To begin developing her Refocus with Progressive Mindfulness plan, Nicole first needed to figure out the following:

- Which foods did she crave and in what amounts? What about when she was stressed?
- Which foods were better for her that she did like?
- What foods were better for her that she didn't like as much but possibly would eat?

- Did she have any specific goals in mind (e.g., eating more fruits or vegetables? Cutting down her saturated fat intake?)

As she was pondering her goals, she kept a log of what and how much she ate during the course of one week—without altering her eating patterns during that week—so that she had a good sense of how she currently was eating. She also charted her stress levels on a 1 to 10 scale (1=no stress, 5=moderate stress and 10=intense and overwhelming stress) throughout the day and noted when her cravings increased, so that she could see how strongly stress influenced her eating patterns. When she completed this task, she reviewed her log and goals, then devised the following list of foods (with portion sizes) and rated them based on how much she craved them or they satisfied her:

NICOLE'S LEVEL OF CRAVINGS AND SATISFACTION FROM CERTAIN FOODS/PORTIONS

Food Item	Craving Intensity/ Satisfaction Level When Eaten
A pint of ice cream	100
3 portions of pasta and meatballs	90
4 slices of a large pizza	90
Double hamburger and large fries	90
Steak with mashed potatoes	85
2 portions of pasta and meatballs	75
½ pint of ice cream	65
2 slices of large pizza	60
Favorite healthy, well-prepared salmon dish (one portion)	50

Lean chicken, veggies, and rice	35
Salad with blue cheese or bacon	30
One slice of large pizza	30
¼ pint of ice cream	25
1 portion of pasta	25
Salad without blue cheese or bacon or excessive dressing	15

From her knowledge of the Reward Center, Nicole knew that the more she ate a particularly satisfying food, the more her brain and body would crave it—and the more of that food she would eat. This meant that she had to change her eating habits slowly and remain aware of her cravings with the Four Steps, especially in times of stress. Otherwise, the desires and cravings would overpower her and cause her to give in (i.e., overeat or eat unhealthy things she craved)—thereby sending her craving and her brain in exactly the wrong direction, back toward square one. The key was to gradually alter her eating habits according to her goals and to stick with her plan. As she did this, she would rewire her brain such that her Habit Center's drive to overeat and her Reward Center's cravings for highly desirable foods would decrease over time.

To begin actually making changes, Nicole needed to define her goals and come up with a reasonable plan she thought she could follow. This is an example of the things she aspired to change:

- Become aware of her cravings and tendency to overeat when stressed
- Eat more healthy foods each day
- Consume less fat and fewer calories each day (Note: She had been eating almost 3,500 calories a day when she was stressed—approximately 1,500 more than her body actually needed!)

With these goals in mind, we devised different commonsense ways Nicole could make changes to her diet based on the medical principle "Start low, go slow." In the case of changing her diet, this meant making small changes at first, rather than cutting something out entirely (i.e., starting with *low* expectations), and making those changes slowly over time, not all at once. For example, with foods that are highly pleasurable, cutting down the portion sizes first, then decreasing the frequency to ensure her cravings did not skyrocket out of control would best serve Nicole and her brain. In contrast, to incorporate more healthy foods, she needed to slowly substitute in the less desirable, but good-for-her foods (like salmon and chicken) for the higher fat, higher calorie favorites she normally would consume (like pizza or hamburgers).

Clearly, she could use the same approach she used with smoking—to slowly cut down the amount she ate by approximately one-quarter per week. She could also use one of the approaches in the table below.

WAYS NICOLE CAN USE REFOCUS WITH PROGRESSIVE MINDFULNESS

Decrease the Frequency	Substitute Healthier Choices
Example: She eats pizza, hamburgers, or steak almost every night, which is increasing her cholesterol.	Example: Less pizza and red meat and more salmon, chicken, and veggies.
Strategy: Slowly decrease the frequency over several weeks, not all at once.	Strategy: Choose a healthier option that still is somewhat appealing to you even if it does not satisfy the craving as fully.
Change eating hamburger and fries/ steak to no more than three times a week for two weeks, then . . .	Start by identifying foods you want to avoid, like fried chicken.

Decrease frequency to twice a week for two weeks, then . . .	When the craving for fried chicken hits, eat a lean, low-fat version of chicken instead.
Decrease to once a week for two weeks, then . . .	When you have a craving for a big steak, choose the salmon that satisfies 50 percent of your craving instead.
Decrease to once every two weeks, then monthly and so on.	When you can't get the thought of pizza out of your head, eat one portion of pasta with meatballs or one slice of pizza instead.

Nicole was successful because she *gradually* made these changes—not in days, but over weeks, and sat with the cravings and desires that arose. Why was this important? It takes time for the Habit Center to rewire and for the brain to "turn off" the strong cravings and impulses for highly desirable foods (or any substance or behavior that releases dopamine or other pleasure-inducing chemicals in the brain) emanating from the Reward Center. Along the path to change, the cravings can be quite intense, which is why slowly decreasing highly desirable foods and incrementally introducing healthier options with Refocus with Progressive Mindfulness is best. As Nicole found out, there were many days when, she says, "the cravings were really strong and I wanted to give in, eat that very thing I was trying to cut down, but I just didn't because I knew what would happen. Instead, I had to sit there with that interminable pain and desire and wait for it to pass. As long as I used the fifteen-minute rule and Refocused on activities I enjoyed and that kept my mind active, like yoga, talking to friends, and the like, I was okay. I just had to keep reminding myself that even though it was painful, I was doing something that would rewire my brain in helpful ways." It does not happen overnight, but with time, as we described previously, the desires and cravings have less hold over you.

In fact, by regularly charting her progress with the desire and satisfaction scale (i.e., seeing how much her cravings ratings changed over time), she could see that her desire for healthy foods increased while her cravings for unhealthy ones decreased over time as her brain rewired. Most encouragingly, she noticed small decreases in her cravings within a few days and clearly noticeable ones within the matter of a few weeks.

The bottom line is this: *Gradually cutting down the activity and sitting with the discomfort that arises—without over-identifying with or excessively focusing your attention on it—is your best option.* As with all uncomfortable physical and emotional sensations, you need to Relabel that craving, Reframe it, and then Refocus on something that is healthy for you without pushing the discomfort and pain away or overly attending to it. Then, whenever possible, Revalue the pain and unsettlingly sensations as related to craving so that you can skillfully deal with it. Determine whether the sensations are related to your true self (i.e., you are grieving the loss of something that is important to you) or are generated by strong biological forces related to deceptive brain messages. Although it is difficult, using Refocus with Progressive Mindfulness in these ways will help you learn to withstand strong cravings/desires/longings, deal with your true emotions, and get to the other side with healthy, wholesome and constructive behaviors.

IN MOST CASES, MODERATION IS KEY

In contrast to smoking or other clearly harmful activities, eating is something we have to do every day. It can also bring us great pleasure that can get us into trouble, including increasing our weight, increasing cholesterol, or causing diabetes. The same goes for alcoholic beverages, playing video games, or any other pleasurable activity that can, if overindulged, lead to you slavishly following cravings and impulses to your detriment.

The truth is that very few foods or drinks are "bad" in and of themselves when taken in moderation and savored as a special treat. There is nothing wrong, for example, with eating pizza once in a while, sharing a bottle of wine with friends, or playing video games a couple times a week. Medical science regularly shows us that foods and even alcohol in moderation can have positive effects for the body. The key, though, is moderation.

As you've seen with Nicole and Steve, when the special treat leads to overwhelming cravings, problems generally ensue. The more they focused on those activities and associated them with significant stress relief (rather than walking, going to yoga, talking to friends), the more automatic and mindless their behaviors became.

When dealing with strong cravings, the goal is to learn how to resist the cravings and see them for what they really are: erroneous biological messages with no real meaning that do not need to be followed. Remember, the cravings become stronger when you continually indulge them. Each time you do this, you are increasing the chances that you will set up strong, enduring brain pathways that cause you to act in automatic, habitual ways that are not always beneficial to you.

This is why we often say with respect to deceptive brain messages: Don't believe everything you think or *feel*. Your body and brain can trick you into thinking that you will feel better if you just act on the craving. While this is true—you will experience a momentary relief or pleasure—giving in can cost you dearly in the long run, as you've seen with Steve.

So, how do you still enjoy some of life's finer pleasures but not set yourself up for unending cravings? Moderation. When you eat pleasurable foods occasionally (as opposed to daily or every time you are stressed), your brain will not ramp up its cravings for those foods and you will be able to resist giving into them automatically. You will have a *choice* in what you do because the craving will not overpower you. You will not be desperately seeking relief or pleasure, but will be enjoying the food because you want to.

The key is to ask yourself: What am I about to do and why? Is it because

I feel overwhelmed, sad, stressed, angry, or down? If the answer to that second question is yes and the reason you want is to eat or drink is to decrease your uncomfortable physical and emotional sensations, then you should use the Four Steps and Refocus with Progressive Mindfulness to help you withstand the craving. In contrast, if the answer to that second question is no and you want to eat or drink for social reasons, for enjoyment, or to celebrate, then use moderation and mindfully enjoy the experience.

RELATIONSHIPS—DON'T DIVE IN OR NEGLECT YOUR TRUE SELF BECAUSE OF CRAVINGS AND LONGINGS

Just as people can be "addicted" to food, drugs, alcohol, video games, sex, or gambling, they can very rapidly become addicted to relationships, too. Whenever you enter into a relationship—romantic or otherwise—solely out of desire (either for something the person possesses, for how you feel when you are with that person, or to avoid the pain of loneliness) and do not see the person for who he or she really is, you are putting your true self at a serious disadvantage because you likely will end up neglecting your needs, thoughts, or values in some way. Like John, you may end up not telling the person how you really feel or push aside your own interests, or you may act like Sarah and continually replay interactions in your head so that you can figure out how to "fix" yourself, thereby ensuring that people like you.

To avoid this brain-based trap, use Refocus with Progressive Mindfulness in the ways John did and acknowledge that, like Nicole, feeling pain related to strong cravings is part of the human condition, but not something to run from or cover up with unhealthy habits. Instead, rely on your Wise Advocate to help you figure out how to constructively deal with people so that your needs are balanced with theirs in a healthy way.

Perfectionism and the Fear of Rejection—Learning How to Make Small Mistakes

Clearly social bonds and acceptance are important to all of us, but there are times when the brain takes over and distorts situations in ways that cause a person to become overrun with fear and insecurity. Sarah and Ed are two clear examples of perfectionism leading to narrowed and chronically stressful lives. In both of their cases, fear of rejection or negative evaluation kept them from living full, active lives. To counteract the deceptive brain messages in their heads and learn how to deal with the ensuing anxiety, they used Refocus with Progressive Mindfulness to help them see that making small, relatively inconsequential mistakes (Sarah) or putting themselves out there (Ed) would expand their worlds, not limit or diminish them. For Ed, this meant that he had to practice asking women out and being more social, even when he was scared to do so. For Sarah it meant that she had to practice deliberately making small mistakes or not rechecking things multiple times and then sitting with the anxiety that arises.

Below is an example of how Sarah used Refocus with Progressive Mindfulness for her perfectionism.

POTENTIAL REFOCUS WITH PROGRESSIVE MINDFULNESS LIST FOR SARAH

Write an e-mail to someone and deliberately spell a few words incorrectly. Do not send the e-mail, but do not fix any of the words or problems in the document, either.
Go to the grocery store and separate your items into three separate checks. Ask the checker to ring up each group separately in the same visit. This may cause the people behind you in line to become impatient—sit with the anxiety this causes but continue to have the clerk check you out in three separate bills.
Write an e-mail to someone you trust (e.g., friend or family member) and do not check to see if you made any errors when you wrote it. Just write it and send it off. Do not look at or check the e-mail after you send it.

Write an e-mail to someone you trust and deliberately make some mistakes in the e-mail. Send it off without correcting it and sit with the anxiety that ensues.
Talk with a friend whom you trust and possibly who knows what you are doing. Deliberately pause several times in the conversation for no reason, or look away from the person many times, as if you are not paying attention.
Complete a project at work and check it only once (rather than five times), then hand it in.

While Sarah's list focused on making mistakes that would induce her anxiety, Ed's list focused on ways he could meet people and be more social while experiencing fear and insecurity. One important aspect of his Refocus with Progressive Mindfulness list is that it is based around *achievable behavioral goals*, rather than specific results that depend on another person's response. When dealing with potential rejection in social situations, achievable behavioral goals allow you to see your progress even if the person is not interested in talking with or dating you. In Ed's case, this meant talking to someone or asking for (but not necessarily receiving) her phone number. In this way, the "outcome" is the achievable behavior (something that is based on Ed's actions), not a specific result that is contingent upon another. Therefore, Ed's Refocus with Progressive Mindfulness list would include many achievable behavioral goals—things that would get him out of the house and meeting people—rather than focusing on how someone may or may not respond to him. (Note: This Refocus with Progressive Mindfulness plan could be merged with the other Refocus with Progressive Mindfulness plan Ed devised in chapter 11 related to avoiding auditions, or they could be done separately.)

POTENTIAL REFOCUS WITH PROGRESSIVE MINDFULNESS LIST FOR ED

Answer an online dating ad (but do not expect a response).
Go to a coffee shop, bar, or other social location and talk with someone.
Take a class where you likely would make mistakes or could be evaluated by others (e.g., foreign language, dancing, group exercise). The achievable behavioral goal is going to the class and participating in it, not anyone's responses.
Go to a social location and ask a woman for her phone number or e-mail address. Do not focus on whether she gives it to you or not—simply ask and you have achieved your goal.
Participate in a speed-dating event. Make your goal learning one fact about each of the women you meet. Again, do not focus on whether you get any phone numbers or dates from the evening, just that you learned one thing about them.

Dealing with Apathy, Depression, Boredom, and Fatigue

As with cravings, you need to begin seeing the low energy, tiredness, diminished interests, and lack of motivation powered by deceptive brain messages as a physical sensation and not a reflection of your true self. Although it may be true that you are tired and do not feel like doing something, you need to acknowledge that these physical sensations are holding you back in some way. They may keep you from completing important (but possibly boring or tedious) tasks, dissuade you from exercising, convince you that staying home is better than hanging out with friends, and so on. In all cases, these kinds of physical and emotional sensations are driven by deceptive brain messages that prevent you from achieving what you want or need to do. In Sarah's case, the "de-energizing" feelings related to her depression caused her to stop exercising, isolate from friends and family, and slow her down at work.

The solution to dealing with the kind of physical inertia Sarah described is to literally move your feet—to get going and get out there. When you are dealing with depression, the best plan is to simply choose something you normally enjoy and go do it. Even if you do not get the same level of pleasure out of the activity as you usually would or do not feel like going, engaging in any kind of physical activity you typically enjoy will help get you out of the rut you are in and back into your normal, healthy routines.

Similarly, Michael, a forty-four-year-old musician and songwriter, found that even when he was interested in his current music project there often were times when his attention would veer off or something would happen in his life that would "deflate" him. In those moments, he would not *feel* like playing or writing, even though he needed to get the job done on time. To combat his brain-based messages urging him to go take a nap or watch another episode of *CSI*, he would Relabel the sensations as fatigue; Reframe them as related to boredom, something else bringing him down emotionally, or a false brain message; and then Refocus by going back to the music he needed to finish. He found that within a few minutes of Refocusing he was back in the groove and those false feelings of fatigue would dissipate on their own.

From Sarah's and Michael's stories, one thing is clear: It does not matter whether the drive to isolate, sit on the couch, or not act is related to depression, boredom, apathy, or wanting to avoid dealing with something. The end result is the same—you withdraw from the world and neglect an important part of yourself. So, whenever lethargy, apathy, boredom, or fatigue strikes, use the Four Steps to constructively deal with it and get moving in some way.

Achieving Optimal Performance

Similar to using constructive "should" statements to motivate you, the Four Steps can assist you in getting work done on time and keep you from excessively worrying about things that are beyond your control. For example, Christine is a twenty-eight-year-old office manager who effectively deals with many crises each day. Sometimes, late at night or early in the morning before going to work, she will worry about what the day will bring and whether she will be able to get it all done on time. The more she goes over potential scenarios in her head, thinking about all the ways something *could* go wrong, the more false expectations she generates and the more anxious she gets. Heading out the door with those negative expectations firmly set in her brain, Christine dreads work and assumes that the day will end up exhausting and overwhelming her.

Rather than engaging in these self-fulfilling prophecies, Christine uses the Four Steps to see the deceptive thoughts and Refocus in ways that make her more productive. For instance, when she is up against a deadline, Christine can view the tension in her body and her quickening heart rate as a friend that is helping her stay more alert, improve her problem-solving skills, allow her to think more clearly, and work more efficiently, not a sign that something is terribly wrong or that the worst-case scenario she dreamed up over her morning coffee is now coming true. By combining this healthy, temporary stress with helpful "should" statements, she will drive herself forward and use her body and brain to support her goals and actions. Then, when things calm down, Christine can balance her work schedule by engaging in a slower, more relaxed pace during the rest of the day (or the next day, depending on her work demands) by taking the entire hour for lunch, focusing on her breath for five minutes around three p.m., getting outside for a ten-minute walk to clear her head, and so on.

SET A TIMER TO REMIND YOURSELF TO MAINTAIN A BALANCED LIFE

Diana Winston, director of the UCLA Mindful Awareness Research Center (MARC) and coauthor of *Fully Present*, recommends setting a timer on your computer or phone to go off every hour during your workday. When the timer goes off, she says, take a few moments (e.g., a minute or two) to remind yourself to focus on your breathing and to gain perspective. These short respites each hour will allow you to tune in to your experiences and ensure that you do not get caught up in endless thought streams that lead to anxiety, excessive (nonoptimal) stress, or other uncomfortable physical and emotional sensations.

Try it and see what happens.

Again, the key is *balance*, not perfection. Working at a breakneck pace all the time or acting in a lackadaisical way most of the time (i.e., not putting in the effort when it's needed) won't work well and will keep Christine away from achieving her true goals in life. Rather, allowing herself to push forward when it's really needed—to take advantage of her body's response to the stress in a healthy way—and to slow her pace when things are calm provides Christine with an optimal performance strategy that benefits her body, brain, and mind.

Changing Unhealthy Habits

As you saw with Nicole's and Michael's examples, you can use Refocus with Progressive Mindfulness to change virtually any unhealthy habit you have. The key is to clearly define reasonable goals you believe you can achieve and to stick with it even when you experience strong cravings (like Nicole) or when you just don't feel like doing something (like Michael).

For example, if you want to start exercising on a regular basis, but are tired at the end of the day, find a truly motivating reason within yourself, such as wanting to sleep better or wanting to be in better shape. As long as the reason is a positive one, based on your true self, not a negative, shame-based reason related to deceptive brain messages, that motivation will help sustain you even on the days you do not feel like going for a run or to the gym. Similarly, if you decide you want to follow a specific diet or exercise routine, you can use that to plan your goals while using the Four Steps to ensure that you remain on your path.

RELAXATION IS GOOD, TOO

We've spent a lot of time telling you to continually apply the Four Steps to deal with deceptive brain messages, uncomfortable sensations, and un-healthy, maladaptive habits. While that is absolutely sound advice, we want to make sure you do not take away from this message that relaxation is bad or that using the Four Steps means you can never take a break.

Nothing could be further from the truth. In fact, if you really listen to your true self, we bet there is a part of you that sees the value in relaxing and knows how important it is. Relaxation helps us recharge and unwind, which is critical to maintaining balance and restoring our energy levels.

So make sure you spend some time each day relaxing and doing healthy, wholesome things that bring you pleasure, satisfaction, and fulfillment.

The Role of Medications

Our discussion of moving forward in your life would not be complete if we did not address the potential role of medications in assisting you on your path. In general, we take a minimalist approach to psychiatric medications and only advocate using them when you cannot recognize that the deceptive brain messages *might* be false or if the struggle to resist acting on deceptive brain messages is causing you significant, marked distress. In other words, medications are necessary when the intensity of the discomfort caused by the deceptive brain message is difficult for you to tolerate or inhibits you from using the Four Steps.

What we do not want you to do is use medications as your only treatment. When medications are used as *the answer*, not as a bridge to self-improvement with therapy (either with a counselor or self-directed with the Four Steps), people often become complacent. This can happen because they feel better with the medication or because they buy into the deceptive brain message telling them that they are now dependent on medications for the rest of their lives.

We can tell you from our countless hours of clinical experience that using medications in this way is a mistake, unless of course you are dealing with a condition that is potentially dangerous when unmedicated, such as bipolar disorder, schizophrenia, chronic suicidal thoughts, serious problems with mood or thought patterns that significantly impair your day-to-day functioning. Therefore, we would prefer you to try the Four Steps without medications unless:

- You are having significant difficulties conceding that the deceptive brain messages *might* be false (i.e., lack of or impaired insight) or
- You are having significant problems functioning without medications.

In those cases where medications are warranted and necessary, use the lowest possible dose to increase your ability to see that the deceptive brain messages possibly are false or to enhance your functioning. As you improve, try to lower the doses with your doctor's permission while continuing to use the Four Steps.[1] Do NOT stop any medications without first talking with your doctor. You will generally find that over weeks and months of using the Four Steps, you may well be able to decrease your dose or be better able to tolerate the upsetting feelings that deceptive brain messages can cause.

Remember: For mild to moderate symptoms, medications should be used as a *bridge* to help you put forth the effort needed to improve your life with the Four Steps or any other kind of therapy. *Medications are helpful, but are not the answer in and of themselves* (again, unless you have a serious and potentially life-threatening psychiatric condition when not properly managed). As we mentioned earlier, even if medications are used, we frequently find in clinical practice that you may well be able to decrease the dose after weeks or months of using the Four Steps.

Summary

As you have seen from the examples in this chapter, you can use the Four Steps to assist with a wide variety of situations, so use your creativity and knowledge of your deceptive brain messages to design Refocus with Progressive Mindfulness plans that get you engaged in the world and following the path of your true self. The key, as Connie learned years ago, is to keep yourself motivated by defining goals that matter to you and to remind yourself that whenever you say, "I can't," what you are really saying is "I won't."

So, continue to Relabel, Reframe, Refocus, and Revalue those false, unhelpful brain messages and keep moving toward your goals. With time,

---

1. Remember: As we mentioned in the Introduction, the Four Steps are designed to help with mild to moderate symptoms. Medications should be used in the case of bipolar disorder, schizophrenia, or chronic suicidal thoughts, and you should always consult with your doctor before changing your medication regimen.

you will rewire your brain in such a way that those new activities become a regular, routine part of your life and those unhealthy habits will increasingly become a thing of the past.

In the final chapter of the book, we will review how to use the Four Steps to enhance your life.

CHAPTER 15

Putting It All Together

We know that learning the Four Steps and aligning your actions with your true self are no easy tasks, but with the skills you have learned in this book, you are well on your way to achieving your goals and shaping your life and brain in the ways you want. Let's review what you have learned.

We started out by introducing you to the concept of deceptive brain messages and how following even seemingly benign deceptive brain messages can result in rewiring your brain in unhelpful, unhealthy ways. From there we emphasized that you are not your brain and that you can and must make healthy choices on your behalf. We taught you how the brain works and showed you that it can be rewired to work *for* you—rather than *against* you—with Hebb's law (neurons that fire together wire together), the quantum Zeno effect (focused, directed attention holds neurons in place so they can fire and wire together), and Self-Directed Neuroplasticity via the Four Steps (sharply focusing your attention shapes your brain to support you). In addition, we explained how the brain learns to ignore, minimize, and neglect many of your true needs and true emotions in childhood and how that process leads to many thinking errors.

To help you along the way, we provided you with two allies who believe in and support your true self:

- Your mind, which enables you and gives you the power to choose what to focus your attention on
- Your Wise Advocate, which empowers you to see yourself from a loving, caring perspective and helps guide your true self in making choices about how to focus your attention

When they work together in your best interest, they are a very powerful twosome and great team advocating for and caring about you!

Combined, this information set the stage for you to learn our powerful Four Step method and find ways to apply it to your life. In Part Two, we drove home the point that while you are not responsible for the thoughts, urges, impulses, sensations, desires, or cravings that arise, you are responsible for how you act and how you focus your attention. We taught you a powerful way to notice your deceptive brain messages and uncomfortable sensations with Step 1: Relabel and explained why they bother you so much with Step 2: Reframe. From there, we again stressed the point that the power is in the focus and that the more you direct your attention toward healthy actions by refusing to let your attention be grabbed repeatedly by the deceptive thoughts, the more you will change your brain in adaptive, wholesome ways.

As we repeated often, Step 3: Refocus is the key to empowering you to change your own brain so that it rewires to work *for* you, not *against* you, because it (along with your Wise Advocate) encourages you to choose constructive, healthy actions that engender supportive brain messages. When these kinds of healthy messages are focused on, they lead your brain to rewire in ways that support positive automatic responses.

In Step 4: Revalue, we explained that progressive mindfulness, the ultimate goal of the Four Steps, is an experiential process that results in you seeing the deceptive brain message as nothing more than a deceptive brain message—something that is inconsequential and not worthy of your attention. Revaluing also helps strengthen your Wise Advocate and its healthy messages, which enables you to further align your actions with your true self.

In the final section of the book, we clarified the difference between emotional sensations and true emotions, explained when "should" statements are helpful, showed you how to use Refocus to its fullest, and discussed the role of medications. Throughout it all, our goal has been to teach you how to notice what happens in your brain so that you can make informed choices about where you focus your attention and thereby shape your brain so that it supports you in healthy, helpful, and adaptive ways. In this final chapter, we will discuss how to begin your work with the Four Steps and how to nurture your true self.

Recommendations for Starting to Use the Four Steps

For the first week or two of using the Four Steps, we recommend that you simply practice Step 1: Relabel and the breathing awareness exercises. While you are working on Step 1, keep the following guidelines and tips in mind:

Relabeling means calling the deceptive thoughts, urges, impulses, desires, and sensations what they are.

- Use mental notes whenever possible to increase your ability to Relabel your deceptive brain messages. This strengthens your powers of observation.
- Identify all the deceptive thoughts, urges, impulses, desires, cravings, physical sensations, and emotional sensations that arise.
- Be vigilant to notice when you are lost in thought and use breath

awareness to pull you back from the endless loops and spirals of thinking that can easily get out of control.

- Being aware of your thoughts, sensations, and experiences takes effort—it is an activity, not merely a state of mind.
- The more you Relabel, the more active your Assessment Center becomes, which helps it quiet the unhelpful parts of your Self-Referencing Center and Uh Oh Center.

Once you are able to effectively Relabel many of your deceptive thoughts, you can start Reframing them with Step 2. Here are a few things to remember:

Reframing asks you to change your perception of the importance of the deceptive brain messages.

- Your default mode has been to see the deceptive brain messages as "a part of me," which makes you unable to see how false your deceptive brain messages are.
- Your goal with Step 2: Reframe is to say *why* these thoughts, urges, impulses, and desires are bothering you so you can change your perception of them.
- To do this, you must use your knowledge of how the brain automatically ignores, minimizes, and neglects your true emotions and needs, how it processes social pain, and how it generates thinking errors so that you can correctly identify what is happening and why you are bothered by these experiences.
- You can Reframe in many ways, including
  - It's the brain, not me!
  - Thinking errors, including: All-or-nothing, Catastrophizing, Discounting the Positive, Emotional Reasoning, Mind Reading, and "Should" Statements
  - False expectations

- Faulty comparisons
- Social pain
- Trying to "get" the 5 A's (Attention, Acceptance, Affection, Appreciation, Allowing) from others
- Reframing can change your Self-Referencing Center from a nagging scold to an empowered enabler, thus calming the Uh Oh Center in the process.

Then, Refocus your attention in healthy, constructive ways with Step 3:

Refocusing means directing your attention toward an activity or mental process that is wholesome and productive—even while the urges, thoughts, impulses, and sensations are present and bothering you.

- Never try to make the feelings go away or try to alter them in the short term.
- With deceptive brain messages, it's not what you think or feel that matters, it's what you do that counts.
- Notice where your *attention* is focused—this is what changes your brain.
- When possible, choose Refocus activities that are enjoyable or strongly engage your attention and interest.
- Ways to Refocus include:
  - Regular Refocus—any activity that is wholesome and captures your interest in a positive way.
  - Regulate & Refocus—breathing or another activity that decreases your emotional or physical sensations as a result of sharply focusing your attention in a positive way.
  - Refocus with Progressive Mindfulness—deliberately encountering a situation that you normally would avoid *and* that is beneficial for you.

- Refocus with Progressive Mindfulness should never be used for dangerous or highly addictive behaviors—use regular Regulate or Regulate & Refocus instead.
- Gratitude lists are an excellent way to Refocus.
- Use the fifteen-minute rule whenever possible.

After working with the first three steps for a few weeks (though some people may jump right in, which is okay if you have enough insight and awareness from prior training or therapy), you likely will be ready to start tackling specific behaviors that you want to change (with Refocus with Progressive Mindfulness) and begin Step 4, where you start Revaluing your experiences:

Revaluing means clearly seeing the thoughts, urges, impulses, and desires for what they are—simply sensations caused by deceptive brain messages that are not true and that have little to no value.

- Progressive mindfulness is the ability to use your Wise Advocate to gain deeper levels of mindful awareness through experience.
- As your capacity to use progressive mindfulness improves, you will be able to view the bothersome, yet useless false thoughts, impulses, desires, cravings, urges, fears, worries, and thinking errors as nothing more than deceptive brain messages.

MAKING THE BRAIN WORK FOR YOU— KEY CONCEPTS

- Habits are hard to break because they are so strongly wired into your brain because of Hebb's law and the quantum Zeno effect.
- You can break the cycle of deceptive brain messages with focused

attention, veto power, and Self-Directed Neuroplasticity (i.e., the Four Steps).

- The key parts of the brain involved in propagating and maintaining deceptive brain messages include the:
  - Drive Center—involved in hunger, thirst, sex, and other basic bodily drives
  - Reward Center—involved in pleasure and obtaining rewards
  - Uh Oh Center—involved in telling you something is wrong; alarm center
  - Habit Center—involved in automatic responses (thoughts and actions)
  - Self-Referencing Center—focuses on information related to you; can cause you to take things too personally at times
- The Assessment Center is involved in rational decision-making and voluntary emotion management and supports the Wise Advocate. It is the part of the brain that is enhanced and recruited more often when you use the Four Steps on a continual basis.

Developing Your Plan

To begin changing your brain-based habits in a more deliberate way, you will want to devise a list or game plan. In chapter 2, we asked you to write down what things you want to stop doing and the activities you would prefer to be doing instead. Look at that list now. Is there anything else that you want to add? For example, when you completed that list, you had not learned about thinking errors, the importance of emotional bonds, or social pain. Now that you know all the ways your brain can hijack you, reformulate your list and include actions, both physical and mental, that you would like to change in the table on page 342.

(e.g., eating carbs when I am stressed out; using alcohol to calm myself after I get into an argument with someone; calling my ex-boyfriend whenever I feel lonely; never doing things for myself, but putting others first; not saying what I think or need; striving for perfection all the time; trying to get the 5 A's from people rather than providing them for myself)

(e.g., eating more healthily; exercising more often; spending more time with friends; meditating to learn how to notice my thoughts and soothe myself; doing more things for myself each day; telling people what I think or need; noticing when I am catastrophizing, and using the Four Steps to deal with it)

With this list in mind, think about which things will be easier to change and which will be harder. Rank them in order in the table below from 1 (the easiest to change) to 10 (the most difficult to change).

THINGS I WANT TO CHANGE WITH THE FOUR STEPS

1.

2.

3.

4.

5.

6.

7.

8.

9.

10.

Obviously, you could start using the Four Steps on anything you want to change, but beginning with something that is easier (#1 on the list above) is your best bet—even if it is not the most pressing or important. Why? It's essential that you learn how to use the Four Steps and have some early successes with applying the method before you tackle more intense sensations or entrenched habits that are strongly wired into your brain. For instance, if you start with something too difficult or that evokes a lot of distress and unsettling emotional sensations, you may feel overwhelmed and not learn how to use the Four Steps effectively. Therefore, start with something small that does not require you to use Refocus with Progressive Mindfulness. With time and repeated use of the Four Steps, you will be able to incorporate Refocus with Progressive Mindfulness plans into your life and tackle almost any difficulty you have.

In short, don't do everything at once, and allow yourself to see the progress you're making by journaling your successes and writing out gratitude lists.

Pay Attention to Your True Self

Along with using the Four Steps to increase your awareness and insight of what is happening in your brain and body, you need to develop and enhance your sense of self with your Wise Advocate and the 5 A's. Doing so will help counteract your brain's natural tendency to ignore, minimize, or neglect your true self or use thinking errors to keep you stuck and unable to stand up for yourself. It will also help you see yourself the way your Wise Advocate does: a good person worthy of living a fulfilling and rewarding life.

To improve your ability to see yourself from the perspective of your true self, try to *incorporate* and *believe* your Wise Advocate's view of you. For example, whenever a thinking error or negative thought about you arises, imagine how your Wise Advocate would respond and try to really take in that message. Allow yourself to consider the possibility that you genuinely are trying your best and are making progress. Remind yourself that it's natural and healthy for you to allow your true emotions to break through that wall of deceptive brain messages that likely has been dominating your life. Acknowledge that the Wise Advocate, that healthy side of you that is strongly aligned with your true self, would advocate for you to allow all of your true feelings, including grief, mobilizing forms of anger, and healthy stress or anxiety, to emerge. Similarly, remember that it is natural and normal to seek out the 5 A's from important people in your life—it's part of what fulfills you and brings meaning to your life. Simultaneously, acknowledge that in most cases you should provide yourself with Attention, Acceptance, Affection, Appreciation, and Allowing so that you remain independent and relate to people in healthy ways.

The definition of respecting your true self and using the Four Steps to its fullest extent is to achieve the following:

- Constructively deal with your true emotions in a way that allows your true self to be honored and represented
- Skillfully deal with deceptive brain messages by allowing the false thoughts, urges, impulses, desires, and sensations to be present, without focusing attention on or overidentifying with them[1]

When you are able to achieve these goals while incorporating and internalizing the view of a loving, caring being who knows how you think and feel but who acts in your best interest into your sense of self, you will be firmly on your way to acting in healthy, wholesome ways that result in lasting changes to your brain and your life.

Best wishes on your journey and in your life. May you be well.

---

1. As always, if in doubt, ask yourself how a reasonable person would respond to the situation currently in front of you and how your Wise Advocate would view the situation.

ACKNOWLEDGMENTS

First and foremost, we want to thank all the people who allowed their stories to be used in this book. Your willingness to share your life and perspective in such a generous way will help many more than you could ever know. We also thank our tireless research assistant and colleague, Poorang Aurasteh, for completing most of the case interviews in this book and enthusiastically helping us with our UCLA Four Step education group.

As with most endeavors, this book is the result of many talented people working together. We begin by thanking two extraordinary people who had the vision and ability to get the project started and see it through to completion. Susan Rabiner, our agent, and Rachel Holtzman, our editor at Avery, were driving forces behind this book. We cannot thank you enough for believing in our ideas and being passionate advocates of our work. We also thank Travers Johnson, assistant editor; Megan Newman, vice president and editorial director of Avery; and William Shinker, president and publisher of Gotham Books/Avery.

In terms of content, we thank Henry P. Stapp, Ph.D., David D. Burns, M.D., Peter G. Levine, and Donald D. Price, Ph.D., for offering their time, knowledge, and pioneering ideas. We also thank the researchers and authors we mention in the book for their groundbreaking work. Finally, we are appreciative of the support from our colleagues at UCLA, including Peter Whybrow, M.D., and everyone at the Mindful Awareness

Research Center (MARC): Diana Winston, Marvin Belzer, Ph.D., Daniel Siegel, M.D., and Susan Smalley, Ph.D.

REBECCA GLADDING

I greatly appreciate my family and friends for their unending support during the writing process and in life in general. Thanks to Darlene Ricker, one of the most amazing writing coaches around. Among her many talents, she had an uncanny ability to help me consistently erase my writer's block and keep me moving forward even when I had no idea where I was headed. I am also indebted to Karin de Weille for helping me find my creative/narrative voice and for assisting in revising chapter 1. To Jennifer Draper, M.D., Keith White, Dana Levy, M.D., Wendy Simon, M.D., Kristen Heiden, Kerry Regan, Donald, Connie, and Curtis Gladding, Melinda Merker, Halary Patch, RN, Iljie Fitzgerald, M.D., Michael Takamura, M.D., Alvin Chan, Shani Delaney, M.D., Jonathan Volk, M.D., Bryan and Vanessa Turner, Luata Bray, LMPc, Stacy Duhon, Alice Rudnick, M.D., and Karen Stone: I couldn't have done this without all of you. Similarly, thanks to my amazing colleagues at UCLA, including the exceptionally talented and hardworking psychiatry residents and everyone in the Adult Eating Disorders Program, particularly Michael Strober, Ph.D., Cynthia Pikus, Ph.D., Maureen Lynch, RN, MSN, and the entire nursing and therapeutic staff, and to the most supportive colleagues imaginable at the University of Washington.

To all of my patients over the years, your willingness to share your life history and emotions taught me more than any textbook ever could. Thank you for allowing me to know you.

Thanks to Jeffrey Schwartz, M.D., for the unsurpassed education you have given me—I have learned so much from you. Thanks also to all of my teachers and mentors over the years, including Phillip Cogen, M.D., Michael Gitlin, M.D., Thomas Strouse, M.D., and John S. Luo, M.D., at UCLA, Lowell Tong, M.D., at UCSF, Karina Uldall, M.D., and Paul Ciechanowski, M.D., at the University of Washington, T. Glen Lawson at Bates College, and Trudy Goodman of InsightLA. You have helped me become the person, clinician, and ardent educator I am today. Finally, thanks to Peet's Coffee in Brentwood, which provided me with a wonderfully relaxing place to write the majority of this book, and especially Warren, who always greeted me with a smile and a perfectly made Americano.

JEFFREY SCHWARTZ

I would like to thank El Shaddai—the Source of it All, Billy Abraham for telling me about the Jesus Prayer, and the Paraclete for being helper, comforter, advocate, counselor, encourager, strengthener, friend. I would also like to thank my parents for their decades of hard labor—the unpayable debt that made it all possible, and Gary, for being an inspiration. Thanks to Mr. Jeffrey Stern for years of dedicated support. And thanks to Becky Gladding, without whom this book would not exist, and those who have provided support through twenty-five years at UCLA.

We are eternally grateful and indebted to everyone who has helped us along the way, including anyone we did not specifically mention. Thank you all for your help, expertise, and support.

RECOMMENDED READING

If you want to learn more about what you read in *You Are Not Your Brain*, you might find these books, most of which we specifically cited and used in the text, interesting and helpful.

The Brain That Changes Itself by Norman Doidge, M.D.
Feeling Good by David D. Burns, M.D.
Fully Present by Susan L. Smalley, Ph.D., and Diana Winston
How to Be an Adult in Relationships by David Richo, Ph.D.
Man's Search for Meaning by Viktor E. Frankl, M.D., Ph.D.
A Mindfulness-Based Stress Reduction Workbook by Bob Stahl, Ph.D., and Elisha Goldstein, Ph.D.
Mindfulness in Plain English by Bhante Henepola Gunaratana
The Relaxation Response by Herbert Benson, M.D., with Miriam Z. Klipper

INDEX

Acceptance: of false messages, 232–35; in healthy emotional connections, 122, 123, 187; true vs. false, 232, 234–35; of uncontrollable circumstances, 233

Accomplishments: acknowledgment of, in refocusing, 271–72; and goal-setting, 43, 44, 53; and motivation, 136–37

Accumbens, 79. *See also* Reward Center

Actions, short-term, vs. long-term goals, 22–23

Activities, as objects of mindfulness, 157. *See also* Healthy behavior/activities

Addiction, treatment of, 260, 340. *See also* Craving(s)

Affection, in healthy emotional connections, 122, 123, 187, 212

Ainsworth, Mary, 106n1

Alcohol: cravings for, 61, 64, 173, 260; excessive consumption of (*see* Drinking); moderation with, 322, 323, 324

Alcoholics Anonymous, 137, 173, 260

All-or-nothing (black-or-white) thinking, 202–4, 215, 218, 220, 221, 298

Allowing, in healthy emotional connections, 123, 187

Amygdala, 76. *See also* Uh Oh Center

Anger: acknowledgment of, as true emotion, 283, 284–87, 299, 300; constructive use of, 47, 298, 299, 300; as dysfunctional emotional response, 286, 287, 298–99, 300; refocusing from, 255–56; reframing of, 226; thinking errors in, 32–33, 47, 298–99, 300, 305

Anterior cingulate, 76. *See also* Uh Oh Center

Anxiety: confrontation of, with refocusing techniques, 259, 261, 264–66, 271, 325–27; as consequence of emotional neglect, 112, 113, 114, 283–84, 285, 286; constructive use of, 303–4, 329–30; deceptive brain messages as source of, 3–7, 83–84; "part of me" mode in, 181; rating of, for refocusing, 262–64, 268–70, 311–12; refocusing techniques with, 251–53, 329, 330; reframing of false messages from, 197–98, 235–36; repetitive thinking in, 179–80; symptoms of, 163–65, 167, 175; thinking errors in, 205–6, 210, 224, 226, 236, 238–39, 261, 303, 304, 328–29; working around vs. stopping, 230–31, 247. *See also* Self-doubt; Stress

Appreciation, in healthy emotional connections, 123, 187

Darwin, Charles, 23

Deceptive brain messages: acceptance of, 232–35; actions caused by, xi–xii, xiii, 21; assessment of damage from, 131–32; biology underlying, 75, 77, 78, 82, 84–85, 86, 341; choice and responsibility regarding, 68–69, 80, 155–56, 336; confusing intensification of, with relapse, 288–89; counteracting, xii–xiii, xiv (*see also* Four Steps; Refocusing; Reframing; Relabeling; Revaluing); counteracting, goal-setting in, 50–57; counteracting, sustaining efforts in, 47–50; cycle of, 9–14, 17–20, 22, 32, 73–74, 75, 95, 340–41; definition of, 4; distinguishing between self and, xiv, 26–27, 121–22, 141–42, 171, 181–82, 183–84 (*see also* False foreign invaders); and emotional neglect, 109–15, 282–83, 284–87; environmental origins of, 104–6, 109–14, 117–20; extent of damage from, 126–31; fusion of self with, 83–84, 86–87, 89, 120, 127, 181–83, 201–2 (*see also* "Part of me" mode); increasing awareness of, 158, 177; intensification of, when starting relabeling, 172–73; interference with relationships, 6–8, 82–84, 118–19, 128–29, 131, 132, 142; medical intervention with, xvii–xviii, 332–33; noncognitive awareness of, in revaluing, 278–80, 336–37, 340; passive focusing on, 66–67; persons triggering, 117–22; physical symptoms from, 6; recognition of, 15–20, 33, 57, 144–45, 146, 290 (*see also* Mindfulness; Relabeling); recognizing falsity of, 154 (*see also* False foreign invaders); refocusing from, 96–97, 98, 142 (*see also* Refocusing; Refocusing with Progressive Mindfulness; Regulate & Refocus); reframing of, 33–34, 91–92, 96, 98, 177, 180, 291, 336, 338–39; relabeling of, 91, 96, 138, 229, 230, 291, 336, 337–38; revaluing of, 94, 98, 171, 274–75, 276; self-treatment of, xvii (*see also* Self-Directed Neuroplasticity); situations triggering, 116–17, 120, 121–22; as source of anxiety, 3–7, 83–84; as source of depression, 6; as source of guilt, 7; as source of perfectionism, 5, 104, 105, 109; as source of self-doubt, 3–4, 103–4, 119–20; as source of stress, 8; veto power over, 35, 69–71, 80; working around vs.

stopping, 95–96, 97–98, 135–36, 139, 191, 192–93, 229–32, 234, 247

Depression: as consequence of emotional neglect, 112, 284, 285, 287; deceptive brain messages as source of, 6; "part of me" mode in, 184–85; patient's efforts in treatment of, 45–46; refocusing toward healthy activity in, 245, 328; reframing of false messages from, 196–97; symptoms of, 166–68, 327, 328; thinking errors in, 227, 301, 302

Desire: creation of false expectations by, 212, 213; as factor in sustained effort, 46–47, 48–50, 57; indiscriminate responses to, 48; origins of, 47–48, 68–69; relabeling of, 48; therapy as fulfillment of, 252, 253, 256. *See also* Craving(s)

Dieting, 315, 319–22, 323–24, 331

Discounting the positive, 206–8, 210–11, 216, 217, 218, 220, 221, 298

Distraction: vs. refocusing, 247, 249; by repetitive thinking, 158–61, 162, 177

Drake Center (Cincinnati), 32, 36

Drinking: control of, 71, 226; cost of, 128–29, 132; and depression, 166; and dysfunctional anger, 298; formation of habit of, 62, 64–65; "part of me" mode in, 185; reframing of false messages from, 196; as response to stress, 8, 60–61, 65, 66, 70–71; selection of refocusing technique for, 260

Drive Center, 48, 75, 78, 82, 341

Eating disorders, 9–10, 22, 73–74, 285. *See also* Food

Effort: estimation of, in goal-setting, 52, 53–56, 57; indispensability of, in successful treatment, 45–50, 133n3, 138–39; in mindfulness, 147–48; selectivity in, 137–38

Ego-dystonic perspective. *See* False foreign invaders

Ego-syntonic perspective. *See* "Part of me" mode

Eisenberger, Naomi, 186–88, 189, 191, 201

Emotional reasoning, 208–9, 216, 217, 218, 220, 221, 227

Emotional sensations: acceptance of, 232, 233, 234; avoidance of, 129, 175–76; bodily manifestations of, 163–68; brain biology underlying, 75–76, 77, 78, 79, 84,

Emotional sensations (*cont.*): 85, 86; confrontation of, with refocusing techniques, 257–59, 260, 261, 264–66, 271; confusing intensification of, with relapse, 288–89; as consequence of emotional neglect, 112; from deceptive brain messages, 9, 10–11, 12, 13, 14, 18, 22, 32, 74, 75, 290; difference between emotions and, 11–12, 281–87, 292, 297–305; distortion of self by, 86–90; examples of, 16–17; expectations as triggers for, 214; impermanence of, 193–95, 280; increasing awareness of, 158, 177; intensification of, when starting relabeling, 173; making mental notes about, 169, 255–26; as objects of mindfulness, 157; rating of, for refocusing, 262–64, 268–70; recognition of false thoughts through, 173, 174; refocusing from, 35, 93–94, 166, 198, 253 (*see also* Refocusing; Refocusing with Progressive Mindfulness; Regulate & Refocus); reframing of, 12, 230 (*see also* Reframing); relabeling of, 12, 32–33, 47, 98, 138, 165, 166, 229, 230, 239, 291, 336, 337–38 (*see also* Relabeling); and relationship anxieties, 83; veto power over, 35, 70–71, 80; working around vs. stopping, 95–96, 97–98, 135–36, 139, 191, 192–93, 229, 230–31, 247

Emotions: anxiety as signal of, 303, 304; attention to thoughts accompanying, 133n3, 139–40; caregiver responses to, and shaping of brain, 111–15; in childhood, 106–9; consequences of dismissiveness toward, 109–14, 123, 212, 282–83, 284–87; difference between emotional sensations and, 11–12, 281–87, 292, 297–305; effects of suppression of, 189–91; healthy cultivation of, 122–24, 187; recognizing neglect of, in bodily symptoms, 163; and respecting true self, 344–45; safe zones for, 107–9, 118; self-care for, 124, 212, 281, 345; surfacing of, in reframing, 197, 198

Executive Center, 75, 77, 78, 82. *See also* Assessment Center; Self-Referencing Center

Exercising, regular, 331

Expectations: all-or-nothing, 203; as factor in sustained effort, 46–47, 48, 49; false (*see* False expectations); taking inventory of, 214–15

Exposure and response prevention, 257–58

Faith. *See* Blind faith; Rational faith

False expectations, 210, 211, 212–13, 216, 217; vs. acceptance, 232; balanced response to, 223–24, 226; emotional consequences of, 32, 47, 299, 300; taking inventory of, 219, 220, 221; in therapy, 32, 47, 249

False foreign invaders: definition of, 181–82; recognition of, 182–83; refocusing from, 184; reframing of, 183, 184, 185, 186, 191–93; relabeling of, 183–84, 185, 192, 193; resulting in social pain, 186–87, 197–98, 200; stemming from brain biology, 186, 195–97, 200; *See also* Deceptive brain messages

Fatigue, overcoming, 327–28

Faulty comparisons, 207–8, 212, 213, 216–17, 219, 220, 221

Feeding the monster, 62, 66, 74, 80, 127–28, 129–30

Fifteen-minute rule, 248–49, 311, 313, 316, 321, 340

Fight-or-flight response, 23, 76n1, 164, 254

5 A's (Attention, Acceptance, Affection, Appreciation, Allowing), 122–24, 126, 137, 187, 212, 222, 228, 272, 281, 299, 301, 302, 339, 344, 345

Focusing of attention: in beginning Four Steps, 138; beneficial, xiv, xv, xvi, 21, 22, 23–24, 33 (*see also* Refocusing; Refocusing with Progressive Mindfulness; Regulate & Refocus); choice in, 67, 70, 71, 95–96; intersection of awareness with, 151–53, 242–44; and neuroplasticity, 38, 39–40, 47, 67; passive, 66–67; in stabilizing brain circuits, 65–67; toward unhealthy behavior, 61–62, 65, 66

Food: moderation with, 322, 323, 324; reducing cravings for, 243, 315, 317–22. *See also* Eating disorders

Fortune-telling. *See* Catastrophizing

Four Steps: counteracting deceptive brain messages with, xii–xiii; developing individualized plan, 341–44; efficacy of, 141–43; life stories illustrating, xiii; medical intervention and, xvii–xviii, 332–33; practicing of, 136–37; research validating, xiv–xvi; self-treatment with, xvii; sequencing of steps in, 337–40, 344; tips for beginners, 135–41. *See also* Refocusing; Refocusing with Progressive Mindfulness;

Relabeling (*cont.*): of false foreign invaders, 183–84, 185, 192, 193; intensification of sensations in, 172–73; making mental notes in, 33, 168–70, 171, 255, 337; mindfulness as foundation of, 146, 149; purpose of, 152, 158, 177, 194; in "reality checks," 228; reframing thinking errors and, 202, 204, 206, 207, 208, 209, 210, 212, 224, 231, 235, 297; in sequence of Four Steps, 337–38; shifting to revaluing from, 278; use with refocusing techniques, 242, 243, 248–49, 250, 252, 265, 266, 271, 328

Relapse, vs. stress, 288–89

Relationships: assertion of true self in, 310–14, 324; biological mechanisms influencing, 85; diminishing influence of deceptive messages in, 91–94; goal-setting for, 43, 53; healthy cultivation of emotions in, 122–24, 187; interference of deceptive brain messages with, 6–8, 82–84, 118–19, 128–29, 131, 132, 142; interference of habitual responses with, 61, 83–84; as satisfaction for cravings, 324; thinking errors in, 203, 206, 210, 212, 224

Relaxation, healthy, 331

Relaxation Response, 253–55

Repetitive behavior: as habitual response, 88, 89–90; identification of, 175; practicing Four Steps as, 136–37; replacement with healthy behavior, 93–94, 142; as response to relationship anxieties, 83–84; weakening of, in reframing, 92

Repetitive thinking: in anxiety, 179–80; becoming lost in, 158–61, 162, 177; dealing with, in refocusing, 160, 249–50; as habitual response, 14, 88, 201; increasing awareness of, 161–63. *See also* Overanalyzing

Revaluing: of deceptive brain messages, 94, 98, 171, 274–75, 276; definition of, xvi, 90, 134, 276; experience as direct object of observation in, 278–80, 336–37, 340; generation of life choices by, 275, 276–77, 280–81; identifying true emotions in, 286–87; mindfulness as foundation of, 146; movement toward true self in, 274–76, 292; and recognition of thinking errors, 228–29, 231; retraining the brain with, 276, 277–78, 281, 322; in sequence of Four Steps, 340

Reward Center: generation of pleasure by, 79,

341; modification of cravings of, 319; origin of craving in, 48, 65, 319, 321; in processing of deceptive brain messages, 78, 82

Richo, David, 122–24

Roosevelt, Eleanor, 133n2

Sadness: acknowledgment of, as true emotion, 12, 283, 285, 287, 299, 301, 302; as consequence of emotional neglect, 110, 111; as false sensation, 12, 301, 302; underlying anger, 299

Safe zones, emotional, 107–9, 118

Schizophrenia, xviii, 332, 333n

Schwartz, Jeffrey M., 65

Self: deception of, xii; distinguishing between symptoms and, xiv, 26–27; distortion by false sensations, 83–84, 86–90; fusion of, with deceptive brain messages, 83–84, 86–87, 89, 120, 127, 181–83, 201–2 (*see also* "Part of me" mode); linkage of false sensations to, 80; restoration of, xii; true (*see* True self)

Self-care: for emotions, 124, 212, 281, 345; goal-setting for, 44, 53; in relationships, 311–13

Self-Directed Neuroplasticity, 24, 315, 335, 341; choosing focus of attention in, 67, 95–96; definition of goals in, 42–45, 50–57; meaningfulness of life and, 40–42, 44; purpose of, 95; sustaining efforts toward goals in, 47–50; time management in, 57–59; treatment of stroke with, 31–43, 47, 48, 57–58, 59

Self-doubt: cost of, 128, 129, 131, 132; deceptive brain messages as source of, 3–4, 103–4, 119–20; thinking errors in, 207, 209–10, 224–25. *See also* Anxiety

Self-hatred, 301, 302

Self-Referencing Center: management of self by, 84, 86, 341; management of social interactions by, 84–85, 86; modulation of, in reframing, 92, 192, 339; modulation of, in relabeling, 98, 170, 189, 192, 338; modulation of, in revaluing, 281; in "part of me" mode, 181; registering of social pain in, 188, 189; reinforcement by Uh Oh Center, 86–90; repetitive thinking as process of, 159; suppression of, in refocusing, 94, 98; and thinking errors, 201, 202, 215

Sensations. *See* Emotional sensations; Physical sensations

"Should" statements, 177, 210–12, 216, 217; balanced response to, 223; emotional consequences of, 32, 47, 298, 299, 300; harm from, 305–6, 307, 308; intent behind, 306, 307; motivation by, 305, 306, 307–8, 329; taking inventory of, 219, 220, 221; in therapy, 249

Shutdown, physical, and emotional sensations, 164, 166

Smiley, Connie, 30–35, 36, 37–38, 39, 40–43, 47, 48, 57–58, 59, 299, 300, 305

Smoking, quitting, 315–16

Social pain: brain activity in, 186–88, 189; from false messages, 186, 197–98, 200, 291; identification of, with self, 188, 189; neurological association of, with physical pain, 187, 198

Stapp, Henry, 65

Stress: cravings as response to, 315, 316, 317, 318, 319, 323–24; deceptive brain messages as source of, 8; formation of habitual responses to, 60–61, 65, 66; refocusing techniques with, 251, 254, 255; vs. relapse, 288–89; suppression of emotions and, 190, 191; vetoing habitual responses to, 70–71. *See also* Anxiety

Stroke: brain damage from, 36–37; prognosis for, 31; symptoms of, 30–31; treatment with Self-Directed Neuroplasticity, 31–43, 47, 48, 57–58, 59

Suicidal thoughts, xviii, 167, 332, 333n

Taper plan, 315–16

Thinking errors: balanced response to, 223–29, 344–45; categories of, 202–13, 215–17; definition of, 200–201; emotional consequences of, 32–33, 47, 298–99, 300, 301, 302, 303, 304, 328–29; recognition of, 180, 186, 198, 200–202, 204, 205, 206, 207, 208, 209, 210, 211–12, 213, 224, 228, 231, 235–36, 239, 291, 297, 338–39; taking inventory of, 217–21

Thinking/thoughts: evaluating truth/falsity of, 177, 181–84, 291 (*see also* False foreign invaders; "Part of me" mode); impairment of, by emotional sensations, 164. *See also* Deceptive brain messages; Overanalyzing; Repetitive thinking

Time management, in meeting goals, 57–59

Timer, pacing work with, 330

True self: aligning choices with, 292–93, 294, 335, 337; assertion of, in relationships, 310–14, 324; vs. biology, 25–26, 322; committing to, 127, 128, 130, 133; deceptive brain messages as diversion from, 4, 5, 7, 8, 21, 125–26, 127–28, 154, 156, 234, 261, 327; definition of, 5–6; discarding of expectations and, 232; emotional consequences of ignoring, 114, 115; "fresh eyes" of, 146; healthy relaxation and, 331; and intention of "should" statements, 307; mind as path to, 22–23; motivation and, 331; movement toward, in revaluing, 274–76, 277, 292; moving from "part of me" mode toward, 185–86; recognition of true emotions and, 297, 299, 300, 301, 302, 303, 304, 305; recognizing neglect of, in bodily symptoms, 163, 174; separating deceptive brain messages from, 26–27, 121–22, 141–42, 171, 181–82, 183–84 (*see also* False foreign invaders); strengthening of, 240–41, 336, 344–45; surfacing of, in reframing, 197, 198; valuing of, 7; Wise Advocate as ally of, 222, 223–24, 228, 229, 235, 336

Twelve Steps (of Alcoholics Anonymous), 137, 173, 243n, 260

Uh Oh Center, 76, 341; appeasement of, with unhealthy behavior, 113, 129; biological modulation of, 85; and childhood emotions, 108–9, 111; and cognitive-behavioral therapy, 258; disarming of, in revaluing, 274, 281; and emotional neglect, 109, 111, 115; evaluating thoughts in response to, 177; modulation of, in reframing, 92, 98, 191, 192, 194, 339; modulation of, in relabeling, 98, 170–71, 189, 192, 255, 338; overattention to, 93, 179–80; in processing of deceptive brain messages, 78, 82; registering of social pain in, 187–88, 189; reinforcement of Self-Referencing Center by, 86–90; stimulation of, by expectations, 213; suppression of, in refocusing, 94, 97, 171; and thinking errors, 201, 202, 208–9, 216

Unhealthy behavior: assessment of damage from, 131–32; brain biology underlying, 76–77, 78; in cycle of deceptive brain messages, 9, 10–11, 13, 22, 74, 75;